LEAD BETTER, DAILY.
LEADING QUESTIONS

366 MEDITATIONS TO TRANSFORM HOW YOU LEAD

DAVID WELLS

Copyright © 2025 by David Wells

All rights reserved.

No portion of this book may be reproduced in any form without written permission from the publisher or author, except as permitted by U.S. copyright law.

> "We make our world significant by the courage of our questions and the depth of our answers."
>
> - Carl Sagan

INTRODUCTION

Why a book of questions about leadership?

Leadership development hinges on three fundamental principles, each strengthened by the transformative power of thoughtful inquiry.

Effective leadership demands profound self-awareness—an understanding of one's values, beliefs, and character—that can only emerge through deliberate introspection. Questions are a primary instrument for this inner work. In his essay Solitude and Leadership, educator and author William Deresiewicz writes, "You have to be prepared in advance. You need to know, already, who you are and what you believe". Deresiewicz asks, "How can you know that unless you've taken counsel with yourself in solitude?"[1] The leader who has not wrestled with fundamental questions about their purpose, values, and identity will find themselves unprepared for the burden of leadership. Questions can create the space for this self-discovery.

Powerful questions can instigate personal transformation. Organisational development consultant Peter Block observes that "transformation comes more from pursuing profound questions than seeking practical answers." Like a sculptor's chisel gradually revealing form from marble, sustained contemplation of meaningful questions reshapes our thinking and perspective. Harvard professor Clayton Christensen explains why this process matters. "Questions

---

[1] *Solitude and Leadership: If you want others to follow, learn to be alone with your thoughts*, William Deresiewicz, The American Scholar, March 1, 2010.

are places in your mind where answers fit." Christensen writes, "If you haven't asked the question, the answer has nowhere to go. It hits your mind and bounces right off. You have to ask the question—you have to want to know—in order to open up the space for the answer to fit." Questions forge cognitive pathways, preparing us to recognise insights when they emerge.

Leadership is fundamentally relational, and questions can build bridges between hearts and minds. "Questions are taken for granted rather than given a starring role in the human drama." psychologist Edgar Schein, whose work spanned decades of organisational consulting, explains. "Yet all my teaching and consulting experience has taught me that what builds a relationship, what solves problems, what moves things forward is asking the right questions."[2] When leaders approach others with genuine curiosity rather than predetermined conclusions, they can create the conditions for trust, understanding, and collaboration. The right question, asked at the right moment, can unlock perspectives that transform teams and organisations.

---
2 *Humble Inquiry: The Gentle Art of Asking Instead of Telling,* Edgar H. Schein, 2013.

These three dimensions—self-knowledge, transformation, and relationship-building—converge through the practice of thoughtful questioning.

This book is therefore not just a collection of questions to consider, it is a means of developing the contemplative and relational muscles that effective leadership requires. The questions in this book are organised around twelve leadership themes, in a day per page format. The source and relevant context is included, as well as a brief biography of the originator.

I hope these questions help you on your leadership journey.

CONTENTS

INTRODUCTION.. iv

JANUARY KNOW THYSELF... 1

FEBRUARY LEAD YOURSELF... 33

MARCH BUILD & LEAD YOUR TEAM..................................... 63

APRIL CULTIVATE & SHARE YOUR VISION.............................. 95

MAY STRENGTHEN PERCEPTION & THOUGHT.............................. 126

JUNE COMMUNICATE WITH IMPACT..................................... 158

JULY WIELD LEVERAGE.. 189

AUGUST SHAPE THE CULTURE... 221

SEPTEMBER SHARPEN THE SAW.. 253

OCTOBER LEAD CHANGE.. 284

NOVEMBER OVERCOME CHALLENGES..................................... 316

DECEMBER LEAVE A LEGACY.. 347

AFTERWORD.. 380

*"One does not begin with answers.
One begins by asking,
'What are our questions?'"
- Peter Drucker*

JANUARY

KNOW THYSELF

JANUARY 1

"What seed was planted when you or I arrived on earth with our identities intact? How can we recall and reclaim those birthright gifts and potentials?"
- Parker J. Palmer[3]

---

[3] *A Hidden Wholeness: The Journey Toward an Undivided Life*, Parker J. Palmer, 2009.

Parker J. Palmer is an author, educator, and activist whose work speaks deeply to people in many walks of life, focusing on issues in education, community, leadership, spirituality, and social change. Author of ten books—including several best-selling and award-winning titles—that have sold nearly two million copies, Palmer is the founder and Senior Partner Emeritus of the Center for Courage and Renewal. An educator, he works with people from all walks of life at the intersection of spiritual, professional, and social change, emphasising the need to acknowledge the inner life of human beings as a source of reality and power. His influential works include "The Courage to Teach" and "Let Your Life Speak," which explore the connection between personal authenticity and effective leadership, teaching, and social engagement.

JANUARY 2

"What is life asking of me?"
- Viktor Frankl[4]

---

[4] "Ultimately, man should not ask what the meaning of his life is, but rather must recognize that it is he who is asked." Frankl writes. "In a word, each man is questioned by life; and he can only answer to life by answering for his own life; to life he can only respond by being responsible." *Man's Search for Meaning*, Viktor E. Frankl, 1946.

Viktor Frankl (1905 – 1997) was an Austrian neurologist, psychiatrist, and Holocaust survivor who developed logotherapy, a form of psychotherapy centred on the search for meaning as the primary human drive. Frankl survived imprisonment in Nazi concentration camps including Auschwitz, where he lost his parents, brother, and pregnant wife. His experiences in the camps formed the basis for his seminal work "Man's Search for Meaning," first published in 1946, which has sold millions of copies worldwide and been named one of the most influential books of the 20th century. In the book, Frankl argues that while we cannot always control what happens to us, we can choose how to respond, and that finding meaning in even the most difficult circumstances is essential for psychological survival and growth. His logotherapy approach posits that the primary motivation in life is not pleasure (as Freud suggested) or power (as Adler proposed), but the pursuit of meaning. After the war, Frankl returned to Vienna where he continued his psychiatric practice, taught at the University of Vienna, and wrote over 30 books. He died in 1997, leaving behind a profound legacy about human resilience, the importance of meaning, and the power of choice even in the face of unimaginable suffering.

JANUARY 3

"What are my strengths? How do I perform? How do I learn? What are my values? Where do I belong? What should I contribute?"
- Peter Drucker[5]

---

[5] "History's great achievers—a Napoléon, a da Vinci, a Mozart—have always managed themselves." Drucker writes. "That, in large measure, is what makes them great achievers. But they are rare exceptions, so unusual both in their talents and their accomplishments as to be considered outside the boundaries of ordinary human existence. Now, most of us, even those of us with modest endowments, will have to learn to manage ourselves. We will have to learn to develop ourselves. We will have to place ourselves where we can make the greatest contribution."

Managing Oneself, Peter F. Drucker, Harvard Business Review, January 2005.

Peter Drucker (1909-2005) was a management consultant, educator, and author widely regarded as the founder of modern management theory. Drucker wrote over 30 books and countless articles that fundamentally shaped how we think about business, leadership, and organisational effectiveness. He coined many concepts that are now management staples, including "management by objectives," "knowledge worker," and the idea that the purpose of business is to create customers. His most influential works include "The Practice of Management" and "The Effective Executive". Drucker emphasised that management is both an art and a science, focusing on people rather than just processes, and he predicted many major business trends including the rise of the information economy and the importance of innovation. Beyond business, he was a prolific social commentator who wrote about democracy, society, and the role of institutions. His insights remain remarkably relevant today, and he's remembered for his practical wisdom and his belief that effective management could make organisations more productive while also making work more meaningful for people.

JANUARY 4

"This, after all is said and done, is the only real problem of life, the only worthwhile occupation preoccupation of man:
What is one's true talent, his secret gift, his authentic vocation?
In what way is one truly unique, and how can he express this uniqueness, give it form, dedicate it to something beyond himself?
How can the person take his private inner being, the great mystery that he feels at the heart of himself, his emotions, his yearnings, and use them to live more distinctively, to enrich both himself and mankind with the peculiar quality of his talent?"
- Ernest Becker[6]

---

[6] *The Denial of Death*, Ernest Becker, 1997.

Ernest Becker (1924 - 1974) was a cultural anthropologist and interdisciplinary thinker best known for his Pulitzer Prize-winning book "The Denial of Death", which explores how the fear of death drives much of human behaviour and culture. Becker argued that humans are uniquely aware of their mortality, and this awareness creates an existential terror that we manage through "immortality projects" - cultural systems, achievements, and beliefs that give us a sense of symbolic immortality and meaning beyond our finite existence. His work synthesised insights from psychology, anthropology, philosophy, and psychoanalysis, drawing heavily on the ideas of Søren Kierkegaard, Otto Rank, and Sigmund Freud. Becker's other notable works include "Escape from Evil" and "The Birth and Death of Meaning." His ideas have profoundly influenced psychology, particularly Terror Management Theory, which has generated extensive research on how death anxiety affects human motivation and behaviour. Though Becker died of cancer in 1974, shortly after winning the Pulitzer Prize, his work continues to influence fields ranging from social psychology to existential therapy, offering deep insights into the human condition and our struggles with meaning, mortality, and authenticity.

JANUARY 5

*"It's not 'What do I want to do?',
it's 'What kind of life do I want to have?'"*
- Arianna Huffington[7]

---

[7] Huffington's question echoes advice from writer Hunter S. Thompson. "... beware of looking for goals:" he writes, "look for a way of life. Decide how you want to live and then see what you can do to make a living WITHIN that way of life."

Thrive: The Third Metric to Redefining Success and Creating a Life of Well-Being, Wisdom, and Wonder, Arianna Huffington, 2015.

Arianna Huffington is an author, businesswoman, and media entrepreneur who co-founded The Huffington Post in 2005, which became one of the most influential news and opinion websites before being sold to AOL in 2011. Born in Greece and educated at Cambridge University, she initially gained prominence as a conservative commentator and author before shifting to more progressive political positions. After leaving The Huffington Post, Huffington founded Thrive Global in 2016, a company focused on wellness and productivity that aims to help individuals and corporations reduce stress and avoid burnout. She's written numerous books, including "The Sleep Revolution" and "Thrive," advocating for the importance of sleep, meditation, and well-being in achieving success. Huffington has been a prominent voice in discussions about work-life balance, women's leadership, and redefining success beyond traditional metrics of money and power.

JANUARY 6

*"What are you being called to do,
and how are you answering your life's call?"*
- Michael Lombardi & George Raveling[8]

---

[8] *Sunday Thinking, The Daily Coach*, August 27, 2023.

Michael Lombardi is a three-time Super Bowl champion as an executive with over 30 years of experience in NFL front offices who recently joined the North Carolina football program as General Manager in December 2024. He has spent 35 years working for the New England Patriots, San Francisco 49ers, the Oakland Raiders and the Cleveland Browns, and has the distinction of the being the only person to make it to the Super Bowl with both the Patriots and 49ers. Beyond his front office work, Lombardi has been a prominent media personality as an NFL analyst, author, and cofounder with George Raveling of The Daily Coach, a newsletter that shares sports and organisational leadership lessons.

George Raveling is a Basketball Hall of Fame coach and Nike executive who has had an extraordinary impact on both basketball and sports marketing. After a successful college coaching career at schools including Washington State, Iowa, and USC, he joined Nike at the request of Phil Knight, where he played an integral role in signing a reluctant Michael Jordan. Raveling has worked as the Director for International Basketball for Nike since his retirement from USC and is known as "the iconic leader who brought Michael Jordan to Nike". Beyond basketball, he has a unique connection to civil rights history and having a personal connection to Martin Luther King Jr.'s "I Have a Dream" speech. Raveling was present at the March on Washington on August 28, 1963, and after Dr. King delivered his speech, King handed Raveling the original typewritten copy.

The two co-founded The Daily Coach newsletter, sharing leadership wisdom from sports and business.

JANUARY 7

"What are you going to do with what you've been given?"
- Rick Warren[9]

---

[9] "What do you have that you've been given?" Warren asks. "Talent, background, education, freedom, networks, opportunities, wealth, ideas, creativity. What are you doing with what you've been given? That, to me, is the primary question about life. That, to me, is what being purpose-driven is all about."
A life of purpose, Rick Warren, TED, February 2006.
Rick Warren is an evangelical Christian pastor and author, best known as the founder and senior pastor of Saddleback Church in Lake Forest, California, which has grown to become one of the largest congregations in the United States. He gained international prominence with his book "The Purpose Driven Life," published in 2002, which became one of the best-selling non-fiction books in history and has been translated into dozens of languages. Warren has been influential in the evangelical movement and has spoken at various high-profile events, including delivering the invocation at President Barack Obama's 2009 inauguration. He's also been involved in global humanitarian efforts, particularly around issues like poverty, disease, and education, and has advocated for what he calls the "P.E.A.C.E. Plan" to address global problems through local churches.

JANUARY 8

"What feels like play to you and work to others?"
- Naval Ravikant[10]

---

[10] Ravikant's question is similar to one attributed to Carl Jung: "What did you do as a child that made the hours pass like minutes? Herein lies the key to your earthly pursuits."

The Almanack of Naval Ravikant: A Guide to Wealth and Happiness, Eric Jorgenson, 2020.

Naval Ravikant is a Silicon Valley entrepreneur, angel investor, and philosopher who has become one of the most influential voices on wealth creation, happiness, and decision-making. He's the co-founder and former CEO of AngelList, the platform that democratised startup investing and job matching in tech. As an angel investor, Naval has backed numerous successful companies including Twitter, Uber, Yammer, and Postmates, establishing himself as one of the most successful early-stage investors in Silicon Valley. Beyond his business success, he's gained a massive following for his philosophical insights on wealth, happiness, and life, often shared through Twitter threads, podcasts, and interviews. His thoughts were compiled into the popular book "The Almanack of Naval Ravikant," compiled by Eric Jorgenson. Naval is known for his aphoristic wisdom and his emphasis on building specific knowledge, taking accountability, and leveraging technology to create value. He advocates for principles like reading voraciously, thinking independently, and focusing on long-term compounding in both wealth and knowledge. His blend of practical business acumen with Eastern philosophy and rational thinking has made him a guru figure for entrepreneurs and investors seeking financial success and personal fulfillment.

JANUARY 9

*"What do I keep coming back to?
What is that telling me?"*
- James Clear[11]

---

11 *3-2-1 Newsletter,* James Clear, April 8, 2021.

James Clear is an author, speaker, and entrepreneur best known for his book "Atomic Habits," which became a bestseller and popularised the concept of making small, incremental changes to build better habits and break bad ones. Clear focuses on the science of habit formation, emphasising how tiny improvements compound over time to create remarkable results. His approach centres on four key principles: making habits obvious, attractive, easy, and satisfying. Before his writing career took off, Clear was a successful entrepreneur and has a background in photography and business. He writes regularly about habits, decision-making, and continuous improvement on his website and newsletter, which has attracted millions of readers. Clear's work draws from psychology, neuroscience, and behavioural economics to provide practical strategies for personal and professional development, making complex research accessible to everyday readers seeking to improve their lives through better systems and habits.

JANUARY 10

"Can you find a kind of work where your ability and interest will combine to yield an explosion of new ideas?"
- Paul Graham[12]

---

[12] Graham suggests, "all you need to do is find something you have an aptitude for and great interest in". It is an idea author Tom Rath expands on, the path of honing your existing natural talents. "The key to human development" Rath writes, "is building on who you already are".

How To Do Great Work, Paul Graham, paulgraham.com, July 2023.

Paul Graham is a computer scientist, entrepreneur, essayist, and venture capitalist who co-founded Y Combinator, the world's most influential startup accelerator. A programmer by training, he co-created Viaweb in the 1990s, one of the first web-based software applications, which was sold to Yahoo for $49 million and became Yahoo Store. Y Combinator has funded over 5,000 startups including Airbnb, Dropbox, Stripe, Reddit, and DoorDash, fundamentally changing how early-stage companies get funded and mentored. Beyond his business ventures, Graham is renowned for his essays on startups, programming, and life, published on his website paulgraham.com. His writing covers topics from technical programming concepts to startup advice to broader philosophical observations, and his essays like "Do Things That Don't Scale" and "Maker's Schedule, Manager's Schedule" have become foundational reading in Silicon Valley. Graham is known for his clear, thoughtful writing style and contrarian insights about entrepreneurship, such as emphasising the importance of building something people want rather than focusing on business plans. He stepped back from day-to-day operations at Y Combinator to focus more on his writing and thinking, but remains one of the most respected voices in the startup ecosystem.

JANUARY 11

"What is it that makes you happy?"
- Joseph Campbell[13]

---

[13] "The way to find out about happiness is to keep your mind on those moments when you feel most happy, when you are really happy — not excited, not just thrilled, but deeply happy." Campbell explains. "This requires a little bit of self-analysis. What is it that makes you happy? Stay with it, no matter what people tell you. This is what is called following your bliss."
Joseph Campbell and the Power of Myth, PBS documentary with Bill Moyers, 1988.

Joseph Campbell (1904 - 1987) was a mythologist, writer, and lecturer who became one of the most influential scholars of comparative mythology and religion in the 20th century. He's best known for his theory of the "monomyth" or "Hero's Journey," which he outlined in "The Hero with a Thousand Faces", arguing that heroic narratives from cultures worldwide follow a similar underlying pattern. Campbell spent decades studying mythologies, religions, and folklore from around the globe, seeking to identify universal themes and structures that reveal shared human experiences and psychological truths. His work gained popular recognition through his televised interviews with Bill Moyers in "The Power of Myth", where he explored how ancient myths remain relevant to modern life. Campbell's ideas have profoundly influenced storytelling in literature, film, and popular culture, with creators like George Lucas citing his work as inspiration for Star Wars.

JANUARY 12

"What's the torture you're comfortable with?"
- Jerry Seinfeld[14]

---

14 "I do the exact same thing now as I did when I was 21 in 1975." Seinfeld's explains. "I sit and play with ideas. I'm never not working on material. Every second of my existence I'm thinking "Could I do something with that". It's like going into the gym every day. You walk in everyday and say "Oh jeeez... I gotta do this again?!". Your blessing in life is when you find the torture you're comfortable with. That's marriage, kids, work, exercise... It is not eating the food you wanna eat... Find the torture you 're comfortable with and you'll do well."
Jerry Seinfeld interview with Howard Stern, 26 June 2013.

Jerry Seinfeld is a comedian, actor, writer, and producer who became one of the most successful entertainers in television history through his groundbreaking sitcom "Seinfeld." He started as a stand-up comedian in the late 1970s before co-creating "Seinfeld" with Larry David, which ran from 1989 to 1998 and became known as "a show about nothing." The series revolutionised television comedy with its focus on the minutiae of daily life and neurotic observations about modern society. After the show ended, he returned to stand-up comedy and created the web series "Comedians in Cars Getting Coffee," where he interviews fellow comedians while driving vintage cars. Beyond entertainment, he's known for his philosophical approach to comedy and life, often discussing the craft of joke-writing and the importance of discipline and consistency in achieving mastery.

JANUARY 13

"Would you be willing to give your life to save the world if no one ever knew your name? If anonymity was the price you would have to pay for significance, would it be too great a price?"
- *Erwin Raphael McManus*[15]

---

[15] "To live a life of courage" McManus explains, "is not a guarantee of prestige or adulation. It only matters if you live and die fulfilling the mission you were born for."

Uprising: A Revolution of the Soul, Erwin Raphael McManus, 2006.

Erwin Raphael McManus is a pastor, author, and cultural thought leader who serves as the lead pastor of Mosaic, a multicultural church in Los Angeles that has become known for its creative and unconventional approach to faith and community. Known as a cultural pioneer for his integration of creativity and spirituality, McManus has written numerous bestselling books including "Soul Cravings," "Chasing Daylight," and "The Artisan Soul," which explore the intersection of faith, creativity, and human potential. His church, Mosaic, is described as a global community of faith built on the belief that every human is created to live a life of purpose, creativity, and courage. Beyond his pastoral work, McManus is a sought-after motivational speaker who has worked with Fortune 100 and Fortune 500 companies including Nike, Sony, Apple, and TED, speaking on topics like reinventing organisations, culture, and community. As a futurist and cultural thought leader, he focuses on helping people experience peace through artful intention and confronting internal battles. His work consistently emphasises the importance of embracing creativity, courage, and authentic living as essential elements of both faith and human flourishing.

JANUARY 14

"Would I be happy with this result if no one other than me and my family could see it, and I didn't compare the result to the appearance of other people's success?"
- Morgan Housel[16]

---

[16] "It's impossible to win the social-comparison game because there's always someone getting richer faster than you." Housel explains. "Once you stop playing the game your attention instantly shifts internally, to what makes you and your family happy and fulfilled. It makes it so much easier to enjoy your money, regardless of how you choose to spend and invest it."
Quiet Compounding, Morgan Housel, collabfund.com, June 17, 2024.
Morgan Housel is a financial writer, investor, and author best known for his bestselling book "The Psychology of Money," which explores how emotions, behaviour, and psychology drive financial decisions more than technical knowledge or intelligence. A former columnist for The Motley Fool and The Wall Street Journal, Housel has become one of the most influential voices in behavioural finance and investment psychology. His writing focuses on the intersection of psychology and money, emphasising that financial success depends more on how you behave than what you know. "The Psychology of Money" became a massive bestseller by making complex financial concepts accessible through storytelling and real-world examples, showing how factors like luck, risk, time, and human nature affect wealth building. Housel is a partner at The Collaborative Fund, a venture capital firm, and continues to write about finance, economics, and human behaviour through his blog and various publications. His work emphasises long-term thinking, the power of compounding, the importance of saving, and understanding that everyone's financial situation and goals are different. He's known for his ability to distil complex financial wisdom into memorable, practical insights that resonate with both novice and experienced investors.

JANUARY 15

"What is so precious to you that you'd never sacrifice it for anything?"
- Gregory Stock[17]

---

17 *The Book of Questions: Revised and Updated*, Gregory Stock, 2013.

Gregory Stock is a biotech entrepreneur, bioethicist, best-selling author and public communicator who is a leading authority on the broad impacts of genomic and other advanced technologies in the life sciences. He founded the influential Program on Medicine, Technology and Society at UCLA's School of Medicine in 1997 and served as its director for ten years while leading a broad effort to explore critical technologies poised to reshape medical science, Stock is the co-founder and former CEO of Signum Biosciences and has held academic positions at institutions including the University of California, Los Angeles (UCLA) and the Icahn School of Medicine at Mount Sinai. Gregory Stock is a scholar in the evolution of humanity as it is and will be, aided by technology. He is in the forefront of the debate on biotech policy, is a frequent speaker at conferences that study the issue, and contributes to scientific journals in the United States and abroad. His work focuses on the intersection of technology and human enhancement, exploring ethical questions around genetic engineering, life extension, and the future of human evolution. His insight at where technology and ethics connect have made him a popular guest on TV and radio, and he has been a prominent voice in discussions about biotechnology policy and the implications of emerging life sciences technologies for society, medicine, and human development.

JANUARY 16

*"If you want to love what you do,
abandon the passion mindset
('what can the world offer me?')
and instead adopt the craftsman mindset
('what can I offer the world?')"*
- Cal Newport[18]

---

[18] "I've always thought of only two questions that have mattered to me personally." system scientist and author Peter Senge explains. "One is what is really needed in the world and the second is what's really important to me and how these two intersect. It's always been a reflective process – spiralling around these two poles."
So Good They Can't Ignore You: Why Skills Trump Passion in the Quest for Work You Love, Cal Newport, 2012.

Cal Newport is a computer science professor at Georgetown University and bestselling author known for his work on productivity, focus, and the intersection of technology with meaningful work. He's written several influential books including "Deep Work," which argues for the importance of sustained, distraction-free concentration in producing valuable work, and "Digital Minimalism," which advocates for a more intentional relationship with technology. Newport is also known for "So Good They Can't Ignore You," where he challenges the conventional wisdom of "follow your passion" and instead argues that passion develops from mastery and that craftsman-like dedication to building rare and valuable skills leads to career satisfaction. Through his books, blog, and podcast, he promotes strategies for managing attention, resisting digital distractions, and creating systems that support focused, high-quality work.

JANUARY 17

"What are you excessively curious about — curious to a degree that would bore most other people?"
- Paul Graham[19]

---

[19] "There's a kind of excited curiosity that's both the engine and the rudder of great work." Graham explains. "It will not only drive you, but if you let it have its way, will also show you what to work on. What are you excessively curious about — curious to a degree that would bore most other people? That's what you're looking for. Once you've found something you're excessively interested in, the next step is to learn enough about it to get you to one of the frontiers of knowledge. Knowledge expands fractally, and from a distance its edges look smooth, but once you learn enough to get close to one, they turn out to be full of gaps. The next step is to notice them. This takes some skill, because your brain wants to ignore such gaps in order to make a simpler model of the world. Many discoveries have come from asking questions about things that everyone else took for granted."

How To Do Great Work, Paul Graham, paulgraham.com, July 2023.

Paul Graham is a computer scientist, entrepreneur, essayist, and venture capitalist who co-founded Y Combinator, the world's most influential startup accelerator. A programmer by training, he co-created Viaweb in the 1990s, one of the first web-based software applications, which was sold to Yahoo for $49 million and became Yahoo Store. Y Combinator has funded over 5,000 startups including Airbnb, Dropbox, Stripe, Reddit, and DoorDash, fundamentally changing how early-stage companies get funded and mentored. Beyond his business ventures, Graham is renowned for his essays on startups, programming, and life, published on his website paulgraham.com. His writing covers topics from technical programming concepts to startup advice to broader philosophical observations, and his essays like "Do Things That Don't Scale" and "Maker's Schedule, Manager's Schedule" have become foundational reading in Silicon Valley. Graham is known for his clear, thoughtful writing style and contrarian insights about entrepreneurship, such as emphasising the importance of building something people want rather than focusing on business plans. He stepped back from day-to-day operations at Y Combinator to focus more on his writing and thinking, but remains one of the most respected voices in the startup ecosystem.

JANUARY 18

*"The question we should be asking ourselves is:
'Who do I need to become?'"*
- Darren Hardy[20]

---

[20] "When most people set out to achieve new goals," Hardy writes, "they ask, 'Okay, I have my goal; now what do I need to do to get it?' It's not a bad question, but it's not the first question that must be tackled either. The question we should be asking ourselves is: 'Who do I need to become?'"
The Compound Effect, Darren Hardy, 2011.
Darren Hardy is an author, keynote speaker, and business mentor who gained prominence as the former publisher of SUCCESS magazine and New York Times best-selling author of books including "The Compound Effect" and "Living Your Best Year Ever." For over 25 years, he served as the central curator of the success media business, founding publisher of SUCCESS magazine, and leader of three television networks, giving him unprecedented access to interview and investigate the most successful entrepreneurs and business leaders in the world. Hardy's philosophy centres on the power of small, consistent daily actions compounding over time to create extraordinary results, which he articulated in "The Compound Effect." He has become a sought-after success mentor to CEOs and high-performance achievers, combining practical business wisdom with motivational speaking to help individuals and organisations achieve breakthrough results.

JANUARY 19

*"... you don't ask what do I want from life?
You ask a different set of questions:
What does life want from me?
What are my circumstances calling me to do?"*
- David Brooks[21]

---

[21] Brooks suggests shifting the focus from personal desires to societal needs when considering one's role in life. Instead of asking "What do I want from life?", he proposes asking, "What does life want from me?" and "What are my circumstances calling me to do?" This perspective emphasises responding to external demands and opportunities rather than solely pursuing personal ambitions. Frances Perkins was an exemplar of this approach: an American workers-rights advocate who served as the fourth United States Secretary of Labor from 1933 to 1945 (Perkins was the first woman ever to serve in a presidential cabinet). She sacrificed everything she had to serve the cause of workers' rights, believing that this cause was calling her.

The Road to Character, David Brooks, 2015.

David Brooks is a prominent American journalist, political commentator, and author who writes for The New York Times, where he has been an op-ed columnist since 2003. Known for his thoughtful analysis of American politics, culture, and society, Brooks often takes a moderate conservative perspective while focusing on themes like community, character, and moral development. He's written several influential books including "The Social Animal," which explores human behaviour and decision-making, "The Road to Character," which examines the difference between résumé virtues and eulogy virtues, and "The Second Mountain," about finding deeper meaning and purpose in life. Before joining the Times, Brooks worked at publications like The Wall Street Journal, The Weekly Standard, and The Atlantic. He's also a regular commentator on PBS NewsHour and NPR, and teaches at Yale University. Brooks is known for his ability to bridge political divides and his interest in how psychology, sociology, and moral philosophy intersect with public policy and everyday life.

JANUARY 20

"All other things being equal, why wouldn't you work on what interests you the most?"
- Paul Graham[22]

---

[22] Graham's question is similar to the one asked by venture capitalist Bill Gurley: "If you've only got one shot, and then it's all over why not do what makes you most happy? *Runnin' Down a Dream: How to Succeed and Thrive in a Career You Love*, University of Texas, September 2018.
When To Do What You Love, Paul Graham, paulgraham.com, September 2024.
Paul Graham is a computer scientist, entrepreneur, essayist, and venture capitalist who co-founded Y Combinator, the world's most influential startup accelerator. A programmer by training, he co-created Viaweb in the 1990s, one of the first web-based software applications, which was sold to Yahoo for $49 million and became Yahoo Store. Y Combinator has funded over 5,000 startups including Airbnb, Dropbox, Stripe, Reddit, and DoorDash, fundamentally changing how early-stage companies get funded and mentored. Beyond his business ventures, Graham is renowned for his essays on startups, programming, and life, published on his website paulgraham.com. His writing covers topics from technical programming concepts to startup advice to broader philosophical observations, and his essays like "Do Things That Don't Scale" and "Maker's Schedule, Manager's Schedule" have become foundational reading in Silicon Valley. Graham is known for his clear, thoughtful writing style and contrarian insights about entrepreneurship, such as emphasising the importance of building something people want rather than focusing on business plans. He stepped back from day-to-day operations at Y Combinator to focus more on his writing and thinking, but remains one of the most respected voices in the startup ecosystem.

JANUARY 21

*"What would you do if you had
a second chance at life?"
- Brian Pennie*[23]

---

[23] Pennie's question channels holocaust survivor and psychologist Viktor Frankl's advice: "So live as if you were living already for the second time and as if you had acted the first time as wrongly as you are about to act now!"

Bonus Time: A true story of surviving the worst and discovering the magic of everyday, Brian Pennie, 2020.

Brian Pennie is a neuroscientist, keynote speaker, resilience specialist, and author who overcame a 15-year heroin addiction to become a doctor and university lecturer. On October 8th 2013, Brian experienced his first day clean after 15 years of chronic heroin addiction, and since then has transformed his life through mindfulness and neuroscience-based practices. In 2017 he graduated with a degree in psychology, winning several awards, including a fully funded PhD scholarship in Trinity College Institute of Neuroscience. He's become a keynote speaker, PhD student, a lecturer in Trinity College and University College Dublin, a life change strategist, a radio presenter, an author and the creator of an online course called "Master Your Self-Talk". He authored the memoir "Bonus Time," sharing his journey from addiction to redemption, providing insights into his transformative experiences and lessons learned. Pennie specialises in "real resilience" and uses his extraordinary personal transformation to show others that change is possible, combining his lived experience with scientific expertise in neuroscience and behavioural change.

JANUARY 22

"Here are a few questions to ask yourself in order to start identifying your values -
deep down, what matters to me?
what relationships do I want to build?
what do I want my life to be about?
how do I feel most of the time?
what kind of situations make me feel most vital?"
- Susan David[24]

---

24 *Emotional Agility: Get Unstuck, Embrace Change, and Thrive in Work and Life*, Susan David, 2016.

Susan David is a Harvard Medical School psychologist, bestselling author, and leading expert on emotional intelligence and resilience. She's best known for her book "Emotional Agility," which introduces a research-based approach to navigating emotions and aligning actions with values rather than being controlled by fleeting feelings. David's work focuses on helping people develop the skills to face challenges, make meaningful changes, and thrive in an uncertain world. She's a frequent contributor to Harvard Business Review and has delivered popular TED Talks on emotional agility and the importance of being honest about difficult emotions rather than forcing positivity. As a consultant and speaker, David works with organisations worldwide to help leaders and teams build psychological resilience and create healthier workplace cultures. Her approach emphasises the importance of acknowledging difficult emotions without being hijacked by them, using values as a compass for decision-making, and making small deliberate adjustments rather than dramatic changes. David's research and practical frameworks have made her a sought-after voice on mental health, leadership, and personal development in both academic and corporate settings.

JANUARY 23

"How do I figure out what is worth suffering for?"
- Graham Weaver[25]

---

[25] "To help my students get clarity, I give them a simple exercise:" Weaver writes, "Imagine you find a lamp, and inside is a genie with one specific power. It can't grant any wish, but it can ensure that whatever career you throw yourself into will eventually work out great. It's going to have ups and downs; it might take longer than you think or be harder than you think. But ultimately, you'll succeed. Whatever you would do if that genie granted you that wish, that's what you would do in your life, absent the fear of failure. And I would argue, in most circumstances that is what you should choose to do with your life."

Three Principles of Leadership, Graham Weaver, grahamweaver.com, 14 December 2023.

Graham Weaver is the founder and managing partner of Alpine Investors, a private equity firm based in San Francisco that specialises in software and services businesses. He started Alpine in his dorm room at Stanford Graduate School of Business, where he earned his MBA in 1999, and has been in private equity for over 20 years. Weaver is also a lecturer at Stanford's Graduate School of Business, where he teaches popular courses and has delivered notable "Last Lectures" to graduating classes. His investment philosophy centres on the belief that exceptional people create exceptional businesses, making Alpine a "people-driven" firm. Beyond his business activities, Weaver is known for his writing and speaking on topics related to entrepreneurship, leadership, and personal development, often sharing frameworks and insights from his extensive experience in both private equity and academia.

JANUARY 24

"What is it on this planet that needs doing that I know something about, that probably won't happen unless I take responsibility for it?"
- Buckminster Fuller[26]

---

[26] The question is linked to a pivotal moment in Fuller's life in 1927, when he contemplated suicide after a series of business failures and the death of his daughter. He ultimately decided against it, choosing instead to live his life as if he had already died and as "an experiment to find what a single individual could contribute to changing the world and benefiting all humanity." The question became a guiding principle for him from that point forward.
Wherever You Go, There You Are, Jon Kabat-Zinn, 2005.
R. Buckminster Fuller (1895-1983) was an engineer, architect, and futurist who developed the geodesic dome, the only large dome that can be set directly on the ground as a complete structure. A renowned 20th century inventor and visionary, Fuller dedicated his life to making the world work for all of humanity, operating as a practical philosopher who demonstrated his ideas as inventions. Fuller developed numerous inventions and architectural designs, and popularised the widely known geodesic dome. Fuller popularised the structure and gained the US patent, erecting models across the United States. The author of more than twenty-eight books and the creator of numerous inventions, he was concerned with the question of whether or not humanity would be able to survive as residents on the planet Earth for an extended amount of time and is recognised as the father of the modern sustainability movement.

JANUARY 25

"Why do I choose to lead?"
- Doug Conant[27]

---

[27] Before attempting to lead others, there is a question that must be answered. It is not "can I lead?" or "do I want to lead?" The question is do I *need* to lead? The brilliant scientist Richard Hamming suggested a way of answering this question: "When your vision of what you want to do is what you can do single-handedly, then you should pursue it. The day your vision, what you think needs to be done, is bigger than what you can do single-handedly, then you have to move toward management [leadership]. And the bigger the vision is, the farther in management [leadership] you have to go."

Leaders, You Can (And Must) Do Better. Here's How., Doug Conant, LinkedIn, June 16, 2016.

Doug Conant is a business executive and leadership expert who served as CEO of Campbell Soup Company from 2001 to 2011, where he led one of the most successful business turnarounds in corporate history. When he took over, Campbell's was struggling with declining sales and low employee engagement, but under his leadership, the company achieved significant growth and became known for its strong workplace culture. Conant is particularly known for his approach to "people-centric leadership" and his belief in the importance of employee engagement and authentic leadership. After leaving Campbell's, he founded ConantLeadership, a leadership development firm, and has written several books on leadership including "TouchPoints" and "The Blueprint." He's also served as chairman of Avon Products and has been involved with various nonprofit organisations. Conant is a frequent speaker on leadership topics and is known for his philosophy that leaders must genuinely care for their people while also delivering strong business results. He emphasises the importance of building trust, inspiring performance, and creating environments where employees can thrive.

JANUARY 26

"What can a person do uncommonly well?"
- Peter Drucker[28]

---

[28] Jim Collins explains a key lesson he learnt from Drucker was "do what you're made for". "One of Drucker's most arresting points is that we are all incompetent at most things." Collins writes. "The crucial question is not how to turn incompetence into excellence, but to ask, "What can a person do uncommonly well?" This leads, inevitably, to a conclusion: your first responsibility is to determine your own distinctive competences—what you can do uncommonly well, what you are truly made for—and then navigate your life and career in direct alignment. "To focus on weakness is not only foolish; it is irresponsible," challenges Drucker. Does Drucker's "Build on strength" imperative mean never confronting our (or others') deficiencies? Yes and no. It means that if you're made to be a distance runner, don't try to be a middle linebacker. At the same time, you must address deficiencies that directly impede full flowering of your strength. When Michael Jordan was reaching the end of his basketball career, he could no longer fly to the basket with the same height and power as when he was younger, so he began to build a strength he'd never previously had: a fade-away jumper. He eradicated a crucial weakness within his strength, turning his fade-away jumper into yet another Jordan-can-kill you-strength on the court. Do what you're made for, yes, but then get better and better; eradicate weakness, yes, but only within strength."

Ten Lessons I Learned from Peter Drucker, Jim Collins, Foreword to the 50th Anniversary Edition of The Effective Executive, May 17, 2016.

Peter Drucker (1909-2005) was a management consultant, educator, and author widely regarded as the founder of modern management theory. Drucker wrote over 30 books and countless articles that fundamentally shaped how we think about business, leadership, and organisational effectiveness. He coined many concepts that are now management staples, including "management by objectives," "knowledge worker," and the idea that the purpose of business is to create customers. His most influential works include "The Practice of Management" and "The Effective Executive". Drucker emphasised that management is both an art and a science, focusing on people rather than just processes, and he predicted many major business trends including the rise of the information economy and the importance of innovation. Beyond business, he was a prolific social commentator who wrote about democracy, society, and the role of institutions. His insights remain remarkably relevant today, and he's remembered for his practical wisdom and his belief that effective management could make organisations more productive while also making work more meaningful for people.

JANUARY 27

*"What does a successful and meaningful life
look like to you?
What is it that I want from this life?"
- Mark Manson*[29]

---

[29] "Personal values" Manson explains, "are the measuring sticks by which we determine what is a successful and meaningful life."

Personal Values: How to Know Who You Really Are, Mark Manson, markmanson.net.

Mark Manson is a bestselling author, blogger, and entrepreneur who has become one of the most influential voices in modern self-help through his irreverent, no-nonsense approach to life's challenges. Manson initially gained attention through his popular blog challenging conventional wisdom about happiness and success with psychology, philosophy, and profanity-laced humour. His breakthrough came with the 2016 publication of "The Subtle Art of Not Giving a F*ck," which became an international bestseller by arguing that the key to a better life is choosing what to care about more carefully and accepting that struggle is inevitable. His writing combines academic research with accessible language and contrarian thinking that challenges typical positive psychology approaches. Instead of promoting endless optimism, Manson advocates for embracing negative emotions, accepting responsibility, and focusing on what truly matters. His work has particularly resonated with those who appreciate his honest, unvarnished take on life's difficulties and rejection of superficial solutions.

JANUARY 28

"What do you love doing so much that the words failure and success essentially become irrelevant?"
- Elizabeth Gilbert[30]

---

[30] Find those activities that are intrinsically rewarding and fulfilling, regardless of external validation or achievement. The question highlights the importance of pursuing passions and creative endeavours not for the sake of success, but for the joy and transformation they bring to one's life. Another test is: "If I were the last person on earth, would I still do it?"
Big Magic: Creative Living Beyond Fear, Elizabeth Gilbert, 2016.

Elizabeth Gilbert is a best-selling author best known for her memoir "Eat, Pray, Love," which became a global phenomenon after its 2006 publication, spending over 200 weeks on the New York Times bestseller list and inspiring a major motion picture. The book chronicled her journey of self-discovery through Italy, India, and Indonesia following a difficult divorce, resonating with millions of readers seeking meaning and transformation. Beyond this blockbuster success, Gilbert has written several novels including "The Signature of All Things," a historical fiction work about a 19th-century botanist, and "City of Girls," demonstrating her versatility as a storyteller. She's also become a prominent voice on creativity and the writing life, delivering a popular TED talk on genius and authoring "Big Magic: Creative Living Beyond Fear," which explores the mysteries and challenges of creative work while encouraging others to embrace curiosity over fear in their creative pursuits.

JANUARY 29

"What is the work you can't not do?"
- Scott Dinsmore[31]

---

[31] Dinsmore shared his journey of quitting a job that made him miserable and spending four years figuring out how to find work that was joyful and meaningful. After following conventional career advice and realising he hated his corporate job, Dinsmore developed three steps for anyone wanting to transform their career or work. The framework focuses on self-discovery as the first step to become a self-expert and understand yourself, followed by identifying your unique strengths and values, and taking action to do work aligned with your passions. Dinsmore emphasises that finding fulfilling work requires deep self-knowledge and the courage to pursue what truly matters to you, rather than simply building an impressive resume.

How to find work you love, Scott Dinsmore, TEDxGoldenGatePark, October 2012.

Scott Dinsmore (1982-2015) was the founder of Live Your Legend, a career and connection platform to inspire people to find their passion. He delivered one of the most watched TED talks of all time "How to Find and Do Work You Love," which has been watched millions of times and is among the top 20 of over 40,000 TED talks. An entrepreneur, coach, and value investor obsessed with adventure, life experiments, and learning, Dinsmore built a global community dedicated to helping people discover meaningful work and surround themselves with supportive people. Tragically, Dinsmore died at age 33 while climbing Mount Kilimanjaro in 2015, during what was meant to be an epic year-long world tour with his wife Chelsea. Despite his brief life, he created lasting impact through Live Your Legend, inspiring tens of thousands of people to pursue careers aligned with their passions and values, with his work continuing through the community he built.

JANUARY 30

"Leadership for what purpose?"
- Peter Drucker[32]

---

[32] Drucker's penetrating question cuts to the heart of authentic leadership by demanding that leaders articulate not merely what they seek to accomplish, but why their leadership matters. Drucker understood that without a compelling purpose that serves something greater than self-interest, leadership becomes sophisticated manipulation and is ultimately hollow. The question forces leaders to confront whether they are leading toward a future worth creating, one that honours human dignity and contributes meaningfully to the communities they serve. Drucker's question echoes scientist Richard Hamming who said, "When your vision of what you want to do is what you can do single-handedly, then you should pursue it. The day your vision, what you think needs to be done, is bigger than what you can do single-handedly, then you have to move toward management. And the bigger the vision is, the farther in management you have to go." From You and Your Research, Transcription of the Bell Communications Research Colloquium Seminar, 7th March 1986. Another (amusing) perspective on this question is Roger McGough's poem The Leader.

A Year with Peter Drucker, Joseph A. Maciariello, 2014.

Peter Drucker (1909-2005) was a management consultant, educator, and author widely regarded as the founder of modern management theory. Drucker wrote over 30 books and countless articles that fundamentally shaped how we think about business, leadership, and organisational effectiveness. He coined many concepts that are now management staples, including "management by objectives," "knowledge worker," and the idea that the purpose of business is to create customers. His most influential works include "The Practice of Management" and "The Effective Executive". Drucker emphasised that management is both an art and a science, focusing on people rather than just processes, and he predicted many major business trends including the rise of the information economy and the importance of innovation. Beyond business, he was a prolific social commentator who wrote about democracy, society, and the role of institutions. His insights remain remarkably relevant today, and he's remembered for his practical wisdom and his belief that effective management could make organisations more productive while also making work more meaningful for people.

JANUARY 31

"If today were the last day of my life, would I want to do what I am about to do today?"
- Steve Jobs[33]

---

[33] Jobs explained, "If the Answer is 'no' for too many days in a row, I know I need to change something." The question was poignant because Jobs shared it just a year after his initial cancer diagnosis, when he had faced the possibility of having only months to live. He used this daily practice as "the most important tool I've ever encountered to help me make the big choices in life" because it stripped away external expectations, pride, and fear, leaving only what truly mattered. The question embodies Jobs' philosophy that confronting mortality clarifies priorities and provides the courage to follow one's heart and intuition rather than living someone else's life. Although at the time of the speech Jobs believed he was free of cancer, sadly he would pass away six years later.

Commencement Address at Stanford University, Steve Jobs, June 12, 2005.

Steve Jobs (1955-2011) was an entrepreneur and visionary who co-founded Apple Inc. and became one of the most influential figures in the technology industry. Known for his perfectionist approach to design and marketing, Jobs helped revolutionise multiple industries through products like the Macintosh computer, iPod, iPhone, and iPad, transforming Apple from a garage startup into one of the world's most valuable companies. His philosophy centred on simplicity, intuitive user experience, famously saying he wanted to create products that were at "the intersection of technology and humanities." After being forced out of Apple in 1985, he founded NeXT and purchased the computer graphics division that became Pixar Animation Studios, which produced groundbreaking films like "Toy Story", before he returned to Apple in 1997. Jobs' demanding leadership style and attention to detail were legendary, as was his ability to anticipate consumer desires and create markets for products people didn't know they wanted, leaving behind a legacy that continues to influence technology design and corporate culture.

FEBRUARY

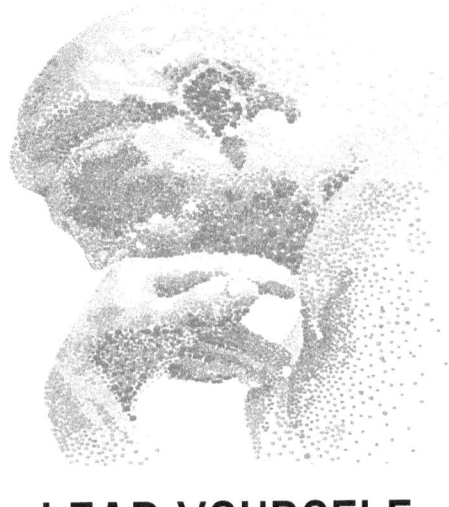

LEAD YOURSELF

FEBRUARY 1

*"If you wouldn't follow yourself,
why should anyone else?"*
- John Maxwell[34]

---

[34] "Here is the very heart and soul of the matter of leadership:" Dee Hock, founder and CEO of Visa writes. "If you seek to lead, invest 50% of your time (attention) leading yourself-your own purpose, ethics, principles, motivation, conduct. Invest at least 20% leading those with authority over you and 15% leading your peers – Use the remainder to induce those you "work for" to understand and practice the theory – If you don't understand that you should be working for your mislabelled "subordinates," then you know nothing of leadership. You know only tyranny - Lead yourself, lead your superiors, lead your peers, and free your people to do the same. All else is trivial."

The 360 Degree Leader: Developing Your Influence from Anywhere in the Organization, John C. Maxwell, 2016.

John C. Maxwell is an author, speaker, and leadership expert widely recognised as one of the world's foremost authorities on leadership development and personal growth. Having written over 100 books, many of which have become New York Times bestsellers, Maxwell has sold more than 31 million copies worldwide, with titles including "The 21 Irrefutable Laws of Leadership," "Developing the Leader Within You," and "The 5 Levels of Leadership" becoming foundational texts in leadership education. A former pastor who transitioned into full-time leadership training, Maxwell founded several organisations including EQUIP and the John Maxwell Team, which have trained millions of leaders across more than 180 countries. His teaching emphasises practical leadership principles, personal development, and the importance of adding value to others, making complex leadership concepts accessible to audiences ranging from corporate executives to community leaders. Maxwell's influence extends globally through his speaking engagements, coaching programs, and mentorship initiatives, establishing him as a pivotal figure in modern leadership development.

FEBRUARY 2

"How can I continually improve the quality of the actions that I repeat every day (as those make up almost all of my life)?"
- Jordan Peterson[35]

---

[35] Peterson echoes coach John Wooden. Wooden was one of the most successful sporting coaches of all time, his teams winning ten NCAA championships in a twelve-year period, including seven in a row. "Don't look for the quick, big improvement." Wooden advised, "Seek the small improvement one day at a time. That's the only way it happens – and when it happens, it lasts."

What are some deep, profound, thought-provoking questions to ponder over?, Jordan B. Peterson, Quora, 2014.

Jordan B. Peterson is a clinical psychologist, professor, and author who gained international prominence for his views on free speech, political correctness, and personal responsibility. He taught at Harvard University and the University of Toronto, specialising in personality psychology, psychopathology, and the psychology of religious and ideological belief. His bestselling book "12 Rules for Life: An Antidote to Chaos" combines psychology, philosophy, and personal anecdotes to offer practical advice for living a meaningful life, emphasizing individual responsibility, self-improvement, and traditional values. His second book, "Beyond Order: 12 More Rules for Life," continues these themes. Peterson's lectures and online content focus on topics like mythology, religion, personal development, and the psychological significance of stories and archetypes.

FEBRUARY 3

"What small thing can you do today that your future self will come back and thank you for?"
- David Whyte[36]

---

[36] Considering your future self when making decisions can make all the difference. Whyte asks some powerful questions. "... how could you be the ancestor of your own future happiness? What conversation could you begin? What promise could you make? What promise, even, could you break, that would make you the ancestor of your future happiness ... and thank yourself for having stepped out on that path into a future which has made both a better world for yourself and the world in which you have given your gifts?" *On Being with Krista Tippett: David Whyte Poetry From the On Being Gathering (Opening Night)*, September 10, 2018.
All The Beautiful Questions That David Whyte Asked Me, Andjelka Jankovic, lifecurator.co, 6 March 2022.

David Whyte is a poet, philosopher, and organisational consultant who has uniquely bridged the worlds of poetry and business leadership. He began his career as a poet and speaker and began taking his poetry and philosophy to larger audiences, including consulting and lecturing on organisational leadership models in the US and UK. Whyte is one of the few poets to take his perspectives on creativity into the field of organisational development, where he works with many American and international companies. His breakthrough book "The Heart Aroused: Poetry and the Preservation of The Soul in Corporate America" topped the business best seller lists. He has written ten volumes of poetry and four books of prose, including the popular "Consolations: The Solace, Nourishment and Underlying Meaning of Everyday Words," which explores the deeper meanings of common words like friendship, gratitude, and regret. Whyte is an associate fellow at Saïd Business School at the University of Oxford and is known for his direct and accessible language that encourages introspection and contemplation. His work centres on helping people find meaning and authenticity in their professional lives, using poetry as a lens to examine work, relationships, and personal identity. He continues to speak and consult with organisations worldwide about bringing soul and creativity into the workplace.

FEBRUARY 4

"What is my code?"
- Doug Conant[37]

---

[37] "As you encounter increasingly challenging decisions, you will need to have a set of principles that provides underlying consistency throughout your interactions." Conant explains. "Without that consistency, you may come across as a chameleon-like leader, mercurial and unreliable. Alternatively, when you have a clear code, people know what you stand for and how you choose to walk in the world. So let's look at how you can delve deep to unearth the code that is lying within you, waiting to be revealed through careful contemplation. Begin by thinking about your childhood. Much of what we consider "the right thing to do" was encoded very early in life. Even before first grade, it's likely we knew how to treat the kids who were smaller than we were, how to deal with bullies, how to share, and what it meant to be responsible. Now, go a little further. Think about how your code continued to evolve over the years as a teacher taught you that high standards were a sign of ethics, a coach helped you learn what it meant to be a real team player, or a boss imparted her code about what it means to take full responsibility for a job." The question echoes NFL coach Pete Carroll's question "what's your philosophy?" Carroll often begins his talks with CEOs, coaches and investors with a question to the audience: "Raise your hand if you have a philosophy for your team or terizerac." Most people do not raise their hand. Carroll follows-up by asking, "Can you describe your philosophy in 25 words or less?"

Leaders: Do You Know What You Stand For?, Douglas R. Conant, conantleadership.com, June 4, 2014.

Doug Conant is a business executive and leadership expert who served as CEO of Campbell Soup Company from 2001 to 2011, where he led one of the most successful business turnarounds in corporate history. When he took over, Campbell's was struggling with declining sales and low employee engagement, but under his leadership, the company achieved significant growth and became known for its strong workplace culture. Conant is particularly known for his approach to "people-centric leadership" and his belief in the importance of employee engagement and authentic leadership. After leaving Campbell's, he founded ConantLeadership, a leadership development firm, and has written several books on leadership including "TouchPoints" and "The Blueprint." He's also served as chairman of Avon Products and has been involved with various nonprofit organisations. Conant is a frequent speaker on leadership topics and is known for his philosophy that leaders must genuinely care for their people while also delivering strong business results. He emphasises the importance of building trust, inspiring performance, and creating environments where employees can thrive.

FEBRUARY 5

*"Who are the people, ideas and books
that magnify your spirit?"*
Maria Popova[38]

---

[38] It is helpful to think about your resilience as a bucket - a leaky bucket with holes in it. The "holes" in your bucket symbolise the stresses of everyday life. They represent outgoings, resilience withdrawals. The actions we can take to reverse stress are what you tip into your bucket to fill it. These are "uplifts". More has to be going in than going out to avoid being drained. "Seek out what magnifies your spirit." Popova writes. "Patti Smith, in discussing William Blake and her creative influences, talks about writers and artists who magnified her spirit — it's a beautiful phrase and a beautiful notion. Who are the people, ideas, and books that magnify your spirit? Find them, hold on to them, and visit them often. Use them not only as a remedy once spiritual malaise has already infected your vitality but as a vaccine administered while you are healthy to protect your radiance." Popova's question echoes poet David Whyte who asks "What is it – just by making contact – that brings me alive?"

18 Life-Learnings from 18 Years of The Marginalian, Maria Popova, The Marginalian, 22 October 2024.

Maria Popova is a writer, literary curator, and the creator of *The Marginalian* (formerly known as *Brain Pickings*), one of the most influential cultural websites on the internet. In 2006, she began the blog Brain Pickings as an email sent each week to seven of her friends. It has since been included in the Library of Congress permanent web archive of culturally valuable materials. What makes Popova's work remarkable is her ability to synthesise ideas across multiple disciplines. For 17 years, she has kept an online literary journal of sorts, a catalogue of what she's been reading, contemplating and grappling with across multiple disciplines: literature, science, art, philosophy, poetry, and what she has called "various other tentacles of human thought and feeling". For nearly two decades, it has remained free and ad-free thanks to patronage from readers. She has no staff, no interns, not even an assistant. Popova has written for publications including The Atlantic, Wired UK, and The Huffington Post. Her work explores the intersection of science, literature, philosophy, and art, often featuring deep dives into the lives and works of historical figures, scientists, artists, and thinkers. She started her site as a personal record of reckoning with her own search for meaning, and it has evolved into one of the most thoughtful and intellectually rich resources on the web, earning her recognition as a leading voice in contemporary cultural criticism and philosophical inquiry.

FEBRUARY 6

"Where is your mindset after something bad happens to you?"
Jay Wright[39]

---

[39] A defining trait separating elite performers isn't talent, it is recovery speed after setbacks. The top athletes master the art of rapid emotional reset, understanding that lingering in negative states destroys downstream performance. Novak Djokovic captures this perfectly: "the difference between the guys who are able to be the biggest champions and the ones that are struggling to get to the highest level is the ability to not stay in those emotions for too long". He acknowledges the emotion, releases it immediately, then bounces back and resets. Meanwhile, struggling players spiral into negative visualisation, hitting exactly where they don't want the ball to go. Josh Waitzkin, master of chess and martial arts explains, "the first mistake rarely proves disastrous but the downward spiral of the second, third and fourth error creates a devastating chain reaction". The key is how rapidly you can regain your composure. Performance effectiveness is inversely related to recovery time. The faster you reset, the better you perform. This applies equally to leading others—your recovery speed directly impacts your team's resilience. Think of maritime rescue vessels, which must right themselves within seconds of capsizing. Train yourself to be self-correcting.

Attitude: Develop a Winning Mindset on and off the Court, Jay Wright, 2017.

Jay Wright is a legendary college basketball coach best known for his highly successful 21-year tenure at Villanova University, where he built one of the most respected programs in college basketball. Under his leadership, the Wildcats won two NCAA national championships (2016 and 2018), with the 2016 title game featuring one of the most iconic moments in tournament history when Kris Jenkins hit a buzzer-beater three-pointer to defeat North Carolina. Wright's teams were known for their disciplined style of play, exceptional three-point shooting, and strong defensive schemes. Beyond the championships, he led Villanova to four Final Four appearances and consistently competed at the highest levels of college basketball. Wright was widely respected for his leadership philosophy, emphasising character development alongside basketball skills, and was known for his impeccable sideline presence - always dressed in sharp suits and maintaining composure under pressure. He was inducted into the Basketball Hall of Fame and received numerous coaching awards throughout his career. In April 2022, Wright surprised the basketball world by announcing his retirement from coaching at age 60, stepping down while still at the peak of his success. Since retiring, he has remained connected to Villanova as a special assistant to the president and has been involved in various basketball-related activities while focusing more on family time and other interests outside of the intense demands of college coaching.

FEBRUARY 7

*"What type of person do you want to become?
What type of values do you want to stand for?
Which actions do you want to become your habits?"*
- James Clear[40]

---

[40] "Decide in your heart of hearts what really excites and challenges you, and start moving your life in that direction." NASA astronaut and writer Chris Hadfield explains. "Every decision you make, from what you eat to what you do with your time tonight, turns you into who you are tomorrow, and the day after that. Look at who you want to be, and start sculpting yourself into that person. You may not get exactly where you thought you'd be, but you will be doing things that suit you in a profession you believe in. Don't let life randomly kick you into the adult you don't want to become." Long after the accolades of your career achievements have faded, your legacy will be who you have become.

The Top Life Regret of Dying Hospital Patients, James Clear, jamesclear.com.

James Clear is an author, speaker, and entrepreneur best known for his book "Atomic Habits," which became a bestseller and popularised the concept of making small, incremental changes to build better habits and break bad ones. Clear focuses on the science of habit formation, emphasising how tiny improvements compound over time to create remarkable results. His approach centres on four key principles: making habits obvious, attractive, easy, and satisfying. Before his writing career took off, Clear was a successful entrepreneur and has a background in photography and business. He writes regularly about habits, decision-making, and continuous improvement on his website and newsletter, which has attracted millions of readers. Clear's work draws from psychology, neuroscience, and behavioural economics to provide practical strategies for personal and professional development, making complex research accessible to everyday readers seeking to improve their lives through better systems and habits.

FEBRUARY 8

"What is your entertainment to education ratio?"
- Darren Hardy[41]

---

[41] Hardy explains that the best leaders spend much of their time on education, as opposed to pure entertainment. The hours invested in learning each week are a lead indicator of future effectiveness and success. Hardy echoes entrepreneur, motivational speaker and author Jim Rohn who explained, "Successful people have libraries. The rest have big screen TV's".

The Compound Effect, Darren Hardy, 2011.

Darren Hardy is an author, keynote speaker, and business mentor who gained prominence as the former publisher of SUCCESS magazine and New York Times best-selling author of books including "The Compound Effect" and "Living Your Best Year Ever." For over 25 years, he served as the central curator of the success media business, founding publisher of SUCCESS magazine, and leader of three television networks, giving him unprecedented access to interview and investigate the most successful entrepreneurs and business leaders in the world. Hardy's philosophy centres on the power of small, consistent daily actions compounding over time to create extraordinary results, which he articulated in "The Compound Effect." He has become a sought-after success mentor to CEOs and high-performance achievers, combining practical business wisdom with motivational speaking to help individuals and organisations achieve breakthrough results.

FEBRUARY 9

"In every interaction, every decision, every moment, let us ask ourselves: Am I being true? Am I aligning my words and my actions with my deepest values and beliefs? Am I using my voice and my influence to champion honesty, authenticity, and integrity?"
- George Raveling[42]

---

[42] Founding CEO of VISA and author Dee Hock put it this way: "The first and paramount responsibility of anyone who purports to manage is to manage self. One's own integrity, character, ethics, knowledge, temperament, words, and acts. It is never-ending, difficult work, largely ignored in most circumstances. The reason it is ignored is not complicated. It is precisely because it is much more difficult than prescribing and controlling the behaviour of others."

What You're Made For: Powerful Life Lessons from My Career in Sports, George Raveling and Ryan Holiday, 2025.

George Raveling is a Basketball Hall of Fame coach and Nike executive who has had an extraordinary impact on both basketball and sports marketing. After a successful college coaching career at schools including Washington State, Iowa, and USC, he joined Nike at the request of Phil Knight, where he played an integral role in signing a reluctant Michael Jordan. Raveling has worked as the Director for International Basketball for Nike since his retirement from USC and is known as "the iconic leader who brought Michael Jordan to Nike". Beyond basketball, he has a unique connection to civil rights history and having a personal connection to Martin Luther King Jr.'s "I Have a Dream" speech. Raveling was present at the March on Washington on August 28, 1963, and after Dr. King delivered his speech, King handed Raveling the original typewritten copy.

FEBRUARY 10

"Am I investing in myself?"
- John Maxwell[43]

---

[43] Investments in yourself, whether they be personal development, nutrition, books, sabbaticals, etc, all pay dividends. "Generally speaking, investing in yourself is the best thing you can do." Warren Buffett says. "Anything that improves your own talents; nobody can tax it or take it away from you. They can run up huge deficits and the dollar can become worth far less. You can have all kinds of things happen. But if you've got talent yourself, and you've maximized your talent, you've got a tremendous asset that can return ten-fold."

Good Leaders Ask Great Questions: Your Foundation For Successful Leadership, John C. Maxwell, 2014.

John C. Maxwell is an author, speaker, and leadership expert widely recognised as one of the world's foremost authorities on leadership development and personal growth. Having written over 100 books, many of which have become New York Times bestsellers, Maxwell has sold more than 31 million copies worldwide, with titles including "The 21 Irrefutable Laws of Leadership," "Developing the Leader Within You," and "The 5 Levels of Leadership" becoming foundational texts in leadership education. A former pastor who transitioned into full-time leadership training, Maxwell founded several organisations including EQUIP and the John Maxwell Team, which have trained millions of leaders across more than 180 countries. His teaching emphasises practical leadership principles, personal development, and the importance of adding value to others, making complex leadership concepts accessible to audiences ranging from corporate executives to community leaders. Maxwell's influence extends globally through his speaking engagements, coaching programs, and mentorship initiatives, establishing him as a pivotal figure in modern leadership development.

FEBRUARY 11

*"What brings out the best in you?
Is it possible to adjust your life so that you show up more often in situations that bring out your best?
Can you change your posture so that the situations you're in a lot bring out your best instead of your worst?"*
- Seth Godin[44]

---

[44] Godin's question picks up on the idea of knowing your "kryptonite" situations, those circumstances, environments, or triggers that consistently neutralise your strengths and undermine your effectiveness. These personal vulnerabilities vary by individual - a confident speaker might crumble in confrontations, a detail-oriented person might falter under tight deadlines, or a team player might struggle working alone. Recognising your kryptonite situations enables you to avoid them when possible, develop coping strategies, or build support systems to compensate for these predictable weaknesses that compromise your usual competence.

What brings out the best in you?, Seth Godin, seths.blog, April 25, 2020.

Seth Godin is a bestselling author, entrepreneur, and marketing guru who has fundamentally changed how people think about marketing, leadership, and the spread of ideas. He's written over 20 books, including influential titles like "Purple Cow," which popularised the concept that businesses must be remarkable to succeed, "The Tipping Point" predecessor "Unleashing the Ideavirus," and "Linchpin," which argues that indispensable employees are those who bring creativity and humanity to their work. Godin founded several companies, including Yoyodyne (one of the first internet marketing companies, sold to Yahoo!) and Squidoo, and the altMBA, an intensive online leadership workshop. His daily blog, which he's maintained for decades, reaches millions of readers with insights on marketing, culture, and human behaviour. Godin is known for coining terms like "permission marketing" (marketing to people who want to be marketed to) and advocating for authentic, story-driven approaches over traditional advertising. His philosophy emphasises that in the modern economy, playing it safe is actually the riskiest strategy, and that success comes from being different, generous, and willing to make a difference. He's also a sought-after speaker who challenges conventional business wisdom and encourages people to embrace change and lead rather than follow.

FEBRUARY 12

"Where in your life or your work are you currently pursuing comfort when what's called for is a little discomfort?"
Oliver Burkeman[45]

---

[45] Burkeman echoes weightlifting champion and author Jerzy Gregorek who explains, "Hard choices easy life, easy choices hard life." Entrepreneur Paul Graham has a similar view. "This is a good plan for life in general." Graham writes. "If you have two choices, choose the harder. If you're trying to decide whether to go out running or sit home and watch TV, go running. Probably the reason this trick works so well is that when you have two choices and one is harder, the only reason you're even considering the other is laziness. You know in the back of your mind what's the right thing to do, and this trick merely forces you to acknowledge it."

Four Thousand Weeks: Time Management for Mortals, Oliver Burkeman, 2021.

Oliver Burkeman is an author and journalist known for his thoughtful, often contrarian approach to productivity and happiness. He wrote the popular "This Column Will Change Your Life" for The Guardian for over a decade, where he explored psychology, productivity culture, and the pursuit of well-being with a healthy dose of scepticism toward self-help orthodoxies. His most acclaimed book, "Four Thousand Weeks: Time Management for Mortals", challenges conventional productivity advice by arguing that our limited time on earth—roughly 4,000 weeks for the average human lifespan—should lead us to embrace our constraints rather than constantly seek optimisation. Burkeman's work stands out in the self-improvement space for its philosophical depth, dry humour, and willingness to question whether the relentless pursuit of efficiency and happiness might actually be counterproductive, offering instead a more realistic and accepting approach to human limitations.

FEBRUARY 13

*"Who have you been,
when you've been at your best?"*
- Keith Yamashita[46]

---

[46] Leaders must be especially aware of emotional contagion. A leader's demeanour and emotional state can be magnified and permeate the whole organisation. Emotions are as contagious as an infectious disease. Entrepreneur and author Chip Conley explains, "Emotions are contagious ..., approximately 50 – 70 percent of the temperament of a work group is influenced by the emotional state of its leader, so a business leader can almost think of herself as the "emotional thermostat" of her work group." If you've ever been in the presence of someone who is relentlessly positive you have felt it as a force multiplier. You want to be around them, to be part of what they are doing – their enthusiasm, energy and optimism are infectious. In his memoirs, General Colin Powell listed his rules for life. The last of Powell's rules is "perpetual optimism is a force multiplier".

Make Your Mark: The Creative's Guide to Building a Business with Impact, Jocelyn K. Glei, 2014.

Keith Yamashita is dedicated to using creativity as a powerful catalyst for change in the world and for the past two decades at SYPartners, has worked with leaders at major companies including Activision Blizzard, Apple, eBay, Emerson Collective, Facebook, IBM, General Electric, Johnson & Johnson, and Oprah Winfrey Network. He is the cofounder and principal of Stone Yamashita Partners (SYP), which was founded in 1994 and began life as a traditional design firm but slowly evolved to resemble a management consultancy as much as a graphic design firm. As a consultant, author and speaker, Yamashita helps companies turn their struggling businesses around and rebrand themselves, encouraging organisations to become stronger by helping their members seek greatness at the individual level, as duos and as members of society. He and his team at SY Partners have spent nearly a quarter century helping individuals and companies transform, working with major brands like Starbucks, IBM, and Target to become better versions of themselves.

FEBRUARY 14

"Is there something I know that I'm supposed to do that I really don't want to do.
Can I make myself do it?
If there is something I know I'm damn well not supposed to do but I want to do it, can I keep myself from it?"
- Nick Saban[47]

---

[47] "All successful people have the habit of doing the things failures don't like to do." Albert E. Gray notes. "They don't like doing them either necessarily. But their disliking is subordinated to the strength of their purpose." *The Common Denominator of Success*, speech delivered by Albert E. Gray to the National Association of Life Underwriters at their annual convention in 1940.
Two Questions Nick Saban Wants You To Ask Yourself, Don Yaeger, Forbes, July 31, 2022.

Nick Saban is widely regarded as one of the greatest college football coaches of all time, having built a dynasty at the University of Alabama that redefined excellence in collegiate athletics. Saban began his coaching career as an assistant before becoming a head coach at Toledo, Michigan State, and LSU, where he won his first national championship in 2003. After a brief stint as head coach of the Miami Dolphins in the NFL, he arrived at Alabama in 2007 and transformed the program into an unprecedented powerhouse. During his tenure with the Crimson Tide, Saban won six national championships (2009, 2011, 2012, 2015, 2017, 2020) and established a culture of relentless preparation and attention to detail that became known as "The Process." His teams were characterised by superior recruiting, meticulous game planning, and an ability to consistently perform in high-pressure situations. Saban's influence extended far beyond wins and losses, as many of his assistant coaches went on to become successful head coaches themselves, creating what became known as the "Saban coaching tree." He retired from Alabama in January 2024 with a career record of 292-71-1 (81%), leaving behind a legacy as a coach who elevated college football to new levels of professionalism and excellence.

FEBRUARY 15

"What is the optimal environment for you to thrive in? What gets in the way of you being the best version of yourself?"
- Owen Eastwood[48]

---

[48] "By his own admission, it is not rocket science," Bishop writes, "but he is surprised time and time again to meet experienced international coaches who have never learned what makes us tick as humans and are unaware of 'the insight that 70% of human behaviour is determined by your environment.' Eastwood is incredulous at how coaches can go through multiple coaching badges without understanding how to build trust, psychological safety and belonging."

Owen Eastwood: *'What gets in the way of you being the best version of yourself?'*, Cath Bishop, The Guardian, 19th November 2023. Also refer to *Belonging: The Ancient Code of Togetherness*, Owen Eastwood, 2022.

Owen Eastwood is a performance coach and author who has become one of the world's most sought-after team culture specialists, working with elite organisations across sports, military, and corporate sectors. He's earned his reputation as the most in-demand team performance coach in the world by delivering breakthrough results with a diverse range of teams from Gareth Southgate's England football team and the England women's team, to the senior leadership team of NATO. Originally a lawyer, his leap to coaching came during a two-year sabbatical at Saatchi & Saatchi in 2008, when the ad agency was asked by Adidas to work on a review of its sponsorship relationship with the All Blacks. His bestselling book "Belonging" reveals his unique ethos, drawing on his own Māori ancestry and weaving together insights from homo sapiens' evolutionary story and collective wisdom. Eastwood's approach is based on an evolutionary understanding of what makes teams of humans strong and weak, reintroducing people to ancient wisdoms about human connection and group dynamics. His philosophy centres on the biological need for belonging, recognising that humans have hormonal reactions in environments where they don't feel they belong, leading to increased anxiety and decreased performance.

FEBRUARY 16

*"What one thing could you do (something you aren't doing now) that, if you did it on a regular basis, would make a tremendous positive difference in your personal life?
What one thing in your business or professional life would bring similar results?"*
- Stephen Covey[49]

---

[49] These questions inform the third of Covey's seven habits. Habit 3 is to 'Put First Things First'. "Putting first things first" Covey explains, "means organizing and executing around your most important priorities. It is living and being driven by the principles you value most, not by the agendas and forces surrounding you."
The 7 Habits of Highly Effective People, Stephen R. Covey, 1989.

Stephen R. Covey (1932-2012) was an educator, author, and businessman who became one of the most influential voices in personal development and leadership through his bestselling book "The 7 Habits of Highly Effective People". His approach emphasised character-based leadership and principle-centred living, arguing that lasting success comes from aligning one's actions with timeless principles like integrity, fairness, and human dignity rather than quick-fix techniques. The seven habits became widely adopted in both corporate and personal settings. Covey founded the Covey Leadership Center (later Franklin Covey) to teach these principles to organisations worldwide and wrote numerous other books, including "First Things First" and "The Leader in Me." His work stood out in the self-help genre for its emphasis on character development over personality techniques, and his concepts like the "Circle of Influence" and "Quadrant II" time management continue to be taught in business schools and leadership programs globally.

FEBRUARY 17

*"I ask myself,
Is this story that I'm telling myself aligned with the best part of me, with who I really want to be in life, my values, my sense of purpose?
Does this story take me where I want to go in life?"*
- Jim Loehr[50]

---

[50] The story you are telling yourself determines your future. "Freedom begins the moment you realize someone else has been writing your story" journalist and former White House press Secretary Bill Moyers writes, "and it's time you took the pen from his hand and started writing it yourself."

Dr. Jim Loehr: Change The Stories You Tell Yourself, The Knowledge Project podcast Episode #193.

Dr. Jim Loehr, renowned performance psychologist and author of 16 books, has spent over three decades studying human achievement. A member of the American Psychological Association with masters and doctorate degrees in psychology, Dr. Loehr's research has led him to a powerful conclusion: character strength is the fundamental driver of success, personal fulfillment, and life satisfaction. His evidence-based insights, drawn from extensive work with high achievers, demonstrate that ethical behaviour and personal integrity are essential to sustained performance in any field.

FEBRUARY 18

*"What are your most vital sources of energy?
What do you love?"*
- Otto Scharmer[51]

---

[51] "Time only has value when it intersects with energy" performance psychologist and author Jim Loehr contends. "Energy, not time, is the fundamental currency of high performance." A leader must balance energy demands, and understand what drains and replenishes their energy. "The most important asset you need to protect in order to manage the demands of a job or an investment portfolio is your production of energy." Jim Loehr explains, "And, just like with money, if you do a great job managing your energy, you'll get a great return. ... Because energy capacity diminishes both with overuse and with underuse, we must balance energy expenditure with intermittent energy renewal." These two questions are part of a broader self-inquiry process that Scharmer outlines to help individuals and teams connect with their deepest sources of inspiration and purpose.
Theory U: Learning from the Future as It Emerges, Otto Scharmer, 2009.
Otto Scharmer is a Senior Lecturer at MIT and Founding Chair of the Presencing Institute. He focuses on awareness-based action research with leaders across various sectors, anchored in the concept of presencing, a method of "learning from the emerging future". Scharmer is the author of several influential books including "Theory U" and "Presence", the latter co-authored with Peter Senge and others, which introduced the groundbreaking concept of "presencing". His Theory U methodology provides a framework for transformational change that moves beyond downloading habitual patterns to accessing deeper sources of knowing and creativity. He chairs the MIT IDEAS program for cross-sector innovation and through the Presencing Institute works with leaders worldwide to address complex social, environmental, and organisational challenges using awareness-based approaches to systems change and regenerative leadership.

FEBRUARY 19

*"Does this activity fill me with energy
or drain me of energy?"*
- James Clear[52]

---

[52] Clear's question echoes entrepreneur Tim Ferriss who advocates a yearly review to identify energy sources and drains. Ferriss explains that this includes –

Create two columns: POSITIVE and NEGATIVE.

Review your calendar week by week from the past year.

Note people, activities, and commitments that triggered peak emotions in each column.

Identify the 20% that produced the most reliable highs and lows.

Schedule more positives immediately—book them now. It's not real until it's in your calendar.

Create a "NOT-TO-DO LIST" with your negative triggers and review it daily for the first few weeks.

Forget New Year's Resolutions and Conduct a 'Past Year Review' Instead (#559), Tim Ferriss, tim.blog, December 27, 2021.

3-2-1 Newsletter, James Clear, February 11, 2021.

James Clear is an author, speaker, and entrepreneur best known for his book "Atomic Habits," which became a bestseller and popularised the concept of making small, incremental changes to build better habits and break bad ones. Clear focuses on the science of habit formation, emphasising how tiny improvements compound over time to create remarkable results. His approach centres on four key principles: making habits obvious, attractive, easy, and satisfying. Before his writing career took off, Clear was a successful entrepreneur and has a background in photography and business. He writes regularly about habits, decision-making, and continuous improvement on his website and newsletter, which has attracted millions of readers. Clear's work draws from psychology, neuroscience, and behavioural economics to provide practical strategies for personal and professional development, making complex research accessible to everyday readers seeking to improve their lives through better systems and habits.

FEBRUARY 20

"Do you measure yourself against the best in the industry/world?"
- Eric Schmidt[53]

---

[53] Bill Campbell would use a format for one-on-one meetings that would include questions aimed at determining whether an individual or organisation is truly striving to be world-class: Are you constantly moving ahead, thinking about how to continually get better? Are you evaluating new technologies, new products, new practices? Do you measure yourself against the best in the industry/world?
Trillion Dollar Coach: The Leadership Playbook of Silicon Valley's Bill Campbell, Eric Schmidt, Jonathan Rosenberg and Alan Eagle, 2019.

Eric Schmidt is a businessman and former computer engineer who was the Chief Executive Officer of Google from 2001 to 2011 and the company's executive chairman from 2011 to 2015. He joined Google in 2001, helping the company grow from a Silicon Valley startup to a global technological leader, and under his leadership, Google dramatically scaled its infrastructure and diversified its product offerings while maintaining a culture of innovation. He holds degrees in electrical engineering from Princeton University and the University of California, Berkeley, where he also earned his PhD. Beyond Google, Schmidt has served as chair of the National Security Commission on Artificial Intelligence and is a prominent philanthropist through Schmidt Futures and other initiatives. He was a member of the President's Council of Advisers on Science from 2009 to 2017 and continues to be influential in technology policy and artificial intelligence research.

FEBRUARY 21

"... major personal decisions should be made not by asking, 'Will this make me happy?', but "Will this choice enlarge me or diminish me?""
- Oliver Burkeman[54]

---

[54] "When stumped by a life choice, choose "enlargement" over happiness." Burkeman writes. "I'm indebted to the Jungian therapist James Hollis for the insight that major personal decisions should be made not by asking, 'Will this make me happy?', but 'Will this choice enlarge me or diminish me?'"

Oliver Burkeman's last column: the eight secrets to a (fairly) fulfilled life, The Guardian, September 2020. The quote from Hollis is from *Finding Meaning in the Second Half of Life: How to Finally, Really Grow Up,* James Hollis, 2005.

Oliver Burkeman is an author and journalist known for his thoughtful, often contrarian approach to productivity and happiness. He wrote the popular "This Column Will Change Your Life" for The Guardian for over a decade, where he explored psychology, productivity culture, and the pursuit of well-being with a healthy dose of scepticism toward self-help orthodoxies. His most acclaimed book, "Four Thousand Weeks: Time Management for Mortals", challenges conventional productivity advice by arguing that our limited time on earth—roughly 4,000 weeks for the average human lifespan—should lead us to embrace our constraints rather than constantly seek optimisation. Burkeman's work stands out in the self-improvement space for its philosophical depth, dry humour, and willingness to question whether the relentless pursuit of efficiency and happiness might actually be counterproductive, offering instead a more realistic and accepting approach to human limitations.

FEBRUARY 22

*"... we all get, maybe, two hours a day ...
and the big important question is:
Who currently gets that time from you?"
- Elizabeth Gilbert*[55]

---

[55] Gilbert echoes educational reformer and slavery abolitionist Horace Mann who wrote, "Lost, yesterday, somewhere between sunrise and sunset, two golden hours, each set with sixty diamond minutes. No reward is offered for they are gone forever." It is the key to productivity and impact – save your most productive time for your most valuable work.
Experts on Expert podcast: Elizabeth Gilbert, Dax Shepherd, June 6, 2019.

Elizabeth Gilbert is a best-selling author best known for her memoir "Eat, Pray, Love," which became a global phenomenon after its 2006 publication, spending over 200 weeks on the New York Times bestseller list and inspiring a major motion picture. The book chronicled her journey of self-discovery through Italy, India, and Indonesia following a difficult divorce, resonating with millions of readers seeking meaning and transformation. Beyond this blockbuster success, Gilbert has written several novels including "The Signature of All Things," a historical fiction work about a 19th-century botanist, and "City of Girls," demonstrating her versatility as a storyteller. She's also become a prominent voice on creativity and the writing life, delivering a popular TED talk on genius and authoring "Big Magic: Creative Living Beyond Fear," which explores the mysteries and challenges of creative work while encouraging others to embrace curiosity over fear in their creative pursuits.

FEBRUARY 23

"What type of leader do you want to be?"
- Michelle Bihary[56]

---

[56] "This question requires us to reflect not only on our skills as leaders, but at a core level, to reflect on our fundamental values and the significant responsibility we take on, in our leadership roles." Bihary explains. "It's an excellent question to use to reflect on how we blend individual aspirations with the collective needs of colleagues and the workplace. As leaders or aspiring leaders, striking this balance is crucial in fostering a supportive, thriving work environment. If we are too much towards our own aspirations, we may become ego centred and at the other end of the spectrum, if we only prioritise being of service to others, we may end up being burnt out and overwhelmed. Questioning the type of leader we want to be affirms that we have a choice about how we want to show up as leaders, that leadership is not totally determined by fixed attributes, but more through applying and developing our skills, insights, and self-awareness."

What Type of Leader Do You Want to Be?, Michelle Bihary, michellebihary.com, 2 May 2024.

Michelle Bihary is a specialist speaker, facilitator and mentor in leadership, self-leadership, creating psychologically safe, emotionally intelligent and vital workplaces that grow potential and productivity. Bihary builds thriving leaders and high performing teams through her expertise in clinical supervision training, leadership courses, and coaching. Her practical and engaging style in applying neuroscience and emerging psychological research is known to be life changing, and she works with organisations to help leaders and teams navigate workplace challenges and stay "above the line" in their behaviours and decision-making. As a coach, author, and speaker on people leadership and workplace resilience, she helps teams navigate the complex ways that humans are challenged by living and working together, focusing on creating psychologically aware, responsible, and safe workplaces where both leaders and teams can thrive.

FEBRUARY 24

"How pro[fessional] are you?"
- Steven Pressfield[57]

---

[57] Pressfield asks the question, "What's the main difference between a pro and an amateur?" His answer: "depth of commitment". "In real life," he writes, "depth of commitment is more important than talent. It's more important than beauty or skill, more important even than luck, because its produce is perseverance, endurance, tenacity."

How Pro are you?, Steven Pressfield, Writing Wednesdays, stevenpressfield.com.

Steven Pressfield is an author best known for his influential book "The War of Art," which explores the psychological barriers that prevent creative people from doing their work. Pressfield had a long and varied career before achieving literary success, working as everything from a truck driver to an advertising copywriter while struggling to establish himself as a writer for decades. His breakthrough came with the historical novel "Gates of Fire", a critically acclaimed retelling of the Battle of Thermopylae that established him as a master of historical fiction. However, it was "The War of Art" that brought him widespread recognition beyond literary circles, as the book resonated deeply with artists, entrepreneurs, and anyone facing creative blocks. In it, Pressfield introduces the concept of "Resistance" - the internal force that sabotages creative endeavours - and offers strategies for overcoming it through discipline and professionalism. He has since written numerous other books including "Turning Pro," "Do the Work," and several other historical novels. Pressfield's work is characterised by his belief in the warrior ethos applied to creative pursuits, emphasising that writing and artistic creation require the same dedication, discipline, and courage as military service.

FEBRUARY 25

"If someone took control of your life tomorrow, what's the first thing they would change?"
- James Clear[58]

---

[58] Clear echoes former Intel CEO Andrew (Andy) S. Grove's famous question, from a thought exercise he went through with Gordon Moore before committing to making a massive change in Intel's business. "I turned back to Gordon and I asked, 'If we got kicked out and the board brought in a new CEO, what do you think he would do?' Gordon answered without hesitation, 'He would get us out of memories.' I stared at him, numb, then said, 'Why shouldn't you and I walk out the door, come back and do it ourselves?'" From *Only the Paranoid Survive: How to Exploit the Crisis Points That Challenge Every Company,* Andrew S. Grove, 1999.

3-2-1 Newsletter, James Clear, March 31, 2022.

James Clear is an author, speaker, and entrepreneur best known for his book "Atomic Habits," which became a bestseller and popularised the concept of making small, incremental changes to build better habits and break bad ones. Clear focuses on the science of habit formation, emphasising how tiny improvements compound over time to create remarkable results. His approach centres on four key principles: making habits obvious, attractive, easy, and satisfying. Before his writing career took off, Clear was a successful entrepreneur and has a background in photography and business. He writes regularly about habits, decision-making, and continuous improvement on his website and newsletter, which has attracted millions of readers. Clear's work draws from psychology, neuroscience, and behavioural economics to provide practical strategies for personal and professional development, making complex research accessible to everyday readers seeking to improve their lives through better systems and habits.

FEBRUARY 26

"What does it mean to be a quiet professional?"
- Rob Shaul[59]

---

[59] Shaul's answer is that it is about mission and team first, before self. "It's not about me." he writes, "… Ambition, angst, jealously have faded and with their evaporation has come a growing sense of solace … Only when I let that go, and put the mission, and others, first, have I begun to realize a budding sense of peace. To be clear. It's not about you. Accept, understand and embrace this. It's liberating."

What Does It Mean to be a Quiet Professional? Mountain Tactical Institute, Rob Shaul, September 2018.

Rob Shaul is a strength and conditioning coach and founder of Mountain Tactical Institute (MTI), specializing in fitness training for tactical and mountain athletes. A 1990 graduate of the U.S. Coast Guard Academy, Shaul started his fitness career with Mountain Athlete in 2007, founded Military Athlete in 2009, and established MTI in 2015. His training philosophy centres on "mission direct" fitness that directly impacts real-world performance rather than traditional gym metrics. Shaul gained recognition by training mountain athletes in Wyoming before military personnel sought his expertise for Afghanistan deployments, eventually expanding to work with first responders and tier 1 operators. His approach emphasises "work capacity" - intense cardiorespiratory and muscular stress at high but sub-maximal levels that mirror dangerous tactical and mountain situations. MTI has become a leading authority in tactical fitness, developing specialised programs for military, law enforcement, and mountain professionals worldwide.

FEBRUARY 27

*"Who do I really want to become?
Which among my various possible selves should I
start to explore now? How can I do that?"*
- Herminia Ibarra[60]

---

[60] "A musician must make music, an artist must paint, a poet must write, if he is to be ultimately at peace with himself." Abraham Maslow explains. "What a man can be, he must be. This need we call self-actualization….It refers to man's desire for self-fulfilment, namely to the tendency for him to become actually in what he is potentially: to become everything one is capable of becoming."

Range: Why Generalists Triumph in a Specialized World, David Epstein, 2019.

Herminia Ibarra is a prominent organisational psychologist and leadership expert who serves as the Charles Handy Professor of Organizational Behaviour at London Business School. She's widely recognised for her research on leadership development, career transitions, and professional identity. Ibarra has authored several influential books, including "Working Identity: Unconventional Strategies for Reinventing Your Career" and "Act Like a Leader, Think Like a Leader," which challenge traditional approaches to career development and leadership. Her work emphasises the importance of taking action and experimenting with new roles and behaviours as a way to develop professionally, rather than simply thinking your way into change. She's also known for her research on gender and leadership, particularly examining barriers that women face in advancing to senior leadership positions. Ibarra is frequently cited as one of the world's top management thinkers and has been recognised by Thinkers50, which ranks the most influential business thinkers globally.

FEBRUARY 28

"What is your life's blueprint?"
- Martin Luther King Jr.[61]

---

[61] The question was part of a speech King delivered to a group of students at Barratt Junior High School in Philadelphia, six months before he was assassinated. "Whenever a building is constructed," King explained, "you usually have an architect who draws a blueprint, and that blueprint serves as the pattern, as the guide, and a building is not well erected without a good, solid blueprint. Now each of you is in the process of building the structure of your lives, and the question is whether you have a proper, a solid, and a sound blueprint. And I want to suggest some of the things that should be in your life's blueprint. Number one in your life's blueprint, should be a deep belief in your own dignity, your own worth and your own somebodiness. Don't allow anybody to make you feel that you are nobody. Always feel that you count. Always feel that you have worth, and always feel that your life has ultimate significance … Secondly, in your life's blueprint you must have as a basic principle the determination to achieve excellence in your various fields of endeavour. You're going to be deciding as the days, as the years unfold what you will do in life — what your life's work will be. And once you discover what it will be, set out to do and to do it well." King implores his audience, "set out to do it as if God Almighty called you at this particular moment in history to do it. don't just set out to do a good job. Set out to do such a good job that the living, the dead or the unborn couldn't do it any better."

What Is Your Life's Blueprint?, Martin Luther King Jr., October 26, 1967.

Martin Luther King Jr. was the most prominent leader of the American civil rights movement in the 1950s and 1960s, advocating for racial equality through nonviolent resistance inspired by Mahatma Gandhi's philosophy. A Baptist minister and gifted orator, he rose to national prominence during the Montgomery Bus Boycott in 1955 and went on to organise pivotal campaigns including the March on Washington in 1963, where he delivered his iconic "I Have a Dream" speech. King's leadership was instrumental in securing landmark legislation like the Civil Rights Act of 1964 and the Voting Rights Act of 1965. He was awarded the Nobel Peace Prize in 1964 at age 35, making him the youngest recipient at the time. His life was tragically cut short when he was assassinated in Memphis, Tennessee, in 1968 at age 39, but his legacy as a champion of justice, equality, and peaceful protest continues to inspire movements worldwide.

FEBRUARY 29

"What kind of leadership is called for at this moment - and am I capable of summoning it?"
- Ed Batista[62]

---

[62] Batista's question reflects situational leadership, the idea that there is no single "best" leadership style or approach. Instead, effective leaders adapt their approach based on the readiness and development level of their followers for specific tasks.

Compasses and Weathervanes (30 Questions for Leaders), Ed Batista, edbatista.com, April 14, 2022.

Ed Batista is an executive coach and former Stanford Graduate School of Business lecturer who has become a prominent voice in leadership development and organisational psychology. He has been an executive coach since 2006, working with senior leaders who are facing challenges or seeking to be more effective or fulfilled in their roles, while spending 15 years as a lecturer and leadership coach at Stanford GSB. Most of his clients are technology company CEOs, though he works with leaders across various fields from investing to healthcare. Batista's approach emphasises self-awareness, emotional intelligence, and the transition from technical expertise to effective leadership. His work addresses complex leadership challenges including managing key relationships, improving team dynamics, and navigating the shift from individual contributor to organisational leader. Known for his thoughtful, research-based approach to coaching, Batista has contributed significantly to discussions about executive development, feedback culture, and the psychological aspects of leadership in high-pressure environments.

MARCH

BUILD & LEAD YOUR TEAM

MARCH 1

"Do you have the right team?"
- Peter Thiel[63]

---

[63] Thiel explains that this is one of seven questions that every business must answer. Thiel's question is similar to the questions author Jim Collins formulated after studying great organisations. "My first question," Collins says, "my first response to every challenge is not what but who. Who am I going to involve in this? Who would be the right people to advise me? Who would be the right people to ..." Former Netflix Chief Talent Officer Patty McCord asks, "If you had to rebuild this team from scratch, who would you hire?" and "Are we limited by the team we have not being the team we should have?" *Powerful: Building a Culture of Freedom and Responsibility,* Patty McCord, 2018.

Zero to One: Notes on Startups, or How to Build the Future, Peter Thiel, 2014.

Peter Thiel is an entrepreneur, venture capitalist, and author who co-founded PayPal and became one of Silicon Valley's most influential and controversial figures. Born in Germany and raised in California, Thiel studied philosophy at Stanford before earning a law degree and working briefly as a securities lawyer and derivatives trader. In 1998, he co-founded PayPal with Max Levchin, which was sold to eBay for $1.5 billion in 2002, establishing him as part of the legendary "PayPal Mafia" of entrepreneurs. Thiel was Facebook's first major outside investor, putting $500,000 into the company in 2004 for a stake that eventually became worth over $1 billion. He founded Palantir Technologies, a data analytics company that works with government agencies, and established Founders Fund, a venture capital firm that has invested in companies like SpaceX, Airbnb, and Stripe. Known for his contrarian thinking, Thiel wrote "Zero to One," a bestselling book about startups and innovation, and has been a vocal advocate for technological progress while critiquing higher education and promoting alternative institutions.

MARCH 2

"If you could invest in someone else and get a % of their earnings for the rest of their lives, what goes through your mind in determining which one you would pick?"
- Warren Buffett[64]

---

[64] Buffett has often said that the qualities Berkshire Hathway look for are intelligence, energy and integrity. "We look for three things when we hire people." he says. "We look for intelligence, we look for initiative or energy, and we look for integrity. And if they don't have the latter, the first two will kill you, because if you're going to get someone without integrity, you want them lazy and dumb."

Warren Buffett, Chairman, Berkshire Hathaway Investment Group, Terry Leadership Speaker Series, Terry College of Business at the University of Georgia, July 18, 2001.

Warren Buffett is an investor, business magnate, and philanthropist widely regarded as one of the most successful investors in history. Known as the "Oracle of Omaha," he serves as chairman and CEO of Berkshire Hathaway, a multinational conglomerate holding company based in Nebraska. Buffett has built his fortune through a disciplined value investing approach, focusing on companies with strong fundamentals, competitive advantages, and long-term growth potential. His investment philosophy emphasises buying undervalued stocks and holding them for extended periods, famously saying his favourite holding period is "forever."

MARCH 3

"Are you an ideal team player?"
- Patrick Lencioni[65]

---

[65] Lencioni explains that the ideal team player is humble, hungry, and smart. "The first and by far the most important is humility." Lencioni explains. "If you want to be an ideal team player and if you want to be successful in life, you really need to be humble. Most of us know what humility is — it means not being arrogant or self-centered but putting others ahead of ourselves. It's such an attractive and powerful thing. When somebody lacks confidence and makes themselves small, that's not humility. To deny our talents is actually a violation of humility, just like it is to exaggerate them. The writer C.S. Lewis said it best when he wrote, 'Humility isn't thinking less of ourselves, it's thinking about ourselves less.' The second is equally simple: You have to be hungry. This simply means having a strong work ethic. People who have an innate hunger about getting work done are typically much more successful on teams and in life. ... Being hungry is not about workaholism, though. Workaholics are people who get their entire identity from their work. People who are hungry just want to go above and beyond what's expected; they have a high standard for what they do, and they never do just the minimum. The third attribute is what I call being smart. But it's not about intellectual smarts; this is about emotional intelligence and having common sense around how we understand people and how we use our words and actions to bring out the best in others."

Are you an ideal team player?, Patrick Lencioni, TEDx University of Nevada, March 2020. Also refer to

The Ideal Team Player: How to Recognize and Cultivate The Three Essential Virtues, Patrick M. Lencioni, 2016.

Patrick Lencioni is an author, speaker, and management consultant who specialises in organisational health and team dynamics. He's the founder and president of The Table Group, a management consulting firm, and has written numerous bestselling business books that focus on leadership and organisational effectiveness. His most famous work is "The Five Dysfunctions of a Team," which presents a model for understanding and overcoming the common pitfalls that prevent teams from working effectively together. Lencioni is known for his fable-style approach to business writing, using fictional narratives to illustrate management concepts in an accessible and engaging way. Other notable books include "The Advantage," "Death by Meeting," and "The Ideal Team Player." His work emphasises the importance of organisational health, the idea that companies succeed not just through strategy and execution, but through creating healthy, functional workplace cultures.

MARCH 4

"What can I do to support you right now?"
- John Gottman[66]

---

[66] This question is similar to the one asked by executive coach and leadership expert Marshall Goldsmith. "One of the ways I did this was asking them to list all the things they could do as a leader to support the people they worked with. I called this the Needs Exercise: What do your people need from you? They'd rattle off the obvious stuff: support, recognition, a sense of belonging and purpose. Then they'd go deeper. People needed to be loved, and heard, and respected. They needed to feel loyal to something and receive loyalty back in return. They needed to be fairly rewarded for doing a good job, not overlooked or discounted. From The Earned Life: Lose Regret, Choose Fulfillment, Marshall Goldsmith, 2022.

The Relationship Cure: A 5 Step Guide to Strengthening Your Marriage, Family, and Friendships, John M. Gottman and Joan Declaire, 2001.

John Gottman is a renowned psychologist and researcher best known for his extensive work on marital stability and relationship dynamics. Based at the University of Washington, he developed the "Love Lab" where he observed thousands of couples and identified specific communication patterns that predict relationship success or failure with remarkable accuracy. Gottman is famous for identifying the "Four Horsemen of the Apocalypse" - criticism, contempt, defensiveness, and stonewalling - as toxic communication behaviours that destroy relationships. His research has shown he can predict divorce with over 90% accuracy by observing couples' interactions for just a few minutes. Beyond his academic work, Gottman has written numerous popular books including "The Seven Principles for Making Marriage Work" and founded the Gottman Institute with his wife Julie, providing relationship therapy training and resources. His evidence-based approach to understanding communication and emotional dynamics has influenced not only couples therapy but also workplace relationship dynamics and leadership communication.

MARCH 5

*"Who is this person, at their core?
Who might this person become, at their best?
What feedback or perspective would help them to get there?"*
- Stephanie Harrison[67]

---

[67] "Max Perkins was one of the most celebrated book editors of all time." Harrison explains. "He discovered Ernest Hemingway; he encouraged F. Scott Fitzgerald to write The Great Gatsby; he helped turn Thomas Wolfe's 1,114-page manuscript into a publishable book. As an editor, he had learned to be a master of feedback. His approach, described in a lecture that he gave to a group of students in 1946, was "so simple." All his job entailed, from his perspective, was unleashing the innate and unique goodness within his authors. "The process is so simple," he said. "If you have Mark Twain, don't try to make him into a Shakespeare or make a Shakespeare into a Mark Twain." Perkins embraced his authors as they were (fighting the publisher to keep swear words in Hemingway's books) and helped them to learn how to become even better (finding ways to cut Wolfe's epic length while maintaining the beauty of his prose.) To give good feedback, we need to follow in Perkins' footsteps and look at how we can embrace who someone really is and help them to become more of themselves. Here's a simple way to put this idea into practice. Before you give feedback, ask yourself these three questions.

Who is this person, at their core?
Who might this person become, at their best?
What feedback or perspective would help them to get there?

It's this type of feedback that helps us to grow, to create new things, to leave a lasting impact. None of us can do great things on our own, and by generously sharing feedback with one another, we can all become who we are meant to be."

The power of feedback, The New Happy podcast, thenewhappy.com, 9 October 2024.

Stephanie Harrison is an expert in the science of happiness and founder of The New Happy, which she founded in 2018 to share a new science-backed philosophy of happiness focused on the idea that lasting happiness comes from understanding yourself and using that knowledge to help others. She holds a master's degree in positive psychology from the University of Pennsylvania and is the author of "NEW HAPPY: Getting Happiness Right in A World That's Got It Wrong" from Penguin Random House. Harrison works as a keynote speaker on happiness and workplace well-being, and her organisation reaches millions of people through its content on well-being and personal development. She combines her background in psychology, writing, and design to challenge conventional wisdom about happiness and promote what she calls a "new philosophy" that emphasises authentic self-understanding and service to others.

MARCH 6

"How can I make the team better?"
- John Wooden[68]

---

[68] This question is actually paraphrased from Wooden who explained, "A player who makes the team great is more valuable than a great player." One famous exemplar is Bill Russell. Russell anchored the Boston Celtics from 1956 to 1969, serving as the cornerstone of the most dominant dynasty in professional sports history, the team winning eleven NBA championships in thirteen seasons, including an unprecedented eight consecutive titles. But Russell's true revolution wasn't just his defensive prowess or rebounding, it was in fundamentally redefining what success meant in team sports. Russell's core philosophy was "creating unselfishness as the most important team attribute." This wasn't merely about passing the ball more, it was about subordinating individual achievement to collective purpose. In an era when basketball was increasingly becoming a showcase for individual stars, Russell insisted that the highest expression of basketball excellence was making teammates better, not accumulating personal statistics. This philosophy manifested in revolutionary ways. Russell measured his own success not by points scored, rebounds grabbed, or blocks recorded, but by a single metric: did the team win? This perspective allowed him to make decisions that traditional basketball logic might have questioned, taking fewer shots to create better opportunities for teammates, sacrificing individual recognition to maximize team chemistry, and viewing every possession through the lens of collective advantage rather than personal glory. Russell's approach anticipated modern basketball analytics by decades, recognising that winning was a complex ecosystem of interdependent contributions rather than the sum of individual performances. His legacy lies not just in the championships, but in proving that the highest form of leadership often involves making others shine brighter than yourself.

Wooden on Leadership: How to Create a Winning Organizaion, John Wooden, 2005.

John Wooden (1910-2010) was a basketball coach and teacher who became a legendary figure in college sports, known as much for his character and wisdom as for his unprecedented success. As head coach at UCLA from 1948 to 1975, he led the Bruins to an extraordinary 10 NCAA championships in 12 years, including seven consecutive titles from 1967 to 1973—a feat unmatched in college basketball. Beyond his coaching achievements, Wooden was revered for his "Pyramid of Success," a philosophical framework emphasizing character traits like industriousness, friendship, and self-control as the foundation for achievement. His famous "Woodenisms"—pithy sayings like "Be quick, but don't hurry" and "Success is peace of mind in knowing you did your best"—became widely quoted principles that transcended sports. Even after retiring from coaching, Wooden continued to inspire through his books and speaking, embodying the ideal of the teacher-coach who viewed developing young people's character as more important than winning games.

MARCH 7

"How do I maximize the talent we already have?"
- Michael Lombardi & George Raveling[69]

---

[69] *"Notes" of an Elder,* The Daily Coach, December 01, 2023.

Michael Lombardi is a three-time Super Bowl champion as an executive with over 30 years of experience in NFL front offices who recently joined the North Carolina football program as General Manager in December 2024. He has spent 35 years working for the New England Patriots, San Francisco 49ers, the Oakland Raiders and the Cleveland Browns, and has the distinction of the being the only person to make it to the Super Bowl with both the Patriots and 49ers. Beyond his front office work, Lombardi has been a prominent media personality as an NFL analyst, author, and cofounder with George Raveling of The Daily Coach, a newsletter that shares sports and organisational leadership lessons.

George Raveling is a Basketball Hall of Fame coach and Nike executive who has had an extraordinary impact on both basketball and sports marketing. After a successful college coaching career at schools including Washington State, Iowa, and USC, he joined Nike at the request of Phil Knight, where he played an integral role in signing a reluctant Michael Jordan. Raveling has worked as the Director for International Basketball for Nike since his retirement from USC and is known as "the iconic leader who brought Michael Jordan to Nike". Beyond basketball, he has a unique connection to civil rights history and having a personal connection to Martin Luther King Jr.'s "I Have a Dream" speech. Raveling was present at the March on Washington on August 28, 1963, and after Dr. King delivered his speech, King handed Raveling the original typewritten copy.

The two co-founded The Daily Coach newsletter, sharing leadership wisdom from sports and business.

MARCH 8

"What is one thing that I currently do that you'd like me to continue to do? What is one thing that I don't currently do frequently enough that you think I should do more often? What can I do to make you more effective?"
- Daniel Coyle[70]

---

[70] Coyle is quoting Laszlo Bock, entrepreneur and former SVP of People Operations at Google.

The Culture Code: The Secrets of Highly Successful Groups, Daniel Coyle, 2018. Refer also *Work Rules! Insights from inside Google that will transform how you live and lead*, Laszlo Bock, 2015.

Daniel Coyle is a New York Times bestselling author known for books including "The Culture Code," "The Talent Code," "The Little Book of Talent," and "The Secret Race." He works as a contributing editor for Outside magazine and serves as a special advisor to the Cleveland Guardians baseball team. Coyle specialises in studying high-performing teams and talent development, spending years observing elite groups around the world to understand how they build culture, develop skills, and achieve success. Winner of the 2012 William Hill Sports Book of the Year Prize (with Tyler Hamilton), he splits his time between Cleveland, Ohio during the school year and Homer, Alaska in the summer with his wife Jen and their four children. His work focuses on translating the science of skill acquisition and team dynamics into practical insights for coaches, leaders, and organisations seeking to unlock human potential and build stronger cultures.

MARCH 9

"Are you beginning to lose other people by keeping this person in the seat?
Do you have a values problem, a will problem or a skills problem?
What's the person's relationship to the window and the mirror? (The right people look out the window when things go right giving credit to others, the wrong people look in the mirror assigning credit to themselves)
Does the person see work as a job or a responsibility?
Has your confidence in the person gone up or down in the past year?
Do you have a bus problem or a seat problem?
How would you feel if the person quit?"
- Jim Collins[71]

---

71 *Jim Collins 7 Questions For People Decisions*, Evolution Partners, 22nd February 2021.

Jim Collins is a bestselling author, business researcher, and management consultant who has spent decades studying what makes companies transition from good to great performance. He's best known for his book "Good to Great," which identified key principles that distinguish exceptional companies from merely good ones, including concepts like Level 5 Leadership, the Hedgehog Concept, and getting the right people on the bus. Collins has written several other influential business books including "Built to Last" (co-authored with Jerry Porras), "How the Mighty Fall," and "Great by Choice." His research methodology involves rigorous data analysis and long-term studies of companies, often spanning decades to identify patterns and principles that drive sustained success. Before his writing career, Collins worked as a faculty member at Stanford Graduate School of Business and served as a consultant to corporations and social sector organisations. His work extends beyond the corporate world to nonprofits and educational institutions through books like "Good to Great and the Social Sectors." Collins is known for his disciplined approach to research, his ability to distil complex business concepts into memorable frameworks, and his focus on timeless principles rather than fleeting management fads.

MARCH 10

"Will this person raise the average level of effectiveness of the group they're entering?"
- Jeff Bezos[72]

---

[72] The context of this question was the following. "It would be impossible to produce results in an environment as dynamic as the Internet without extraordinary people. Working to create a little bit of history isn't supposed to be easy, and, well, we're finding that things are as they're supposed to be! We now have a team of 2,100 smart, hard-working, passionate folks who put customers first. Setting the bar high in our approach to hiring has been, and will continue to be, the single most important element of Amazon.com's success.

During our hiring meetings, we ask people to consider three questions before making a decision:

- Will you admire this person? If you think about the people you've admired in your life, they are probably people you've been able to learn from or take an example from. For myself, I've always tried hard to work only with people I admire, and I encourage folks here to be just as demanding. Life is definitely too short to do otherwise.

- Will this person raise the average level of effectiveness of the group they're entering? We want to fight entropy. The bar has to continuously go up. I ask people to visualize the company 5 years from now. At that point, each of us should look around and say, "The standards are so high now -- boy, I'm glad I got in when I did!"

- Along what dimension might this person be a superstar? Many people have unique skills, interests, and perspectives that enrich the work environment for all of us. It's often something that's not even related to their jobs."

Amazon 1998 Letter to Shareholders, Customers, and Employees, Jeffrey P. Bezos, April 1999.

Jeff Bezos is an entrepreneur and business magnate who founded Amazon in 1994 and transformed it from an online bookstore into one of the world's largest and most influential companies. Bezos worked on Wall Street before starting Amazon from his garage in Bellevue, Washington, initially focusing on selling books online. Under his leadership as CEO until 2021, Amazon expanded into virtually every sector of commerce, revolutionising retail through innovations like one-click purchasing, Prime membership, and same-day delivery, while also becoming a dominant force in cloud computing through Amazon Web Services. Bezos became the world's richest person at various points, accumulating wealth that made him a symbol of both entrepreneurial success and income inequality debates. Beyond Amazon, he founded the space exploration company Blue Origin in 2000 with the goal of making space travel more accessible, and he's been involved in various philanthropic efforts including climate change initiatives. Known for his long-term thinking, customer obsession, and willingness to experiment and fail, Bezos has been credited with fundamentally changing how people shop and businesses operate in the digital age..

MARCH 11

"If an employee is considering leaving, would you fight to retain them?"
- Reed Hastings[73]

---

[73] There are multiple versions of what is often referred to as the "Keeper Test" question. Hastings explains, "We try to apply the Keeper Test to everyone, including ourselves. Would the company be better off with someone else in my role? The goal is to remove any shame for anyone let go from Netflix. Think of an Olympic team sport like hockey. To get cut from the team is very disappointing, but the person is admired for having had the guts and skill to make the squad in the first place. When someone is let go at Netflix, we hope for the same. We all stay friends and there is no shame."

No Rules Rules: Netflix and the Culture of Reinvention, Reed Hastings, 2020.

Reed Hastings is an entrepreneur and technology executive best known as the co-founder and former CEO of Netflix, where he transformed the company from a DVD-by-mail service into the world's leading streaming entertainment platform. Under his leadership from 1997 to 2023, Netflix pioneered the subscription-based streaming model and became a major producer of original content, fundamentally disrupting the traditional television and film industries. Prior to Netflix, Hastings founded Pure Software, a debugging tools company that he sold in the 1990s. He's recognised for his data-driven approach to business decisions and his willingness to cannibalise Netflix's own DVD business to focus on streaming. Hastings has also been active in education reform, serving on various boards and advocating for charter schools, and he stepped down as Netflix CEO in 2023 to focus on philanthropy while remaining executive chairman of the company.

MARCH 12

"What's on your mind?"
- Michael Bungay Stanier[74]

---

[74] Bungay Stanier calls this the "The Kickstart Question". The reason it works so well is that it is an open question and it's "An almost fail-safe way to start a chat that quickly turns into a real conversation" Bungay Stanier explains. "It's something of a Goldilocks question," he writes, "walking a fine line so it is neither too open and broad nor too narrow and confining."

The Coaching Habit: Say Less, Ask More & Change the Way You Lead Forever, Michael Bungay Stanier, 2016.

Michael Bungay Stanier is an author, leadership coach, and business consultant best known for his bestselling book "The Coaching Habit: Say Less, Ask More & Change the Way You Lead Forever." He founded Box of Crayons, a learning and development company that helps organisations transform from advice-driven to curiosity-led, and currently leads MBS.works, a place where people find clarity, confidence and community to be a force for change. His work focuses on helping leaders develop better coaching skills through practical, science-backed approaches that emphasise asking powerful questions rather than giving advice. His philosophy is captured in his haiku-like summary: "Tell less and ask more. Your advice is not as good as you think it is." Known as a compelling speaker and facilitator who combines practicality, humour, and high audience engagement, Stanier has become a prominent voice in the leadership development space, helping countless managers and executives shift from being advice-givers to becoming more effective coaches who unlock potential in their teams through curiosity and thoughtful questioning.

MARCH 13

"What's the thing you see me doing that's helping me best contribute to the team or organization? What's the thing I do that's detracting from our success?"

- Tasha Eurich[75]

---

[75] *Insight: The Surprising Truth About How Others See Us, How We See Ourselves, and Why the Answers Matter More Than We Think*, Tasha Eurich, 2017.

Tasha Eurich is an organisational psychologist, researcher, and bestselling author who specialises in self-awareness and its impact on leadership and success. She's best known for her book "Insight: The Surprising Truth About How Others See Us, How We See Ourselves, and Why the Answers Matter More Than We Think," which presents research showing that while most people believe they are self-aware, only 10-15% actually are. Eurich's work distinguishes between internal self-awareness (understanding our own values, passions, and impact on others) and external self-awareness (understanding how others see us), arguing that both are crucial for effective leadership and personal fulfilment. She conducts extensive research on leadership effectiveness, emotional intelligence, and workplace dynamics, and works as a consultant helping executives and organisations develop greater self-awareness. Eurich is a popular keynote speaker and has been featured in Harvard Business Review, where she's written about the myths and realities of self-awareness. Her approach combines rigorous research with practical tools and strategies, helping people bridge the gap between how they see themselves and how others actually perceive them, ultimately leading to better relationships and more effective leadership.

MARCH 14

"Will you build your unit into a pocket of greatness?"
- Jim Collins[76]

[76] "One thing I gained greater appreciation for at West Point is that great leadership at the top doesn't amount to very much without exceptional leadership at the unit level." Collins explains. "This is the cellular structure. This is where great things get done. When I look at how the good-to-great CEOs became CEO, they did it by not focusing on their career. They focused on their unit of responsibility. At every stage of their career, whatever they were running, whether it be a little accounting department or whether it be a manufacturing facility, controllership, they built their unit into a pocket of greatness. That is why they were tapped. Focus on your unit, not on your career. Every responsibility you get, make it a pocket of greatness. If you do that, you are more likely to die of indigestion from too much responsibility than starvation from too little. And focusing on your unit means above all being a First Who leader rather than a First What leader. And that the #1 executive skill for building a pocket of greatness of any size is figuring out who should be in the key seats on the bus, to be rigorous about your people decisions. And we've spoken about this before, but it also means not being ruthless. Be rigorous, not ruthless. That means taking care of your people. For in the end, life is people. One of our greatest living military leaders, a four-star, told me a story of how early in his career after graduating from West Point, he worried a lot about promotions and how, perhaps, he might not be advancing as fast as he had hoped. Then he had an epiphany, and he changed his focus from taking care of his career to taking care of his people. And at that point, he said, everything changed. 'They would not let me fail.' Life is people."

Jim's Seven Questions: Learning From Young Leaders Full Talk, Global Leadership Summit, 2015.

Jim Collins is a bestselling author, business researcher, and management consultant who has spent decades studying what makes companies transition from good to great performance. He's best known for his book "Good to Great," which identified key principles that distinguish exceptional companies from merely good ones, including concepts like Level 5 Leadership, the Hedgehog Concept, and getting the right people on the bus. Collins has written several other influential business books including "Built to Last" (co-authored with Jerry Porras), "How the Mighty Fall," and "Great by Choice." His research methodology involves rigorous data analysis and long-term studies of companies, often spanning decades to identify patterns and principles that drive sustained success. Before his writing career, Collins worked as a faculty member at Stanford Graduate School of Business and served as a consultant to corporations and social sector organisations. His work extends beyond the corporate world to nonprofits and educational institutions through books like "Good to Great and the Social Sectors." Collins is known for his disciplined approach to research, his ability to distil complex business concepts into memorable frameworks, and his focus on timeless principles rather than fleeting management fads.

MARCH 15

*"One of the things you should always ask is,
'If this person joined my company,
would you join?'"*
- Keith Rabois[77]

---

[77] This question could be called the "gravity" test. A person's gravity is their ability to attract other high quality people into their orbit.
High Growth Handbook: Scaling Startups from 10 to 10,000 People, Elad Gil, 2018.

Keith Rabois is a prominent Silicon Valley entrepreneur and venture capitalist known for his roles in building several major tech companies. He served as an executive at PayPal during its early growth phase, was COO at Square where he helped scale the payments company, and held a senior position at LinkedIn. As an investor, Rabois has been a general partner at Khosla Ventures and Founders Fund, backing numerous successful startups including Airbnb, Lyft, and DoorDash. He's recognised for his operational expertise in scaling companies and his often provocative commentary on business strategy and Silicon Valley culture. Rabois is also known for mentoring entrepreneurs and for his active presence on social media, where he shares insights about startups, investing, and technology trends.

MARCH 16

"Do you make others better?"
- Randall Stutman[78]

---

[78] After studying leadership and working with leaders for decades, Stutman distils leadership to its essence: it is about making people and situations better. The idea echoes Roman stoic philosopher Lucius Annaeus Seneca who wrote, "Happy is the man who can make others better, not merely when he is in their company, but even when he is in their thoughts!"
Do You Make Others Better?, The Daily Stoic.
The Essence of Leadership with Randall Stutman, The Knowledge Project #95.
Dr. Randall K. Stutman is the founder of the Admired Leadership Institute and CRA (formerly CRA Inc.), widely recognised as an authority in leadership strategy and style. He began his career at the University of Illinois teaching and conducting research on managing conflict in relationships, groups, and organisations, and is co-author of the award-winning book "Working Through Conflict". Labelled by Goldman Sachs as the most experienced advisor and executive coach on Wall Street, he has served as a Principal Advisor to more than 2,000 Senior Executives working with major firms including Bank of America Merrill Lynch, Capital One, Deutsche Bank, Goldman Sachs, State Farm, Morgan Stanley, BorgWarner, and PerkinElmer. As a leadership scientist, Stutman focuses on exploring the behavioural practices and routines that distinguish exceptional leaders, emphasizing practical, behavioural approaches over psychological methods to develop what he terms "admired leadership."

MARCH 17

"What makes people give the very best of themselves?"
- Doug Conant[79]

---

[79] Conant's question relates to the quote from Carly Fiorina, former CEO of Hewlett-Packard, who said, "The highest calling of leadership is to unlock the potential of others."

Leaders, You Can (And Must) Do Better. Here's How., Doug Conant, LinkedIn, June 16, 2016.

Doug Conant is a business executive and leadership expert who served as CEO of Campbell Soup Company from 2001 to 2011, where he led one of the most successful business turnarounds in corporate history. When he took over, Campbell's was struggling with declining sales and low employee engagement, but under his leadership, the company achieved significant growth and became known for its strong workplace culture. Conant is particularly known for his approach to "people-centric leadership" and his belief in the importance of employee engagement and authentic leadership. After leaving Campbell's, he founded ConantLeadership, a leadership development firm, and has written several books on leadership including "TouchPoints" and "The Blueprint." He's also served as chairman of Avon Products and has been involved with various nonprofit organisations. Conant is a frequent speaker on leadership topics and is known for his philosophy that leaders must genuinely care for their people while also delivering strong business results. He emphasises the importance of building trust, inspiring performance, and creating environments where employees can thrive.

MARCH 18

"What could I do or stop doing that would make it easier to work with me?"
- Kim Scott[80]

---

[80] Scott recommends having a "go-to question" for soliciting feedback. "Your question must sound like you — something you would naturally say." Scott says. "If you sound like Kim Scott and not yourself, people won't believe you really want to hear what they have to say. The question I like to use is, "What I could do or stop doing that would make it easier to work with me?" However, If those words don't fall easily off your tongue, find words that do." Scott provides some examples -

Fred Kofman, author, philosopher and vice president at LinkedIn, has suggested a question like, "Is there anything I could do or stop doing that would make it easier to work with me?" Andy Grove, former Intel CEO, asked, "I want to ask you a favor. It's a big one, and it is the most important thing you can do for me. I really need you to tell me what I am doing wrong, how I am screwing up?" Bill Berry of Tacoma Power says, "Give me some advice."

Scott also provides some additional variations -

"How can I support you on this project?"

"What's bothering you?"

"What's the one thing you've been wanting to tell me but have been holding back?"

The Go-To Question, Brandi Neal, radicalcandor.com.

Radical Candor: Be a Kick-Ass Boss Without Losing Your Humanity, Kim Malone Scott, 2017.

Kim Scott is a former Apple and Google executive who became a bestselling author and leadership expert through her concept of "Radical Candor." Scott defines radical candour as feedback that incorporates both praise and criticism, and her book "Radical Candor: Be a Kick-Ass Boss Without Losing Your Humanity" became a New York Times and Wall Street Journal bestseller. At Google and Apple, she worked with teams to develop classes on effective management, drawing from these experiences to create her management philosophy. Her approach centers on three principles: making relationships personal, getting things done, and understanding why work matters. Scott now runs Candor, Inc. and has built her career around creating work environments where people can do their best work while maintaining their humanity. Her framework emphasises giving specific, sincere praise and kind but clear criticism to help build better workplace relationships and more effective teams.

MARCH 19

"How do we accelerate the process of building mutual trust?"
- Graham Duncan[81]

---

[81] The trust and quality of a relationship at any point is a function of all the exchanges up to that point. Spotify founder Tobi Lutke describes the idea of the "trust battery" to help think about this. The trust battery is –

being charged when commitments are met, when there is collaboration. It is a measure of what you *do*.

being discharged when appointments are missed, expectations aren't met or when we don't keep our word. It is a measure of what you *say*.

Net charge is the ratio of charge (deposits) versus discharge (withdrawals), the accumulation of all the interactions up to that point. Or more simply what we do versus what we say.

Current questions I find interesting, Graham Duncan, grahamduncan.blog.

Graham Duncan is a successful investor and talent spotter who co-founded East Rock Capital, a multi-family office investment firm that manages $2 billion for a small number of families and their charitable foundations. Before starting East Rock, Duncan worked at two other investment firms and started his career by co-founding an independent Wall Street research firm. A Yale graduate with a degree in ethics, politics, and economics, Duncan has become known as a "talent whisperer" for his unique ability to identify and nurture emerging investment talent. Duncan's unusual ability to wait out the moment is one of his defining characteristics as an investor, with colleagues noting that he's "not susceptible to impatience the way most people are" when it comes to seeding new investment managers. He also co-chairs The Sohn Investment Conference, which raises money for paediatric cancer research. Duncan maintains an active presence as a thoughtful writer and commentator on investment philosophy, human development, and talent identification, sharing insights through his blog and social media about the intersection of psychology and investing. His approach emphasises patience, deep understanding of human potential, and the importance of allowing talent to develop naturally rather than forcing growth.

MARCH 20

"*Do you judge others by higher or lower standards than you judge yourself?*"
- *Gregory Stock*[82]

---

[82] *The Book of Questions: Revised and Updated*, Gregory Stock, 2013.
Gregory Stock is a biotech entrepreneur, bioethicist, best-selling author and public communicator who is a leading authority on the broad impacts of genomic and other advanced technologies in the life sciences. He founded the influential Program on Medicine, Technology and Society at UCLA's School of Medicine in 1997 and served as its director for ten years while leading a broad effort to explore critical technologies poised to reshape medical science, Stock is the co-founder and former CEO of Signum Biosciences and has held academic positions at institutions including the University of California, Los Angeles (UCLA) and the Icahn School of Medicine at Mount Sinai. Gregory Stock is a scholar in the evolution of humanity as it is and will be, aided by technology. He is in the forefront of the debate on biotech policy, is a frequent speaker at conferences that study the issue, and contributes to scientific journals in the United States and abroad. His work focuses on the intersection of technology and human enhancement, exploring ethical questions around genetic engineering, life extension, and the future of human evolution. His insight at where technology and ethics connect have made him a popular guest on TV and radio, and he has been a prominent voice in discussions about biotechnology policy and the implications of emerging life sciences technologies for society, medicine, and human development.

MARCH 21

"Are my people better off as a result of their time with me?"
- David Dye[83]

---

[83] Effective leadership can instil energy, confidence, and belief in those being led. Robert Greenleaf, the founder of servant leadership, wrote: "It is part of the enigma of human nature that the "typical" person - immature, stumbling, inept, lazy - is capable of great dedication and heroism if wisely led. ... Many otherwise able people are disqualified to lead because they cannot work with and through the half-people who are all there are. The secret of institution building is to be able to weld a team of such people by lifting them up to grow taller than they would otherwise be."

7 Practical Questions That Will Multiply Your Influence, David Dye, leadchangegroup.com, July 14, 2012.

David M. Dye is the Founder and President of Trailblaze, Inc., that works with leaders and managers who want to get more done, build teams that care, and meet their goals. He is a former executive and elected official who serves as lead trailblazer of the leadership-consulting firm, Trailblaze, Inc. Dye is the author of "The Seven Things Your Team Needs to Hear You Say" and focuses on practical leadership development for managers and executives. He holds a master's degree in nonprofit management, is a member of the American Society of Trainers and Developers and the National Speakers Association, and has been listed with leadership thought-leaders including Seth Godin, Tom Peters, Kouses & Posner, and John Maxwell. His work emphasises helping leaders create high-performing teams through clear communication, accountability, and building environments where team members feel valued and motivated. Dye regularly speaks and writes about effective leadership principles and practices for organisational success.

MARCH 22

"Do those served grow as persons? Do they, while being served, become healthier, wiser, freer, more autonomous, more likely themselves to become servants?"
- Robert Greenleaf[84]

---

[84] "The servant-leader is servant first" Greenleaf explains. "It begins with the natural feeling that one wants to serve, to serve first. Then conscious choice brings one to aspire to lead. That person is sharply different from one who is leader first, perhaps because of the need to assuage an unusual power drive or to acquire material possessions. For such it will be a later choice to serve — after leadership is established. The leader-first and the servant- first are two extreme types. Between them there are shadings and blends that are part of the infinite variety of human nature. The difference manifests itself in the care taken by the servant-first to make sure that other people's highest priority needs are being served. The best test, and difficult to administer, is: Do those served grow as persons? Do they, while being served, become healthier, wiser, freer, more autonomous, more likely themselves to become servants? And, what is the effect on the least privileged in society; will they benefit, or, at least, not be further deprived?"

The Leader as Servant, Robert K. Greenleaf, 1970.

Robert Greenleaf (1904-1990) was a management consultant, writer, and philosopher who developed the influential concept of "servant leadership." After a 38-year career at AT&T, where he rose to the position of Director of Management Research, Greenleaf became deeply interested in how organisations could be more effectively led through service rather than traditional command-and-control methods. His seminal 1970 essay "The Servant as Leader" introduced the idea that the best leaders are servants first, motivated by a natural desire to serve others rather than to accumulate power or material possessions. Greenleaf's servant leadership philosophy emphasises that effective leaders prioritise the growth and well-being of their followers and communities, asking themselves whether those they serve grow as persons and become more capable, autonomous, and likely to become servants themselves. His work was influenced by Hermann Hesse's novel "Journey to the East," which features a character who serves his companions on a journey and is later revealed to be their true leader. After leaving AT&T, Greenleaf founded the Center for Applied Ethics (later renamed The Greenleaf Center for Servant Leadership) and spent his later years writing, consulting, and teaching about leadership principles. His ideas have profoundly influenced business leaders, educators, and organisations worldwide, with many companies and institutions adopting servant leadership principles as core to their management philosophies. His writings continue to be studied and applied in leadership development programs across various sectors.

MARCH 23

"What would I need to reach across and blend into myself?"
- Peter Kauffman[85]

---

[85] Peter Drucker believed, "The task of leadership is to create an alignment of strengths in ways that make a system's weaknesses irrelevant." Like blending different materials together to obtain a superior alloy, people can be combined in a team in ways that create a powerful force multiplier. Drucker explains, "the task is to make people capable of joint performance, to make their strengths effective and their weaknesses irrelevant. The first secret of effectiveness is to understand the people you work with and depend on so that you can make use of their strengths, their ways of working, and their values. Working relationships are as much based on the people as they are on the work." In his talk Kauffman uses metallurgy to explain. "Copper on the Mohs' scale is only a three." he says. "If we have a 1.5 over there and a three over here. ... in nature, for whatever reason, tin and copper are not generally found in the geographic proximity of one another. ... Does anybody know what you get when you blend tin and copper ... You get bronze. Now, does anybody know what bronze is on the Mohs' scale of hardness? ... It's a 6. Iron is 5.5. Can you imagine taking two independent characteristics, neither of which is all that powerful, and putting them together in just the right way, and getting a 6? Now, in physics, they have a name for this. It's called a leaping emergent effect. Now, what if in your own life you could put together some characteristics and become bronze yourself? Become a 6? What would you need to do? Well, you need to identify what kind of a person am I? Am I tin? Am I copper? What would I need to reach across and blend into myself?"

Peter Kauffman speech *An Unsung Hero* about Frederick Taylor Gates, The Redlands Forum 16th January 2020.

Peter Kaufman is Chairman and CEO of Glenair, Inc., a manufacturer of electrical and fiber optic components and assemblies primarily for aerospace applications. He first started working for Glenair while in college nearly 40 years ago, and has been CEO for many decades. He was a longtime director of Wesco Financial, a unit of Berkshire Hathaway, and is a current director of Daily Journal Corp. As the steward of "Poor Charlie's Almanack: The Wit and Wisdom of Charles T. Munger", Kaufman has learned from some of the brightest minds in business and is known for his multidisciplinary approach to thinking and investing, closely aligned with the principles of Charlie Munger.

MARCH 24

"How can I help?"
- Doug Conant[86]

---

[86] This has been called "the ultimate leadership question".
Ask "How Can I Help?" and Other Tips to Lead Positive, Lead Positive profile: Doug Conant, founder and CEO of ConantLeadership (Part 1), Psychology Today, July 17, 2014.
Doug Conant is a business executive and leadership expert who served as CEO of Campbell Soup Company from 2001 to 2011, where he led one of the most successful business turnarounds in corporate history. When he took over, Campbell's was struggling with declining sales and low employee engagement, but under his leadership, the company achieved significant growth and became known for its strong workplace culture. Conant is particularly known for his approach to "people-centric leadership" and his belief in the importance of employee engagement and authentic leadership. After leaving Campbell's, he founded ConantLeadership, a leadership development firm, and has written several books on leadership including "TouchPoints" and "The Blueprint." He's also served as chairman of Avon Products and has been involved with various nonprofit organisations. Conant is a frequent speaker on leadership topics and is known for his philosophy that leaders must genuinely care for their people while also delivering strong business results. He emphasises the importance of building trust, inspiring performance, and creating environments where employees can thrive.

MARCH 25

*"Is everyone singing the same hymn?
How do leader's lead?
Who gets to drink from the information reservoir?
Is this an organisation of teams or of stars
and satellites?
How does the organisation evaluate
employee's performance?"*
- Howard Stevenson[87]

---

[87] Stevenson suggests that company culture can be accurately assessed through these five questions -

Ask team members about purpose, values, and goals. Disparate or generic answers reveal fragmented culture where everyone pulls in different directions.

Do leaders' actions match their words? Misalignment creates dysfunctional culture through conflicting "informal rules".

Who has access to key information? Healthy cultures share bad news openly and cultivate divergent opinions through total communication.

Organisations built around stars with supporting casts limit collaboration and full team potential, unlike true team-based cultures.

Healthy cultures use transparent, objective measures against clear goals and benchmarks. Subjective evaluations create confusion and undermine trust.

Howard's Gift: Uncommon Wisdom to Inspire Your Life's Work, Eric Sinoway and Merrill Meadow, 2012.

Howard Stevenson is a prominent figure in entrepreneurship education and research, best known for his long tenure at Harvard Business School where he served as the Sarofim-Rock Baker Foundation Professor of Business Administration. He's often referred to as the "godfather of entrepreneurship studies" at Harvard and played a pivotal role in establishing entrepreneurship as a legitimate academic discipline. Stevenson developed influential frameworks for understanding entrepreneurship, including his widely-cited definition of entrepreneurship as "the pursuit of opportunity beyond resources controlled." He has authored numerous books and articles on entrepreneurship, venture capital, and business strategy, and has been instrumental in shaping how entrepreneurship is taught in business schools worldwide. Throughout his career, he has also been involved with various entrepreneurial ventures and has served on numerous boards, bridging the gap between academic theory and practical business application.

MARCH 26

"What do you need?"
- Stanley McChrystal[88]

---

[88] The context for this question was McChrystal explaining how he decentralised his military command in order to combat a more nimble, protean enemy. "Eventually a rule of thumb emerged: "If something supports our effort, as long as it is not immoral or illegal," you could do it. Soon, I found that the question I most often asked my force was "What do you need?" We decentralized until it made us uncomfortable, and it was right there—on the brink of instability—that we found our sweet spot."
Team of Teams: New Rules of Engagement for a Complex World, Stanley McChrystal, 2015.
Stanley McChrystal is a retired U.S. Army four-star general who became one of America's most respected military leaders and organisational transformation experts. McChrystal spent 34 years in the Army, rising to become the commander of U.S. and International Security Assistance Forces in Afghanistan from 2009 to 2010. He is perhaps best known for leading Joint Special Operations Command (JSOC) from 2003 to 2008, where he revolutionised counterterrorism operations in Iraq and Afghanistan by transforming traditional military hierarchies into agile, networked organisations capable of rapid decision-making and execution. McChrystal's leadership philosophy centres on what he calls "Team of Teams" - the idea that in complex, rapidly changing environments, organisations must become networks of small, empowered teams rather than traditional command-and-control structures. This approach, detailed in his bestselling book "Team of Teams: New Rules of Engagement for a Complex World," has been widely adopted by businesses and organisations seeking to become more adaptive and responsive. After retiring from the military, McChrystal founded the McChrystal Group, a leadership consulting firm that helps organisations apply military-tested leadership principles to business challenges. He has also written several other influential books, including "Leaders: Myth and Reality," which examines different leadership styles throughout history, and "My Share of the Task," a memoir of his military service. McChrystal currently teaches at Yale University and serves on various boards, continuing to share insights about leadership, teamwork, and organisational change.

MARCH 27

"How will I affect the space I am about to enter?"
- Adam Fraser[89]

---

[89] The "Third Space" is the transitional moment between the role or environment you're leaving (the first space) and the one you're about to enter (the second space). Fraser emphasises the importance of this in-between space as an opportunity to reset and prepare oneself mentally and emotionally for the next interaction or task. Fraser outlines a three-step process to navigate this transition effectively -

Reflect: Consider what has just occurred and acknowledge any emotions or thoughts associated with it.

Rest: Take a moment to relax and release any tension or stress.

Reset: Set a clear intention for how you want to approach the upcoming space or interaction.

By consciously engaging in this process, leaders can improve their performance and relationships, ensuring they bring their best selves to each new situation. The idea aligns with the concept of "leadership presence" and "leadership shadow".

The Third Space: Using Life's Little Transitions to Find Balance and Happiness, Adam Fraser, 2012.

Dr. Adam Fraser is a peak performance researcher, author, and keynote speaker who holds a PhD in Biomedical Science. He is the author of three best-selling books, including "The Third Space" and "Strive", and serves as director of the e-lab, a research company that partners with various Universities throughout Asia Pacific to elevate knowledge of what drives high performance. His unique research focuses on working with elite athletes and sporting teams, special forces soldiers and business leaders. In the last decade, Dr. Fraser has delivered more than 1,500 presentations to over half a million people globally. His work centres on helping teams, organisations and individuals optimise their wellbeing, culture and leadership to achieve peak performance.

MARCH 28

"What more can I be doing to facilitate the team's progress and minimize its setbacks?"
- Hal Gregersen[90]

---

90 *Questions Are the Answer: A Breakthrough Approach to Your Most Vexing Problems at Work and in Life*, Hal Gregersen, 2018.

Hal Gregersen is an organisational behaviour expert, innovation researcher, and executive educator who specialises in leadership development and fostering creative thinking in organisations. He is a Senior Lecturer at MIT Sloan School of Management and the founding Executive Director of the MIT Leadership Center, where he focuses on helping leaders develop the skills needed to navigate uncertainty and drive innovation. Gregersen is co-author of several influential books, including "The Innovator's DNA" (with Clayton Christensen and Jeff Dyer), which identifies five key skills that distinguish innovative leaders: questioning, observing, networking, experimenting, and associational thinking. His research emphasises the power of asking better questions as a catalyst for breakthrough thinking and organisational change. Through his work with executives and organisations worldwide, Gregersen advocates for creating cultures where curiosity is valued and where leaders regularly challenge assumptions through disciplined inquiry. His approach combines rigorous research with practical frameworks, helping leaders develop what he calls "question bursts" and other techniques to unlock creative potential in themselves and their teams.

MARCH 29

"How can I use myself to serve best?"
- Robert Greenleaf [91]

---

[91] Greenleaf's question echoes author Jim Collins who explains that effectiveness is, "anyone who seeks how best to self-deploy on the few priorities that will make the biggest impact."
The Leader as Servant, Robert K. Greenleaf, 1970.
Robert Greenleaf (1904-1990) was a management consultant, writer, and philosopher who developed the influential concept of "servant leadership." After a 38-year career at AT&T, where he rose to the position of Director of Management Research, Greenleaf became deeply interested in how organisations could be more effectively led through service rather than traditional command-and-control methods. His seminal 1970 essay "The Servant as Leader" introduced the idea that the best leaders are servants first, motivated by a natural desire to serve others rather than to accumulate power or material possessions. Greenleaf's servant leadership philosophy emphasises that effective leaders prioritise the growth and well-being of their followers and communities, asking themselves whether those they serve grow as persons and become more capable, autonomous, and likely to become servants themselves. His work was influenced by Hermann Hesse's novel "Journey to the East," which features a character who serves his companions on a journey and is later revealed to be their true leader. After leaving AT&T, Greenleaf founded the Center for Applied Ethics (later renamed The Greenleaf Center for Servant Leadership) and spent his later years writing, consulting, and teaching about leadership principles. His ideas have profoundly influenced business leaders, educators, and organisations worldwide, with many companies and institutions adopting servant leadership principles as core to their management philosophies. His writings continue to be studied and applied in leadership development programs across various sectors.

MARCH 30

"Whenever you are about to find fault with someone, ask yourself the following question: What fault of mine most nearly resembles the one I am about to criticize?"
- Marcus Aurelius[92]

---

[92] This question hints at a key part of human nature, the tendency to see faults in others but not ourselves. Research suggests that while 95% of people think they are self-aware, less than 15% are. Claire Hughes Johnson, previously a VP at Google and the COO of Stripe, says a sign of low self-awareness is constantly receiving feedback that you disagree with, revealing others perceive you differently to how you perceive yourself.

Meditations, Marcus Aurelius, Book 10, Section 30. Marcus Aurelius penned his thoughts in a personal journal, never thinking his inner dialogue would be published and appreciated by countless readers over ensuing millennia. Written as reflections and self-help advice as Marcus struggled to make sense of the Universe, the book is regarded as one of the greatest philosophical works of all time, a literary monument. Meditations has become a favourite of millions of readers, from ordinary people to world leaders. Classicist, researcher, and author Michael Grant described it as "the best book ever written by a major ruler", and Marcus as "the noblest of all the men who, by sheer intelligence and force of character, have prized and achieved goodness for its own sake and not for any reward."

Marcus Aurelius (121 – 180 AD) was a Roman Emperor who ruled from 161 to 180 CE and is remembered as the last of the "Five Good Emperors" and one of history's most important Stoic philosophers. Born in 121 CE, he was originally named Marcus Annius Verus and was adopted by Emperor Antoninus Pius, eventually ascending to the throne during a period of relative peace and prosperity in the Roman Empire. Despite his imperial duties, Marcus Aurelius is best known for his philosophical work "Meditations," a collection of personal reflections and moral exercises written during military campaigns. These writings, never intended for publication, reveal his struggles to live according to Stoic principles while managing the enormous responsibilities of ruling an empire. His philosophy emphasised virtue, duty, acceptance of fate, and the impermanence of life, offering timeless insights on leadership, resilience, and personal conduct. Marcus Aurelius died in 180 CE, likely from plague, and his reign marked the end of the Pax Romana, as the empire would face increasing challenges under his less capable successors.

MARCH 31

"The final test of a leader is the feeling you have when you leave his presence ... Have you a feeling of uplift and confidence?"
- Bernard Montgomery[93]

---

[93] In his book *The Captain Class*, journalist Sam Walker notes, "Studies have shown that a team leader who is in a positive mood can increase a group's enthusiasm, help it to channel anger more constructively, and even coax it to perform better on specific tasks." The effect on a team or organisation can be profound. Researchers Emma Seppälä and Kim Cameron found, "the greatest predictor of success for leaders is not their charisma, influence, or power. It is not personality, attractiveness, or innovative genius. The one thing that supersedes all these factors is positive relational energy: the energy exchanged between people that helps uplift, enthuse, and renew them." There have been many famous exemplars, including in military leadership where the leader's presence can act as a powerful force multiplier. The Duke of Wellington recalled, "I used to say of Napoleon that his presence on the field made the difference of forty thousand men". There is a wonderful scene in the movie "Master and Commander" where Captain Jack Aubrey (played by Russell Crowe) recalls meeting Admiral Nelson. He recounts Nelson declining a cloak on a cold evening because he was kept warm by his passion for King and country. Some of crew scoff at this and Aubrey acknowledges it sounds absurd, but he says, with Nelson, "you felt your heart glow".

Monty: The Making of a General, 1887-1942 v. 1: Life of Montgomery of Alamein, Nigel Hamilton, 1981.

Field Marshal Bernard Law Montgomery (1887 – 1976), known as "Monty," was one of Britain's most prominent military commanders during World War II. He gained fame leading the British Eighth Army to victory against Erwin Rommel's forces at the Second Battle of El Alamein in 1942, marking a crucial turning point in the North African campaign. Montgomery later commanded British forces during the D-Day landings in Normandy and led the 21st Army Group through the liberation of Western Europe. He was famous for his meticulous planning, cautious approach, and emphasis on thorough preparation before battle. After the war, he served as Chief of the Imperial General Staff and later as NATO's Deputy Supreme Allied Commander Europe until his retirement.

APRIL

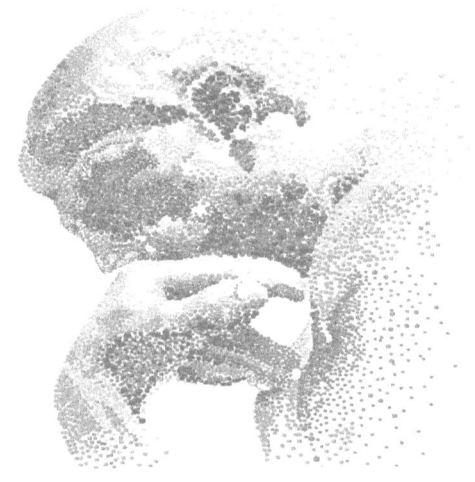

CULTIVATE & SHARE YOUR VISION

APRIL 1

"What would you attempt to do if you knew you could not fail?"
- Robert Schuller[94]

---

[94] A leader's belief in the vision is paramount. "The secret of leadership is simple" author and entrepreneur Seth Godin says, "Do what you believe in. Paint a picture of the future. Go there. People will follow." People can sense belief, or the absence of it. It cannot be faked. Pulitzer Prize winning writer Robert Caro has written for decades on power and observes, "what convinces is conviction. You simply have to believe in the argument you are advancing: if you don't, you're as good as dead. The other person will sense that something isn't there."

In his autobiography "Shoe Dog", Nike founder Phil Knight recalled the impact that his belief had on others, "Driving back to Portland I'd puzzle over my sudden success at selling. I'd been unable to sell encyclopedias, and I'd despised it to boot. I'd been slightly better at selling mutual funds, but I'd felt dead inside. So why was selling shoes so different? Because, I realized, it wasn't selling. I believed in running. I believed that if people got out and ran a few miles every day, the world would be a better place, and I believed these shoes were better to run in. People, sensing my belief, wanted some of that belief for themselves. Belief, I decided. Belief is irresistible."

Tough Times Never Last, But Tough People Do!, Robert H. Schuller, 1983.

Robert H. Schuller (1926-2015) was a Reformed Church pastor who became one of the most influential television evangelists of the 20th century. Born on a farm near Alton, Iowa, as the youngest of five children, Schuller revolutionised modern Christian ministry by founding the Crystal Cathedral in Garden Grove, California. He dedicated his spectacular worship space, the Crystal Cathedral, in 1980, working with renowned architect Philip Johnson to create a building with both glass walls and a glass ceiling. He was best known for his television program "Hour of Power," which he founded in 1970 and hosted until 2010, reaching millions of viewers worldwide with his message of possibility thinking and positive Christianity. Schuller's ministry emphasised reaching the "unchurched" through innovative approaches, including drive-in services, and his Crystal Cathedral became an architectural landmark that demonstrated the potential of modern megachurch ministry.

APRIL 2

"What would you still do if you knew you would fail?"
- Seth Godin[95]

---

[95] "I know of no better life purpose than to perish in attempting the great and impossible." Philosopher Friedrich Nietzsche notes. "The fact that something seems impossible shouldn't be a reason to not pursue it. That's exactly what makes it worth pursuing, where would the courage and greatness be if success was certain and there was no risk. The only true failure is shrinking away from life's challenges."
The Icarus Deception: How High Will You Fly?, Seth Godin, 2012.
Seth Godin is a bestselling author, entrepreneur, and marketing guru who has fundamentally changed how people think about marketing, leadership, and the spread of ideas. He's written over 20 books, including influential titles like "Purple Cow," which popularised the concept that businesses must be remarkable to succeed, "The Tipping Point" predecessor "Unleashing the Ideavirus," and "Linchpin," which argues that indispensable employees are those who bring creativity and humanity to their work. Godin founded several companies, including Yoyodyne (one of the first internet marketing companies, sold to Yahoo!) and Squidoo, and the altMBA, an intensive online leadership workshop. His daily blog, which he's maintained for decades, reaches millions of readers with insights on marketing, culture, and human behaviour. Godin is known for coining terms like "permission marketing" (marketing to people who want to be marketed to) and advocating for authentic, story-driven approaches over traditional advertising. His philosophy emphasises that in the modern economy, playing it safe is actually the riskiest strategy, and that success comes from being different, generous, and willing to make a difference. He's also a sought-after speaker who challenges conventional business wisdom and encourages people to embrace change and lead rather than follow.

APRIL 3

*"You only get one life.
Why not do something huge?"
- Paul Graham*[96]

---

[96] People have a deep need to be part of something larger than themselves, to commit themselves to a magnificent cause, or pursue a grand vision. Jesuit priest, scientist, theologian, philosopher, and teacher Pierre Teilhard de Chardin explained, "There is an almost sensual longing for communion with others who have a larger vision. The immense fulfillment of the friendships between those engaged in furthering the evolution of consciousness has a quality almost impossible to describe." The need to be part of something larger than oneself gives life meaning, and enables a person to transcend their own self-centredness. "This is the true joy in life, being used for a purpose recognized by yourself as a mighty one." playwright George Bernard Shaw wrote. "Being a force of nature instead of a feverish, selfish little clod of ailments and grievances, complaining that the world will not devote itself to making you happy." It is impossible to overstate the power of being part of something bigger than oneself.

Some Heroes, Paul Graham, paulgraham.com, April 2008.

Paul Graham is a computer scientist, entrepreneur, essayist, and venture capitalist who co-founded Y Combinator, the world's most influential startup accelerator. A programmer by training, he co-created Viaweb in the 1990s, one of the first web-based software applications, which was sold to Yahoo for $49 million and became Yahoo Store. Y Combinator has funded over 5,000 startups including Airbnb, Dropbox, Stripe, Reddit, and DoorDash, fundamentally changing how early-stage companies get funded and mentored. Beyond his business ventures, Graham is renowned for his essays on startups, programming, and life, published on his website paulgraham.com. His writing covers topics from technical programming concepts to startup advice to broader philosophical observations, and his essays like "Do Things That Don't Scale" and "Maker's Schedule, Manager's Schedule" have become foundational reading in Silicon Valley. Graham is known for his clear, thoughtful writing style and contrarian insights about entrepreneurship, such as emphasising the importance of building something people want rather than focusing on business plans. He stepped back from day-to-day operations at Y Combinator to focus more on his writing and thinking, but remains one of the most respected voices in the startup ecosystem.

APRIL 4

"What do we want to create?"
- Peter Senge[97]

---

[97] "It's not what the vision is, it's what the vision does ..." Senge explains. "A shared vision is not an idea. It is not even an important idea such as freedom. It is, rather, a force in people's hearts, a force of impressive power. It may be inspired by an idea, but once it goes further - if it is compelling enough to acquire the support of more than one person - then it is no longer an abstraction. It is palpable. People begin to see it as if it exists. Few, if any, forces in human affairs are as powerful as shared vision. At its simplest level, a shared vision is the answer to the question, "What do we want to create?"

The Fifth Discipline: The Art and Practice of the Learning Organization, Peter M. Senge, 1990.

Peter Senge is a systems scientist, organisational learning expert, and senior lecturer at MIT Sloan School of Management who revolutionised how organisations think about learning and change. He is best known for his groundbreaking book "The Fifth Discipline: The Art and Practice of the Learning Organization," which introduced the concept of learning organisations, companies that continually expand their capacity to create their future rather than just react to events. Senge's work integrates systems thinking, personal mastery, mental models, shared vision, and team learning into a comprehensive framework for organisational transformation. Through his research at MIT and his work with the Society for Organizational Learning, he has helped countless companies move from traditional hierarchical structures to more adaptive, learning-focused organisations. His systems thinking approach emphasises understanding the interconnectedness of organisational elements rather than focusing on isolated problems, making him one of the most influential management thinkers of the past several decades and a pioneer in applying complexity science to business challenges.

APRIL 5

"How can we do the most good?"
- Will MacAskill[98]

---

[98] As part of his approach to maximising impact, MacAskill asks some other thought provoking questions: "How can we ensure that, when we try to help others, we do so as effectively as possible?" and "How can I make the biggest difference I can?"

What are the most important moral problems of our time? Will MacAskill, TED April 2018. Also refer *Doing Good Better: How Effective Altruism Can Help You Help Others, Do Work That Matters, and Make Smarter Choices about Giving Back*, William MacAskill, 2016.

William MacAskill is an Associate Professor in Philosophy and Research Fellow at the Global Priorities Institute at the University of Oxford, and at the time of his appointment, he was the youngest associate professor of philosophy in the world. He is one of the co-founders of the effective altruism movement, which is about trying to use evidence and reason to help others as much as possible with our time and money. MacAskill co-founded several influential organisations including Giving What We Can, the Centre for Effective Altruism, and 80,000 Hours, which together have moved over $300 million to effective charities. He is the author of "Doing Good Better" and "What We Owe the Future", and co-author of "Moral Uncertainty". His work focuses on applying philosophical reasoning to practical questions about how individuals and institutions can do the most good with their resources and careers.

APRIL 6

"What would you do if you were not afraid?"
- David Brooks[99]

---

[99] "Each day befriend a single fear," author Sam Keen writes, "and the miscellaneous terrors of being human will never join together to form such a morass of vague anxiety that it rules your life from the shadows of the unconscious. We learn to fly not by being fearless, but by the daily practice of courage."
How to Know a Person: The Art of Seeing Others Deeply and Being Deeply Seen, David Brooks, 2023.

David Brooks is a prominent journalist, political commentator, and author who writes for The New York Times, where he has been an op-ed columnist since 2003. Known for his thoughtful analysis of American politics, culture, and society, Brooks often takes a moderate conservative perspective while focusing on themes like community, character, and moral development. He's written several influential books including "The Social Animal," which explores human behaviour and decision-making, "The Road to Character," which examines the difference between résumé virtues and eulogy virtues, and "The Second Mountain," about finding deeper meaning and purpose in life. Before joining the Times, Brooks worked at publications like The Wall Street Journal, The Weekly Standard, and The Atlantic. He's also a regular commentator on PBS NewsHour and NPR, and teaches at Yale University. Brooks is known for his ability to bridge political divides and his interest in how psychology, sociology, and moral philosophy intersect with public policy and everyday life.

APRIL 7

"What if you could?"
- Alan Cohen[100]

---

[100] "There is no comparison between that which is lost by not succeeding" Francis Bacon writes, "and that which is lost by not trying."

A Deep Breath of Life: Daily Inspiration for Heart-Centered Living, Alan Cohen, 1996.

Alan Cohen is a prolific inspirational author, speaker, and life coach who has written over 30 books focusing on personal growth, spirituality, and self-empowerment. His works include titles like "A Deep Breath of Life," "The Dragon Doesn't Live Here Anymore," and "I Had It All the Time," which blend practical wisdom with spiritual insights to help readers find greater fulfillment and authenticity in their lives. Cohen's writing style is accessible and often incorporates humour, personal anecdotes, and simple yet profound teachings drawn from various spiritual traditions. He conducts workshops, retreats, and coaching programs worldwide, emphasising themes like following one's passion, overcoming fear, and living from the heart rather than the ego. His approach combines elements of New Thought spirituality, psychology, and practical life advice, making complex spiritual concepts relatable to everyday situations. Cohen is known for his warm, encouraging tone and his ability to help people shift from limitation-based thinking to possibility-focused living. Cohen is also contributing writer for the best-selling series *Chicken Soup for the Soul*.

APRIL 8

"What future is being imagined here?"
- James Bridle[101]

---

[101] How does management differ from leadership? Leadership is about people. Admiral Grace Hopper expressed the difference as "Manage things, lead people". But the difference also concerns time. Management is largely focussed on the present, and supporting what is, whereas leadership is concerned with forging the future. Psychologist and MIT Professor Edgar H. Schein defines leadership as, "wanting to do something new and better, and getting others to go along."
Ways of Being: Animals, Plants, Machines: The Search for a Planetary Intelligence, James Bridle, 2023.

James Bridle is an artist, writer, and technologist known for exploring the intersection of technology, politics, and society through both visual art and critical writing. Their work often examines how digital technologies shape our understanding of the world, from surveillance systems to artificial intelligence. Bridle has exhibited internationally and written several influential books, including "New Dark Age: Technology and the End of the Future," which critiques how our increasing reliance on complex technological systems can obscure rather than illuminate our understanding of reality. They frequently address themes of algorithmic governance, digital infrastructure, and the unintended consequences of technological progress in contemporary life.

APRIL 9

"By 'why', I mean:
What's your purpose?
What's your cause?
What's your belief?
Why does your organization exist?
Why do you get out of bed in the morning?
And why should anyone care?"
- Simon Sinek[102]

---

[102] "The mystery of human existence lies not in just staying alive," Fyodor Dostoyevsky writes, "but in finding something to live for."
How great leaders inspire action, Simon Sinek, TEDxPuget Sound, 2009.
Simon Sinek is an author, motivational speaker, and organisational consultant best known for popularizing the concept of "Start With Why" through his famous 2009 TED Talk, which has become one of the most-watched TED presentations of all time. The central idea is that great leaders and organisations inspire action by communicating their purpose and beliefs (the "why") before explaining what they do or how they do it. Sinek has written several bestselling books including "Start With Why," "Leaders Eat Last," and "The Infinite Game," which explore leadership, organisational culture, and sustainable success. He argues that the best leaders create environments of trust and safety where people feel valued and motivated to contribute their best work. Sinek works with organisations ranging from startups to Fortune 500 companies and government agencies, helping them clarify their purpose and build stronger, more inspiring cultures. His approach combines insights from anthropology, psychology, and biology to explain human behaviour in organisational settings, emphasising that people don't buy what you do, they buy why you do it.

APRIL 10

"We could if ...?"
- Edgar Schein[103]

---

[103] The question is attributed to Edgar Schein as a key aspect of his concept of "Humble Inquiry". Humble Inquiry is about asking questions rather than telling, which can build stronger relationships and lead to better communication and problem-solving. Schein writes, "Humble Inquiry is the fine art of drawing someone out, of asking questions to which you do not already know the answer, of building a relationship based on curiosity and interest in the other person." He emphasises, "The time when Humble Inquiry is often most needed is when we observe something that makes us angry or anxious. It is at those times that we need to slow down, to ask ourselves and others "What's really going on?" in order to check out the facts. Then we ask ourselves how valid our reactions are before we make a judgment and leap into action."

Humble Inquiry: The Gentle Art of Asking Instead of Telling, Edgar H. Schein, 2013.

Edgar H. Schein (1928 - 2023) was a pioneering organisational psychologist and management theorist who fundamentally shaped our understanding of organisational culture and leadership. Schein spent most of his distinguished academic career at MIT Sloan School of Management, where he was a professor emeritus until his death in 2023. He is best known for developing the influential three-level model of organisational culture, which describes culture as consisting of artifacts (visible structures and processes), espoused beliefs and values, and underlying assumptions that truly drive behaviour. His seminal work "Organizational Culture and Leadership" became one of the most cited texts in management literature and established him as the foremost expert on corporate culture. Schein also made significant contributions to the field of career development, coining the concept of "career anchors" - the self-perceived talents, motives, and values that guide career decisions. His approach to organisational consulting emphasised process consultation, where consultants help organisations solve their own problems rather than providing direct solutions. Throughout his career, Schein worked with numerous Fortune 500 companies and government agencies, helping them navigate cultural change and leadership challenges. His humanistic approach to management, which emphasised the importance of psychological safety and authentic relationships in the workplace, influenced generations of leaders and consultants. Schein authored over 30 books and countless articles, leaving an enduring legacy in organisational psychology and management theory.

APRIL 11

"What should exist?
To me, that's the most exciting question imaginable.
What do we need that we don't have?
How can we realise our potential?"
- Paul Allen[104]

---

104 *Paul Allen on Invention*, Big Think, January 21, 2014.

Paul G. Allen (1953-2018) was the co-founder of Microsoft Corporation with his childhood friend Bill Gates, which was followed by the microcomputer revolution of the 1970s and 1980s. An investor and philanthropist, Allen left Microsoft in the 1980s due to illness but remained involved in various ventures. Beyond technology, he was a prolific collector and investor who owned the Seattle Seahawks NFL team and Portland Trail Blazers NBA team. Allen founded Ai2 in 2014 to find transformative ways to develop AI to address some of the world's biggest challenges. He left a legacy in technology, sports ownership, philanthropy, and cultural institutions including Seattle's Museum of Pop Culture.

APRIL 12

"Have you identified a unique opportunity that others don't see?"
- Peter Thiel[105]

---

[105] Thiel echoes writer and businessman William C. Taylor. "IDEO's Tom Kelly likes to quote French novelist Marcel Proust, who famously said, "The real act of discovery consists not in finding new lands but in seeing with new eyes." Taylor explains. "What goes for novelists goes for leaders searching to discover a novel game plan for the future. The most successful companies don't just out-compete their rivals. They redefine the terms of competition by embracing one-of-a-kind ideas in a world of me-too thinking. If you believe that what you see shapes how you change, then the challenge for leaders is to see opportunities that other leaders don't see. That's the virtue of vuja dé–it reframes how organizations make sense of their situation and build for the future." From *Ten Questions Every Game Changer Must Answer*, William C. Taylor, Fast Company, January 4, 2011.

Zero to One: Notes on Startups, or How to Build the Future, Peter Thiel and Blake Masters, 2014.

Peter Thiel is an entrepreneur, venture capitalist, and author who co-founded PayPal and became one of Silicon Valley's most influential and controversial figures. Born in Germany and raised in California, Thiel studied philosophy at Stanford before earning a law degree and working briefly as a securities lawyer and derivatives trader. In 1998, he co-founded PayPal with Max Levchin, which was sold to eBay for $1.5 billion in 2002, establishing him as part of the legendary "PayPal Mafia" of entrepreneurs. Thiel was Facebook's first major outside investor, putting $500,000 into the company in 2004 for a stake that eventually became worth over $1 billion. He founded Palantir Technologies, a data analytics company that works with government agencies, and established Founders Fund, a venture capital firm that has invested in companies like SpaceX, Airbnb, and Stripe. Known for his contrarian thinking, Thiel wrote "Zero to One," a bestselling book about startups and innovation, and has been a vocal advocate for technological progress while critiquing higher education and promoting alternative institutions.

APRIL 13

*"The question is:
What kind of impact do you want to make?"
- Jane Goodall*[106]

---

[106] "The greatest danger to our future is apathy." Goodall writes. "We can't all save the world in a dramatic way, but we can each make our small difference, and together those small differences add up. Every single person makes an impact on the planet every single day."

Reason for Hope: A Spiritual Journey, Jane Goodall and Phillip Berman, 2000.

Jane Goodall is a primatologist, ethologist, and anthropologist who revolutionised the study of chimpanzees and became one of the world's most respected conservationists. She began her groundbreaking research at what is now Gombe National Park in Tanzania in 1960, when she was just 26 years old, studying wild chimpanzees in their natural habitat. Her observations challenged existing scientific beliefs about what makes humans unique—she discovered that chimpanzees make and use tools, have complex social relationships, and display distinct personalities and emotions. Goodall's work fundamentally changed our understanding of primates and redefined the relationship between humans and animals. She founded the Jane Goodall Institute in 1977 and later created the Roots & Shoots program to engage young people in conservation efforts. Now in her 90s, Goodall continues to travel extensively as an advocate for environmental conservation, animal welfare, and sustainable living. She has received numerous honors including being made a Dame by Queen Elizabeth II and is considered one of the most influential scientists and conservationists of the modern era.

APRIL 14

"How you will you change the lives of others? How will some people's lives be better and different because you were here on this Earth?"
- Jim Collins[107]

---

[107] Referring to a discussion he had with Peter Drucker, Collins recalls Drucker asking an even more fundamental question, "how can you be useful?" Collins also recounts Dr. Martin Luther King, Jr. saying, "life's most persistent and urgent question is, 'what are you doing for others?'".

Jim's Seven Questions: Learning From Young Leaders Full Talk, Global Leadership Summit, 2015.

Jim Collins is a bestselling author, business researcher, and management consultant who has spent decades studying what makes companies transition from good to great performance. He's best known for his book "Good to Great," which identified key principles that distinguish exceptional companies from merely good ones, including concepts like Level 5 Leadership, the Hedgehog Concept, and getting the right people on the bus. Collins has written several other influential business books including "Built to Last" (co-authored with Jerry Porras), "How the Mighty Fall," and "Great by Choice." His research methodology involves rigorous data analysis and long-term studies of companies, often spanning decades to identify patterns and principles that drive sustained success. Before his writing career, Collins worked as a faculty member at Stanford Graduate School of Business and served as a consultant to corporations and social sector organisations. His work extends beyond the corporate world to nonprofits and educational institutions through books like "Good to Great and the Social Sectors." Collins is known for his disciplined approach to research, his ability to distil complex business concepts into memorable frameworks, and his focus on timeless principles rather than fleeting management fads.

APRIL 15

*"Why do you exist?
For what would you be willing to die?"
- Arthur Brooks*[108]

---

[108] "As a social scientist, I believe that happiness should be understood as a combination of three phenomena: enjoyment, satisfaction, and meaning." Brooks explains. "Enjoyment is pleasure consciously and purposefully experienced, so it can create a positive memory. Satisfaction is the joy of an achievement, the reward for a job well done. And then, there's meaning. You can make do without enjoyment for a while, and even without a lot of satisfaction. But without meaning, you will be utterly lost. That is the psychiatrist and Holocaust survivor Viktor Frankl's argument in his classic book *Man's Search for Meaning*. Without a sense of meaning—a sense of the *why* of our existence–our lives cannot be endured. Here is a quick diagnostic tool I sometimes use to find out if someone has a good sense of their life's meaning. I ask them two questions:

1. Why do you exist?
2. For what would you be willing to die?

There is no greater joy than seeing someone you love find their answers."

America Is Pursuing Happiness in All the Wrong Places, Arthur C. Brooks, The Atlantic, November 16, 2022.

Arthur C. Brooks is the Parker Gilbert Montgomery Professor of the Practice of Public and Nonprofit Leadership at the Harvard Kennedy School, and Professor of Management Practice at the Harvard Business School, where he teaches courses on leadership, happiness, and nonprofit management. Before joining the Harvard faculty in July of 2019, he served for ten years as president of the American Enterprise Institute (AEI), a public policy think tank in Washington, DC. Brooks is the author of 11 books, including the national bestsellers "Love Your Enemies", "The Conservative Heart", and "The Road to Freedom". He is a columnist for The Atlantic, and specialises in using the highest levels of science and philosophy to provide people with actionable strategies to live their best lives, focusing particularly on happiness research and social entrepreneurship.

APRIL 16

"What is the real goal?"
- Eliyahu Goldratt[109]

---

[109] Goldratt's question is central to his Theory of Constraints and serves as the foundational inquiry in his groundbreaking business novel "The Goal". In the book, the protagonist Alex Rogo, a plant manager facing the closure of his factory, is challenged by his former physics professor Jonah to identify what the true goal of his business actually is. This seemingly simple question forces Alex to look beyond common metrics like efficiency, utilisation, and cost reduction to recognize that the goal of a business is to make money, specifically, to increase net profit while simultaneously increasing return on investment and cash flow. Goldratt uses this question to expose how organisations often optimise for local improvements rather than global performance, creating systems that appear efficient but fail to deliver real results. The inquiry becomes a diagnostic tool that reveals constraints and bottlenecks preventing the achievement of the true goal. By constantly returning to "What is the real goal?" leaders are forced to align all activities and decisions with the fundamental purpose of their organisation, rather than getting lost in operational metrics that may actually work against overall success. This question has become a cornerstone of systems thinking and lean management practices worldwide.

The Goal: A Process of Ongoing Improvement, Eliyahu M. Goldratt, 1984.

Eliyahu M. Goldratt (1947-2011) was a business management guru and physicist who revolutionised manufacturing and operations management through his Theory of Constraints. Best known for his influential novel "The Goal", Goldratt introduced the concept that every system has bottlenecks that limit overall performance, and that identifying and optimising these constraints is key to improving efficiency. His approach shifted focus from local optimisation to system-wide thinking, emphasising throughput over traditional cost accounting metrics. Beyond manufacturing, Goldratt applied his constraint-based methodology to project management through Critical Chain Project Management and to other business areas, leaving a lasting impact on operations research and business process improvement worldwide.

APRIL 17

"What is the best that can happen?"
- Mo Gawdat[110]

---

110 *Solve for Happy: Engineer Your Path to Joy*, Mo Gawdat, 2017.
Mo Gawdat is the former Chief Business Officer of Google [X]; host of the popular podcast, Slo Mo: A Podcast with Mo Gawdat; author of the international bestselling books Solve for Happy; Scary Smart; That Little Voice in Your Head; and Unstressable; founder of One Billion Happy; and Chief AI Officer of Flight Story. A remarkable thinker and the Chief Business Officer at Google's [X], an elite team of engineers that comprise Google's futuristic "dream factory", Gawdat applied his engineering mindset to the challenge of happiness after realizing in 2001 that despite his incredible success, he was desperately unhappy. After a 30-year career in tech and serving as Chief Business Officer at Google [X], Google's 'moonshot factory' of innovation, Gawdat has made happiness his primary topic of research, diving deeply into literature and conversing on the topic with some of the wisest people in the world. His ambitious goal is "1 billion happy people", viewing this as essential for humanity's continued progress.

APRIL 18

"What are you trying to do?"
- Robert Greenleaf[11]

---

111 "'What are you trying to do?' is one of the easiest to ask and most difficult to answer of questions." Greenleaf writes. "A mark of leaders, an attribute that puts them in a position to show the way for others, is that they are better than most at pointing the direction. As long as one is leading, one always has a goal. It may be a goal arrived at by group consensus, or the leader, acting on inspiration, may simply have said, 'Let's go this way.' But the leader always knows what it is and can articulate it for any who are unsure. By clearly stating and restating the goal the leader gives certainty and purpose to others who may have difficulty in achieving it for themselves. The word goal is used here in the special sense of the overarching purpose, the big dream, the visionary concept, the ultimate consummation which one approaches but never really achieves. It is something presently out of reach; it is something to strive for, to move toward, or become. It is so stated that it excites the imagination and challenges people to work for something they do not yet know how to do, something they can be proud of as they move toward it. Every achievement starts with a goal — but not just any goal and not just anybody stating it. The one who states the goal must elicit trust, especially if it is a high risk or visionary goal, because those who follow are asked to accept the risk along with the leader. Leaders do not elicit trust unless one has confidence in their values and competence (including judgment) and unless they have a sustaining spirit (entheos) that will support the tenacious pursuit of a goal. Not much happens without a dream. And for something great to happen, there must be a great dream. Behind every great achievement is a dreamer of great dreams. Much more than a dreamer is required to bring it to reality; but the dream must be there first.

The Servant as Leader, Robert K. Greenleaf, 1970.

Robert Greenleaf (1904-1990) was a management consultant, writer, and philosopher who developed the influential concept of "servant leadership." After a 38-year career at AT&T, where he rose to the position of Director of Management Research, Greenleaf became deeply interested in how organisations could be more effectively led through service rather than traditional command-and-control methods. His seminal 1970 essay "The Servant as Leader" introduced the idea that the best leaders are servants first, motivated by a natural desire to serve others rather than to accumulate power or material possessions. Greenleaf's servant leadership philosophy emphasises that effective leaders prioritise the growth and well-being of their followers and communities, asking themselves whether those they serve grow as persons and become more capable, autonomous, and likely to become servants themselves. His work was influenced by Hermann Hesse's novel "Journey to the East," which features a character who serves his companions on a journey and is later revealed to be their true leader. After leaving AT&T, Greenleaf founded the Center for Applied Ethics (later renamed The Greenleaf Center for Servant Leadership) and spent his later years writing, consulting, and teaching about leadership principles. His ideas have profoundly influenced business leaders, educators, and organisations worldwide, with many companies and institutions adopting servant leadership principles as core to their management philosophies.

APRIL 19

*"Every team member has four
questions for the leader -
"Where are we going?
How do we get there?
Have you got my back?
Do you care about me?"
- Mark Scharenbroich*[112]

---

[112] Mark Scharenbroich is an Emmy Award-winning motivational speaker, humourist, and author who has built his career around helping people make meaningful connections in both professional and personal settings.
Four Questions Every Leader Must Answer, Mark Scharenbroich, LinkedIn, February 21, 2019.
The questions are relayed by Scharenbroich from Dan Dye, CEO of Ardent Mills. Dan Dye is the former CEO of Ardent Mills, one of North America's premier flour milling and ingredient companies. As CEO, Dan led an extensive network of more than 40 locations that specialise in flour, quinoa, pulses, organic and gluten-free products that drive flour and emerging nutrition plant-based ingredients across the U.S., Canada and Puerto Rico. Prior to leading Ardent Mills, Dye spent three decades at Cargill, serving as president of Horizon Milling and Cargill AgHorizons, U.S. Under his leadership, Ardent Mills established itself as what he describes as a "people-first, values-based business" with a mission to transform how the world is nourished. Beyond his corporate role, Dye has been actively involved in industry leadership, lending his experience and expertise to various executive and Board positions, including the North American Millers' Association, American Bakers Association and Partners in Food Solutions. His decade-long tenure at Ardent Mills focused on building sustainable food systems, advancing employee and community development, and improving access to nutritious ingredient solutions across local and global markets.

APRIL 20

"What do you wish existed that doesn't?"
"What's missing from the world?"
- Paul Graham[113]

---

[113] If you can answer these questions, you will possess the fuel to endure the inevitable challenges. An inspiring exemplar is Sir James Dyson who invented the bagless vacuum cleaner and founded the Dyson company. Dyson explained, "My tale is one of not being brilliant, I wasn't even trained as an engineer or scientist. I did, however, have the bloody-mindedness not to follow convention, to challenge experts and to ignore Doubting Thomases. I am also someone who is prepared to slog through prototype after prototype searching for the breakthrough. He developed no less than 5,127 prototypes of the cyclonic vacuum cleaner between 1979 and 1984. If a slow starter like me could succeed, surely this might encourage others." "In order to fix it," Dyson said, "you need a passionate anger about something that doesn't work well."

An interview with investor Paul Graham of Y Combinator, TechCrunch, September 2, 2006 and *How To Get Startup Ideas*, Paul Graham, paulgraham.com, November 2012.

Paul Graham is a computer scientist, entrepreneur, essayist, and venture capitalist who co-founded Y Combinator, the world's most influential startup accelerator. A programmer by training, he co-created Viaweb in the 1990s, one of the first web-based software applications, which was sold to Yahoo for $49 million and became Yahoo Store. Y Combinator has funded over 5,000 startups including Airbnb, Dropbox, Stripe, Reddit, and DoorDash, fundamentally changing how early-stage companies get funded and mentored. Beyond his business ventures, Graham is renowned for his essays on startups, programming, and life, published on his website paulgraham.com. His writing covers topics from technical programming concepts to startup advice to broader philosophical observations, and his essays like "Do Things That Don't Scale" and "Maker's Schedule, Manager's Schedule" have become foundational reading in Silicon Valley. Graham is known for his clear, thoughtful writing style and contrarian insights about entrepreneurship, such as emphasising the importance of building something people want rather than focusing on business plans. He stepped back from day-to-day operations at Y Combinator to focus more on his writing and thinking, but remains one of the most respected voices in the startup ecosystem.

APRIL 21

"What possibility do you see?"
- Seth Godin[114]

---

[114] "The very essence of leadership is you have a vision." priest and academic Theodore M. Hesburgh writes. "It's got to be a vision you articulate clearly and forcefully on every occasion. Whatever you value, be committed to it and let nothing distract you from this goal. The uncommitted life, like Plato's unexamined life, is not worth living."

Failing On Our Way To Mastery: Seth Godin on The Knowledge Project, Shane Parrish, 23 February 2021.

Seth Godin is a bestselling author, entrepreneur, and marketing guru who has fundamentally changed how people think about marketing, leadership, and the spread of ideas. He's written over 20 books, including influential titles like "Purple Cow," which popularised the concept that businesses must be remarkable to succeed, "The Tipping Point" predecessor "Unleashing the Ideavirus," and "Linchpin," which argues that indispensable employees are those who bring creativity and humanity to their work. Godin founded several companies, including Yoyodyne (one of the first internet marketing companies, sold to Yahoo!) and Squidoo, and the altMBA, an intensive online leadership workshop. His daily blog, which he's maintained for decades, reaches millions of readers with insights on marketing, culture, and human behaviour. Godin is known for coining terms like "permission marketing" (marketing to people who want to be marketed to) and advocating for authentic, story-driven approaches over traditional advertising. His philosophy emphasises that in the modern economy, playing it safe is actually the riskiest strategy, and that success comes from being different, generous, and willing to make a difference. He's also a sought-after speaker who challenges conventional business wisdom and encourages people to embrace change and lead rather than follow.

APRIL 22

"When I look out the window, what is visible but not yet seen by others?"
- Frances Hesselbein[115]

---

[115] *Work is Love Made Visible: A Collection of Essays About the Power of Finding Your Purpose From the World's Greatest Thought Leaders* , Frances Hesselbein, Marshall Goldsmith, Sarah McArthur, 2018.

Frances Hesselbein (1915 - 2022) was a transformational leader who became one of America's most respected authorities on leadership and management through her groundbreaking work with the Girl Scouts of the USA. She served as CEO of the Girl Scouts from 1976 to 1990, where she revolutionised the organisation by transforming it from a traditional to a modern institution capable of serving girls from all backgrounds. Starting as a volunteer troop leader in 1960 despite having no daughters, Hesselbein rose through the ranks and applied principles she learned from management guru Peter Drucker to create innovative organisational models focused on mission, leadership development, and inclusivity. Hesselbein was awarded the Presidential Medal of Freedom, America's highest civilian honour, by President Clinton in 1998 for her leadership as CEO and her service as "a pioneer for women, volunteerism, diversity". After leaving the Girl Scouts, she became the founding president and CEO of the Peter F. Drucker Foundation for Nonprofit Management (later renamed the Leader to Leader Institute), where she continued her work helping nonprofit organisations achieve excellence. Hesselbein authored several influential books on leadership and was widely regarded as one of the most effective nonprofit executives in American history, demonstrating that principled, mission-driven leadership could create lasting organisational and social change. She passed away in 2022 at age 107, leaving behind a legacy of servant leadership and organisational transformation.

APRIL 23

"Who is served by the work that we do?"
- David Burkus[116]

---

[116] David Burkus contends that "most people are less inspired by a compelling answer to 'why?' and more motivated by a clear answer to the question 'who?' ... as in 'who is served by the work we do?'" Burkus uses KPMG as an example. Their initial 'We Shape History' campaign highlighted the firm's role in major historical events including certifying the election of Nelson Mandela, but their breakthrough came with the '10,000 Stories Challenge,' where employees shared personal stories about how their individual work made a difference. They received 42,000 responses with specific examples like 'I combat terrorism because I help banks prevent money laundering' or 'I help farmers grow because I support the farm credit system'. Supporting research from university call centers showed that when student fundraisers spent just five minutes meeting scholarship recipients, their performance doubled, making twice as many calls and generating over five times as much revenue each week. People are more motivated by understanding specifically *who* benefits from their work (pro-social motivation) than by grandiose corporate purpose statements. Leaders should become "chief storytelling officers", helping employees connect their daily tasks to the real people they serve.

A simple way to inspire your team, David Burkus, TEDxReno, May 2022.

David Burkus is an author, award-winning podcaster, and management professor who challenges conventional business wisdom through research-backed insights. A best-selling author, an award-winning podcaster, and associate professor of management at Oral Roberts University, Burkus has written several influential books including "Under New Management," "The Myths of Creativity," "Friend of a Friend," and "Leading from Anywhere." Drawing on decades of research, Burkus has found that not only are many of our fundamental management practices wrong and misguided, but they can be downright counter-productive. His work focuses on debunking popular management myths and revealing what actually works in modern organisations. "Under New Management" examines how leading companies are abandoning traditional practices in favour of more effective approaches to leadership, team dynamics, and organisational culture. Through his books, speaking engagements, and podcast, Burkus translates complex organisational psychology research into practical insights for leaders and managers. His evidence-based approach helps organisations move beyond outdated assumptions about how people work best together.

APRIL 24

*"Why?
Why not?
Why not you?
Why not now?"
- Jim Rohn*[117]

---

[117] *Take Charge of Your Life: Unlocking Influence, Wealth, and Power*, Jim Rohn, 2024.

Jim Rohn (1930-2009) was an entrepreneur, author and motivational speaker who became one of the most influential figures in the personal development industry. His parents owned and worked a farm in Caldwell, Idaho, where Rohn grew up as an only child. A successful entrepreneur, author, and motivational speaker, he achieved his first million by 31, thanks to his dedication, resilience, and keen insights. His rags to riches story played a large part in his work, which influenced others in the personal development industry, and he was the recipient of the 1985 National Speakers Association CPAE Award for excellence in speaking. He frequently stressed the notion that in order to attain success an individual must continually strive to improve themselves, firmly believing that investing in self-education, self-reflection, skill development is the gateway to unleashing a person's capabilities. Rohn is remembered for his philosophy of personal responsibility and his famous quote: "Formal education will make you a living; self-education will make you a fortune."

APRIL 25

"And what else?"
- Michael Bungay Stanier[118]

---

[118] Bungay Stanier writes, "I know they seem innocuous. Three little words. But 'And What Else?'—the AWE Question—has magical properties. With seemingly no effort, it creates more—more wisdom, more insights, more self-awareness, more possibilities—out of thin air."

The Coaching Habit: Say Less, Ask More & Change the Way You Lead Forever, Michael Bungay Stanier, 2016.

Michael Bungay Stanier is an author, leadership coach, and business consultant best known for his bestselling book "The Coaching Habit: Say Less, Ask More & Change the Way You Lead Forever." He founded Box of Crayons, a learning and development company that helps organisations transform from advice-driven to curiosity-led, and currently leads MBS.works, a place where people find clarity, confidence and community to be a force for change. His work focuses on helping leaders develop better coaching skills through practical, science-backed approaches that emphasise asking powerful questions rather than giving advice. His philosophy is captured in his haiku-like summary: "Tell less and ask more. Your advice is not as good as you think it is." Known as a compelling speaker and facilitator who combines practicality, humour, and high audience engagement, Stanier has become a prominent voice in the leadership development space, helping countless managers and executives shift from being advice-givers to becoming more effective coaches who unlock potential in their teams through curiosity and thoughtful questioning.

APRIL 26

*"There are two questions a man must ask himself:
The first is 'Where am I going?' and the second is
'Who will go with me?'
If you ever get these questions in the wrong order
you are in trouble."*
- Sam Keen[119]

---

[119] Leadership is articulating a better future. The clearer the vision is, the more compelling it will be for followers. Psychologist David McClelland explains, "Whatever the source of the leader's ideas, he cannot inspire his people unless he expresses vivid goals which in some sense they want. Of course, the more closely he meets their needs, the less "persuasive" he has to be, but in no case does it make sense to speak as if his role is force submission. Rather it is to strengthen and uplift, to make people feel that they are the origins, not the pawns, of the socio-political system."
Fire in the Belly: On Being a Man, Sam Keen, 1991.
Sam Keen (1931 - 2025) was a philosopher, author, and public intellectual best known for his exploration of masculinity, spirituality, and human development. With a PhD from Harvard, he gained prominence through his work at Psychology Today magazine and his influential book "Fire in the Belly: On Being a Man," which became a cornerstone of the 1990s men's movement. Keen's writing combines philosophical inquiry with psychological insights, examining themes like authentic selfhood, the stages of love, and the importance of wonder throughout life. He was an international speaker and workshop leader, and emphasised asking meaningful questions over providing easy answers, helping people live more examined and purposeful lives.

APRIL 27

"What is my highest future possibility?"
- Otto Scharmer[120]

---

[120] Scharmer asks, "Isn't there a way to break the patterns of the past and tune into our highest future possibility—and to begin to operate from that place?" Set high expectations. "A lot of times people don't do great things because it's not really expected of them and nobody demands they try." Steve Jobs writes. "Nobody says "Hey that's the culture here, to do great things." If you set that up, people will do things that are greater than they ever thought they could."
Theory U: Learning from the Future as It Emerges, C. Otto Scharmer, 2007.
Otto Scharmer is a Senior Lecturer at MIT and Founding Chair of the Presencing Institute. He focuses on awareness-based action research with leaders across various sectors, anchored in the concept of presencing, a method of "learning from the emerging future". Scharmer is the author of several influential books including "Theory U" and "Presence", the latter co-authored with Peter Senge and others, which introduced the groundbreaking concept of "presencing". His Theory U methodology provides a framework for transformational change that moves beyond downloading habitual patterns to accessing deeper sources of knowing and creativity. He chairs the MIT IDEAS program for cross-sector innovation and through the Presencing Institute works with leaders worldwide to address complex social, environmental, and organisational challenges using awareness-based approaches to systems change and regenerative leadership.

APRIL 28

"What cause do you serve?"
- Jim Collins[121]

---

[121] "I've been asked many times whether people can become Level 5, and if so, how?" Collins writes, "Yes, and the best spark to ignite such leadership in yourself is to wrestle with a hard, simple question: What cause do you serve? What cause are you willing to sacrifice and suffer for, when you must make decisions that cause pain for yourself and others to advance that cause? What cause will infuse your life with meaning? It might be a grand, highly visible cause or a more private, less-visible cause; what matters is that you lead in service to that cause, rather than in service to yourself."

Jim's Seven Questions: Learning From Young Leaders Full Talk, Global Leadership Summit, 2015.

BE 2.0 (Beyond Entrepreneurship 2.0): Turning Your Business Into an Enduring Great Company, Jim Collins and William Lazier,

Jim Collins is a bestselling author, business researcher, and management consultant who has spent decades studying what makes companies transition from good to great performance. He's best known for his book "Good to Great," which identified key principles that distinguish exceptional companies from merely good ones, including concepts like Level 5 Leadership, the Hedgehog Concept, and getting the right people on the bus. Collins has written several other influential business books including "Built to Last" (co-authored with Jerry Porras), "How the Mighty Fall," and "Great by Choice." His research methodology involves rigorous data analysis and long-term studies of companies, often spanning decades to identify patterns and principles that drive sustained success. Before his writing career, Collins worked as a faculty member at Stanford Graduate School of Business and served as a consultant to corporations and social sector organisations. His work extends beyond the corporate world to nonprofits and educational institutions through books like "Good to Great and the Social Sectors." Collins is known for his disciplined approach to research, his ability to distil complex business concepts into memorable frameworks, and his focus on timeless principles rather than fleeting management fads.

APRIL 29

Hans Selye, the pioneer in the understanding of human stress, was often asked the following question -
'What is the most stressful condition a person can face?'
His unexpected response -
'Not having something to BELIEVE in.'[122]

---

[122] The question echoes Viktor Frankl who, in his book "Man's Search for Meaning" writes, "Those who have a 'why' to live, can bear almost any 'how'". Attributed to philosopher Friedrich Nietzsche, this idea encapsulates Frankl's theory of logotherapy, which emphasises the importance of finding meaning in life, even amidst suffering. Frankl's experiences in Nazi concentration camps during World War II deeply influenced his perspective, leading him to believe that a sense of purpose is crucial for enduring hardship.

From Dream to Discovery: On Being a Scientist, Hans Selye, 1964.

Hans Selye (1907-1982) was a pioneering endocrinologist and physician who is widely regarded as the father of stress research. revolutionised our understanding of how the body responds to stress through his groundbreaking work on what he termed the "General Adaptation Syndrome" (GAS). His research demonstrated that the body has a predictable three-stage response to stress: alarm, resistance, and exhaustion. Selye's most significant contribution was identifying stress as a nonspecific response of the body to any demand placed upon it, whether physical, emotional, or psychological. He distinguished between "eustress" (beneficial stress that motivates and energises) and "distress" (harmful stress that can lead to illness and dysfunction). His work showed that chronic stress could lead to serious health problems including cardiovascular disease, immune system suppression, and various other ailments. After completing his medical degree and PhD, Selye spent most of his career at McGill University in Montreal, where he conducted extensive research and wrote prolifically. He authored over 1,700 scholarly papers and 39 books, including the influential "The Stress of Life", which brought his scientific findings to the general public. His research laid the foundation for the modern field of stress physiology and has had profound implications for medicine, psychology, and our understanding of the mind-body connection. Selye's work continues to influence how we approach stress management, health, and wellness today.

APRIL 30

"What will the world look like after you change it?"
- William McRraven[123]

---

[123] "Visionary statements and actions come from a completely different place in the human psyche from predictions, forecasts, scenarios, or cynical, downer assertions of political impossibility." systems theorist Donella Meadows explains. "They come from commitment, responsibility, confidence, values, longing, love, treasured dreams, our innate sense of what is right and good. A vision articulates a future that someone deeply wants, and does it so clearly and compellingly that it summons up the energy, agreement, sympathy, political will, creativity, resources, or whatever to make that future happen."

Admiral William H. McRaven Commencement speech, The University of Texas, May 17, 2014. Also refer *Make Your Bed: Little Things That Can Change Your Life... and Maybe the World*, William H McRaven, 2017.

William McRaven is a retired U.S. Navy four-star admiral who served as the ninth commander of U.S. Special Operations Command from 2011 to 2014, overseeing all special operations forces across the military branches. He is best known for planning and overseeing the 2011 Navy SEAL raid that killed Osama bin Laden in Pakistan, a mission that required meticulous coordination and demonstrated his expertise in special operations leadership. McRaven spent 37 years in the Navy, much of it with the SEALs, and became widely recognized beyond military circles after his 2014 University of Texas commencement speech, which went viral and became a bestselling book. Since retiring, he has served as chancellor of the University of Texas System, authored several books on leadership and resilience, and remains a prominent voice on national security issues and the values of military service.

MAY

STRENGTHEN PERCEPTION & THOUGHT

MAY 1

"How do I know I'm right?"
- Ray Dalio[124]

---

[124] Dalio recalls how, decades earlier, he had incorrectly predicted an economic downturn and lost everything. He had been so sure he was right. "I gained a humility that I needed in order to balance my audacity." he reflects. Dalio became a proponent of radical transparency and idea meritocracy. "I wanted to find the smartest people who would disagree with me to try to understand their perspective or to have them stress test my perspective. I wanted to make an idea meritocracy. In other words, not an autocracy in which I would lead and others would follow and not a democracy in which everybody's points of view were equally valued, but I wanted to have an idea meritocracy in which the best ideas would win out. And in order to do that, I realized that we would need radical truthfulness and radical transparency." "To be effective", he says, "you must not let your need to be right be more important than your need to find out what's true. If you are too proud of what you know or of how good you are at something you will learn less, make inferior decisions, and fall short of your potential."

How to build a company where the best ideas win, Ray Dalio, TED 2017.

Ray Dalio is an investor, hedge fund manager, and author who founded Bridgewater Associates in 1975, which became the world's largest hedge fund. Known for his systematic, principle-based approach to investing and management, Dalio developed unique strategies that helped Bridgewater navigate major economic crises while delivering consistent returns for decades. His investment philosophy centres on understanding economic cycles, diversification, and what he calls "radical transparency", a management approach emphasising open, honest feedback and meritocratic decision-making. Dalio gained broader public recognition through his bestselling book "Principles: Life and Work", where he outlined the systematic principles that guided his personal and professional success, and his economic writings on debt cycles and societal change. Beyond finance, he has become an influential voice on economic inequality, geopolitics, and the rise and fall of nations, using historical analysis to understand contemporary global shifts.

MAY 2

"What would convince me I am wrong?"
- Philip Tetlock[125]

---

[125] "Scientists must be able to answer the question 'What would convince me I am wrong?'" Tetlock explains. "If they can't, it's a sign they have grown too attached to their beliefs." The question "What would convince me I am wrong?" is central to Tetlock's broader message: that highquality forecasting—like good science—depends on testing hypotheses, embracing uncertainty, and being willing to update your beliefs in light of new evidence.

Superforecasting: The Art and Science of Prediction, Philip E. Tetlock and Dan Gardner, 2015.

Philip E. Tetlock is a renowned psychologist and political scientist who is the Annenberg University Professor at the University of Pennsylvania, holding appointments in both the Wharton School and the School of Arts and Sciences. He is best known for his groundbreaking research on forecasting and prediction, particularly through The Good Judgment Project (GJP), which he co-created to "harness the wisdom of the crowd to forecast world events". From 2011-2015, the GJP participated in a massive Intelligence Advanced Research Projects Activity (IARPA) competition involving 500 questions and over a million forecasts, ultimately emerging as the undisputed winner. Tetlock demonstrated that generally, the accuracy of our predictions is no better than chance, but certain people are able to make predictions far more accurately than others. These individuals he termed "superforecasters." He is the author of influential books including "Superforecasting: The Art and Science of Prediction" and "Expert Political Judgment," which challenge conventional wisdom about expertise and forecasting ability, showing how systematic approaches can dramatically improve predictive accuracy.

MAY 3

"Don't just read it; fight it! Ask your own question, look for your own examples, discover your own proofs. Is the hypothesis necessary? Is the converse true? What happens in the classical special case? What about the degenerate cases? Where does the proof use the hypothesis?"
- Paul Halmos[126]

---

[126] Extreme objectivity includes trying to disconfirm our own ideas and prove ourselves wrong. To be able to challenge our "belief confidence" and put our thoughts on trial. "The life of Darwin" Charlie Munger explains, "demonstrates how a turtle may outrun the hares, aided by extreme objectivity, which helps the objective person end up like the only player without a blindfold in a game of Pin the Tail on the Donkey. One of the most successful users of an antidote to first conclusion basis was Charles Darwin. He trained himself, early, to intensively consider any evidence tending to disconfirm any hypothesis of his, more so if he thought his hypothesis was a particularly good one. The opposite of what Darwin did is now called confirmation bias, a term of opprobrium. Darwin's practice came from his acute recognition of man's natural cognitive faults arising from Inconsistency-Avoidance Tendency. He provides a great example of psychological insight used correctly to advance some of the finest mental work ever done". *Poor Charlie's Almanack: The Essential Wit and Wisdom of Charles T. Munger*, Charles T. Munger, Peter D. Kaufman (editor), 2005.

I Want to be a Mathematician: An Automathography, Paul Halmos, 1985.

Paul R. Halmos (1916-2006) was a mathematician who made fundamental advances in the areas of logic, probability, statistics, operator theory and functional analysis. He is best known for some of his text-books and for his collection of mathematicians' photographs. While at the Institute, Halmos wrote his first book "Finite Dimensional Vector Spaces", which immediately established his reputation as a fine expositor of mathematics. He taught at several prestigious institutions and became renowned not only for his mathematical contributions but also for his exceptional ability to communicate mathematics clearly and engagingly. According to current records, Paul Halmos has 22 students and 1132 descendants in the mathematical genealogy, reflecting his significant influence as a teacher and mentor in the mathematical community.

MAY 4

*"Always ask: What am I missing?
And listen to the answer."*
- Strauss Zelnick[127]

---

[127] "Your personal experiences make up maybe 0.00000001% of what's happened in the world," Morgan Housel writes, "but maybe 80% of how you think the world works. ... We're all biased to our own personal history. ... Start with the assumption that everyone is innocently out of touch and you'll be more likely to explore what's going on through multiple points of view, instead of cramming what's going on into the framework of your own experiences. It's hard to do."
Tribe of Mentors: Short Life Advice from the Best in the World, Tim Ferriss, 2017.

Strauss Zelnick is the Chairman and CEO of Take-Two Interactive Software, one of the world's largest video game publishers. Before joining Take-Two in 2007, Zelnick had an extensive career in entertainment and media, including serving as President and CEO of BMG Entertainment and holding executive positions at 20th Century Fox and Columbia Pictures. He's also the founder of ZelnickMedia, a private equity firm focused on media and entertainment investments. Known for his business acumen and strategic vision, Zelnick has been credited with transforming Take-Two from a struggling company into one of the most successful and profitable gaming companies in the industry. He's also noted for his unique approach to executive compensation, often tying his pay directly to the company's stock performance, and for his focus on building long-term value rather than just short-term gains.

MAY 5

*"One way to open your eyes is to ask yourself,
What if I had never seen this before?
What if I knew I would never see it again?"*
- Rachel Carson[128]

---

[128] *Silent Sprint*, Rachel Carson, 1962.

Rachel Carson (1907-1964) was a marine biologist and author whose groundbreaking book "Silent Spring" catalysed the modern environmental movement and fundamentally changed how society views the relationship between human activity and the natural world. Trained in biology, Carson was adept at the kind of long-term observation required to document shifts in the behaviour and ecosystems caused by chemical pesticides, particularly Dichlorodiphenyl-trichloroethane (DDT). Carson's thesis throughout Silent Spring was that pesticides and chemicals used to kill pests on crops bleed into the environment and affect our water sources. Her work demonstrated how "minute amounts of chemicals were being bio-magnified in the system," showing the interconnectedness of ecological systems through compelling examples like robins dying after eating contaminated earthworms. Silent Spring launched an environmental movement, not only helping to create the department that would become the Environmental Protection Agency, but also inspiring the Clean Air Act (1963), the Clean Water Act (1964), the Toxic Substances Control Act (1976), and led to a nationwide ban of DDT. Despite fierce opposition by chemical companies, the book swayed public opinion and led to a reversal in US pesticide policy.

MAY 6

"Can I believe this?"
- Thomas Gilovich[129]

---

[129] Gilovich explains that "For desired conclusions, we ask ourselves, 'Can I believe this?', but for unpalatable conclusions we ask, 'Must I believe this?'"

How We Know What Isn't So: The Fallibility of Human Reason in Everyday Life, Thomas Gilovich, 1991.

Thomas Gilovich is a prominent social psychologist and professor at Cornell University, best known for his groundbreaking research on human judgment, decision-making, and cognitive biases. He gained widespread recognition through his influential book "How We Know What Isn't So", which explores how people form false beliefs and make systematic errors in reasoning. Gilovich has extensively studied phenomena like the "hot hand" fallacy in sports, overconfidence in personal judgments, and various statistical misconceptions that affect every day thinking. His work bridges academic psychology and practical understanding, making complex research accessible to general audiences while contributing significantly to the field of behavioural economics and the psychology of decision-making.

MAY 7

"Do you ever prove yourself wrong?
Do you take precautions to avoid fooling yourself?
Do you have any good critics?"
- Julia Galef[30]

---

130 Entrepreneur, writer, and professor Margaret Heffernan described the case of epidemiologist Doctor Alice Stewart who was conducting research in the 1950's on the rising incidents of childhood leukemia. She identified the likely cause as pregnant women who had been x-rayed, but prior to publishing her hypothesis, Alice worked closely with statistician George Kneale. When asked by a colleague to describe his role, Kneale said, "It is my job to prove that Dr. Stewart's theories are wrong." Kneale's job was disconfirmation, to challenge her findings.

In the absence of a thinking partner we need to challenge ourselves. *Dare to disagree*, Margaret Heffernan, TEDGlobal, June 2012.

The Scout Mindset: Why Some People See Things Clearly and Others Don't Hardcover, Julia Galef, 2021.

Julia Galef is a writer, speaker, and researcher focused on reasoning, decision-making, and cognitive biases. She's the co-founder and former president of the Center for Applied Rationality (CFAR), an organisation dedicated to improving human reasoning and decision-making skills. Galef is best known for her book "The Scout Mindset: Why Some People See Things Clearly and Others Don't," which explores the difference between the "soldier mindset" (defending existing beliefs) and the "scout mindset" (seeking truth and accuracy). She hosts the popular podcast "Rationally Speaking," where she interviews experts on topics related to reasoning, science, and philosophy. Galef is also known for her engaging TED talks and presentations about motivated reasoning and how to think more clearly. Her work draws from psychology, philosophy, and behavioural economics to help people make better decisions and form more accurate beliefs. She's particularly interested in how people can overcome their natural cognitive biases and improve their ability to update their beliefs when presented with new evidence.

MAY 8

"Is that assumed or confirmed?"
- Jeanne Torre[131]

---

131 "Don't act as though your limited experience represents universal truths." music publisher Herb Cohen cautions. "It doesn't. Force yourself to go outside your own experience by vigorously testing your assumptions."
From *3-2-1 Newsletter,* James Clear, March 28, 2024.

Jeanne Torre is a health and wellness coach with over 25 years of coaching experience who works in both corporate settings and private practice, with particular focus on coaching teachers and support staff. She holds a Master's degree in Social Work and is a National Board Certified Health & Wellness Coach. Torre specialises in helping educators and professionals navigate the challenges of maintaining well-being while managing demanding careers, drawing on her extensive background in social work to provide holistic support that addresses both personal and professional dimensions of health. Her coaching approach emphasises sustainable wellness practices that can be integrated into busy professional lives, particularly for those in education and helping professions who often prioritise others' needs over their own well-being.

MAY 9

"How's the water?"
- David Foster Wallace[132]

---

[132] In "This is Water", the 2005 commencement address delivered at Kenyon College, Wallace explored themes of awareness, choice, and consciousness in daily life. The speech starts with, "There are these two young fish swimming along and they happen to meet an older fish swimming the other way, who nods at them and says 'Morning, boys. How's the water?' And the two young fish swim on for a bit, and then eventually one of them looks over at the other and goes 'What the hell is water?'". The phrase "This is water" serves as a metaphor for the invisible forces that shape our thoughts, attitudes, and experiences, and for the freedom we have in how we interpret and respond to the world. The question is echoed in Y Combinator founder Paul Graham's question: "Did you ever notice...?" *How To Do Great Work*, Paul Graham, paulgraham.com, July 2023.

2005 Kenyon Commencement Address, David Foster Wallace, May 21, 2005

David Foster Wallace (1962-2008) was an American novelist, essayist, and short story writer celebrated for his intellectual brilliance, linguistic virtuosity, and profound exploration of contemporary American culture and consciousness. His masterpiece, "Infinite Jest", a sprawling 1,000-page novel about addiction, entertainment, and the search for meaning in postmodern America, established him as one of the most important writers of his generation. Wallace's work was characterised by footnotes, experimental structure, and an ability to blend high literary art with pop culture references, mathematical concepts, and philosophical inquiry. Beyond fiction, his nonfiction essays, including "Consider the Lobster" and his Kenyon College commencement speech demonstrated his capacity to find profound meaning in everyday experiences while grappling with depression, anxiety, and the overwhelming complexity of modern life. His tragic suicide at age 46 cut short a career that had already fundamentally changed contemporary American literature.

MAY 10

"What am I subject to, what's water in my fishbowl to me, what can I not make object and clearly see?"
- Graham Duncan[133]

---

[133] Your view of the world is just one version of reality. What you see depends not only on what you are looking at, but also on where you look from. The problem is that we see things from one angle. The solution is to acquire "fresh eyes". Writer Blas Moros says fresh eyes are "those outside your system due to age, experience, background, expertise and/or wisdom". Moros' advice echoes Novelist Marcel Proust who wrote, "The only true voyage of discovery, the only fountain of Eternal Youth, would be not to visit strange lands but to possess other eyes, to behold the universe through the eyes of another, of a hundred others …".

Current questions I find interesting, Graham Duncan, grahamduncan.blog.

Graham Duncan is a successful investor and talent spotter who co-founded East Rock Capital, a multi-family office investment firm that manages $2 billion for a small number of families and their charitable foundations. Before starting East Rock, Duncan worked at two other investment firms and started his career by co-founding an independent Wall Street research firm. A Yale graduate with a degree in ethics, politics, and economics, Duncan has become known as a "talent whisperer" for his unique ability to identify and nurture emerging investment talent. Duncan's unusual ability to wait out the moment is one of his defining characteristics as an investor, with colleagues noting that he's "not susceptible to impatience the way most people are" when it comes to seeding new investment managers. He also co-chairs The Sohn Investment Conference, which raises money for paediatric cancer research. Duncan maintains an active presence as a thoughtful writer and commentator on investment philosophy, human development, and talent identification, sharing insights through his blog and social media about the intersection of psychology and investing. His approach emphasises patience, deep understanding of human potential, and the importance of allowing talent to develop naturally rather than forcing growth.

MAY 11

"Am I seeing the situation clearly?
Do I feel like I am overreacting here?
Do you see this differently?
You know, I have been wrong before.
What are your thoughts?"
- Greg McKeown[134]

---

[134] In their book *Superforecasting*, Philip Tetlock and Dan Gardner describe aggregation of perspectives using the analogy of dragonfly eyes. Dragonflies have the largest compound eyes of any insect, with each eye containing up to 30,000 facets. Each facet within the eye points in a slightly different direction, meaning they have a spherical field of vision - they can see in all directions simultaneously. Tetlock and Gardner explain that super forecasters use "dragonfly forecasting". By remaining actively open-minded they can collect and synthesise a large number of perspectives, including dissonant information, which dramatically improves prediction accuracy. Engaging others magnifies intelligence. In the words of computer scientist and author Astro Teller, "a change in perspective is sometimes more powerful than being smart". Teller says, "Perspective shifts will unlock more than smartness will."

Two Phrases That can Change Your Life, Greg McKeown, gregmckeown.com, December 4, 2014.

Greg McKeown is a business writer, consultant, and bestselling author. McKeown is the author of two New York Times bestsellers, "Essentialism: The Disciplined Pursuit of Less" and "Effortless: Make It Easier to Do What Matters Most," which together have sold 3 million copies and been published in 40 languages. His core philosophy of Essentialism teaches people to focus on what truly matters by eliminating the non-essential from their lives and work. McKeown has become one of the most sought-after public speakers in the world, speaking to hundreds of organisations while traveling to more than 45 countries, with clients including Apple, Amazon, Google, and Microsoft. He also hosts a popular podcast and runs the Essentialism Academy, helping individuals and organisations apply his principles to achieve greater impact through more disciplined choices about where to invest their time and energy.

MAY 12

"The two most powerful questions leaders and organizations can ask themselves are -
What am I not seeing? and
What else might be true?"
- Tony Schwartz[135]

---

[135] Describing Abraham Lincoln's ability to bring the smartest people into his cabinet team, including some of his biggest political rivals, author Doris Kearns Goodwin explains, "Good leadership requires you to surround yourself with people of diverse perspectives who can disagree with you without fear of retaliation." *Team of Rivals: The Political Genius of Abraham Lincoln*, Doris Kearns Goodwin, 2005.

What It Takes to Think Deeply About Complex Problems, Tony Schwartz, Harvard Business Review, May 09, 2018.

Tony Schwartz is an author, business consultant, and entrepreneur who has dedicated his career to transforming how people approach work and productivity. In 2003, Schwartz founded The Energy Project, a consulting firm that focuses on the improvement of employee productivity and counts Facebook as one of its clients, after previously co-authoring "The Power of Full Engagement: Managing Energy Not Time" with Jim Loehr. His groundbreaking philosophy centres on the idea that managing energy, rather than time, is the key to peak performance and sustained productivity. Through his years of intensive work consulting to companies including Procter & Gamble, Sony, Toyota, Microsoft, Ford and Ernst & Young, with his firm The Energy Project, Schwartz has developed a powerful program for changing the way we are working that greatly boosts our engagement and our satisfaction with our work and increases our performance. His bestselling book "The Way We're Working Isn't Working" argues that the modern workplace model is counterproductive, sapping employees of their physical, emotional, mental, and spiritual energy. Schwartz's approach focuses on four core human needs that he believes organisations must address to create high-performing, engaged workforces. His work has influenced countless companies to rethink their approach to employee well-being, productivity, and organisational culture, making him a leading voice in the movement toward more sustainable and human-centered approaches to work.

MAY 13

*"What do you most yearn for?
Do you yearn to defend your beliefs?
Or do you yearn to see the world as clearly as you possibly can?"*
- Julia Galef[36]

---

[136] Galef describes the soldier and scout mindsets. Whereas the soldier acts reflexively, "The scout's job is not to attack or defend." Galef says. "The scout's job is to understand. The scout is the one going out, mapping the terrain, identifying potential obstacles. And the scout may hope to learn that, say, there's a bridge in a convenient location across a river. But above all, the scout wants to know what's really there, as accurately as possible."

Why you think you're right - even if you're wrong, Julia Galef, TEDxPSU, February 2016.

Julia Galef is an American writer, speaker, and researcher focused on reasoning, decision-making, and cognitive biases. She's the co-founder and former president of the Center for Applied Rationality (CFAR), an organisation dedicated to improving human reasoning and decision-making skills. Galef is best known for her book "The Scout Mindset: Why Some People See Things Clearly and Others Don't," which explores the difference between the "soldier mindset" (defending existing beliefs) and the "scout mindset" (seeking truth and accuracy). She hosts the popular podcast "Rationally Speaking," where she interviews experts on topics related to reasoning, science, and philosophy. Galef is also known for her engaging TED talks and presentations about motivated reasoning and how to think more clearly. Her work draws from psychology, philosophy, and behavioural economics to help people make better decisions and form more accurate beliefs. She's particularly interested in how people can overcome their natural cognitive biases and improve their ability to update their beliefs when presented with new evidence.

MAY 14

"When my information changes, I change my mind. What do you do?"
- John Maynard Keynes[137]

---

[137] The question is paraphrased by Nobel prize winner Paul Samuelson from John Maynard Keynes' 1924 essay titled "Investment Policy for Insurance Companies" in "The Nation and Athenaeum" of London.

John Maynard Keynes (1883-1946) was a British economist whose revolutionary ideas fundamentally transformed economic theory and government policy in the 20th century. He is best known for "The General Theory of Employment, Interest and Money", which challenged classical economic assumptions and argued that economies could remain stuck in prolonged periods of high unemployment without automatic self-correction. Keynes advocated for active government intervention through fiscal and monetary policy to manage economic cycles, particularly during recessions when he believed government spending could stimulate demand and restore full employment. His economic philosophy, known as Keynesian economics, became the dominant macroeconomic framework for decades and heavily influenced government policies during the Great Depression and World War II. Beyond economics, Keynes was a member of the influential Bloomsbury Group of intellectuals and artists, served as a British representative at the Bretton Woods Conference that established the post-war international monetary system, and was elevated to the House of Lords as Baron Keynes in 1942.

MAY 15

"Is it true?
Can you absolutely know that it's true?
How do you react when you believe that thought?
Who would you be without the thought?"
- Byron Katie[138]

---

[138] Four questions which Katie refers to as a process of self-inquiry called "The Work".
Loving What Is, Byron Katie and Stephen Mitchell, 2021.

Byron Katie is a spiritual teacher and author who developed a simple yet profound method of self-inquiry called "The Work" that has helped millions of people around the world question their stressful thoughts and find inner peace. Born Byron Kathleen Reid, she experienced a dramatic spiritual awakening in 1986 after years of severe depression, agoraphobia, and suicidal thoughts. This awakening led her to realise that her suffering was caused not by circumstances themselves, but by her thoughts about those circumstances. The Work consists of four questions and a turnaround that Katie encourages people to apply to any stressful thought. The process is designed to help individuals examine the validity of their beliefs and discover the freedom that comes from questioning rather than automatically accepting their thoughts. Katie's approach is notable for its simplicity and accessibility - it requires no special training, religious beliefs, or complex philosophical understanding. She has written several bestselling books, including "Loving What Is," "I Need Your Love - Is That True?" and "A Thousand Names for Joy," which outline her method and philosophy. Katie travels extensively, conducting workshops and facilitating public demonstrations of The Work, often working with audience members in real-time to show how the inquiry process works. Her teaching emphasises radical acceptance of reality and the idea that arguing with what is causes all human suffering. Her work has been embraced by people from all walks of life, from business leaders to inmates in maximum-security prisons, demonstrating the universal applicability of her method for finding peace through self-inquiry.

MAY 16

"Look back ten years and you can probably identify a few blind spots or mistaken beliefs you held at the time. Now, fast forward ten years from today... what are likely to be your current blind spots? What are you not spending enough time thinking about or perhaps even wilfully ignoring?"
- James Clear[139]

---

[139] "One of the surprising discoveries of modern psychology is how easy it is to be ignorant of your own ignorance." philosopher and cognitive scientist Daniel Dennett warns. "You are normally oblivious of your own blind spot, and people are typically amazed to discover that we don't see colors in our peripheral vision. It seems as if we do, but we don't, as you can prove to yourself by wiggling colored cards at the edge of your vision - you'll see motion just fine but not be able to identify the color of the moving thing."

3-2-1 Newsletter, James Clear, October 12, 2023.

James Clear is an author, speaker, and entrepreneur best known for his book "Atomic Habits," which became a bestseller and popularised the concept of making small, incremental changes to build better habits and break bad ones. Clear focuses on the science of habit formation, emphasising how tiny improvements compound over time to create remarkable results. His approach centres on four key principles: making habits obvious, attractive, easy, and satisfying. Before his writing career took off, Clear was a successful entrepreneur and has a background in photography and business. He writes regularly about habits, decision-making, and continuous improvement on his website and newsletter, which has attracted millions of readers. Clear's work draws from psychology, neuroscience, and behavioural economics to provide practical strategies for personal and professional development, making complex research accessible to everyday readers seeking to improve their lives through better systems and habits.

MAY 17

"How did you come to believe that?"
- David Brooks[140]

---

[140] "First, in political journalism, which I do, I don't ask people anymore: What do you think about this issue?" Brooks explains. "I ask: How did you come to believe that? That's a way of getting them into narrative mode. They start telling you about an experience or a person who was important to shaping their values and suddenly they're in storytelling mode. You learn a lot more. We're most accurate when talking about ourselves in narrative mode, not in argument mode."
Journalist David Brooks reveals the essential questions to deepen any relationship, Jenna Abdou, Fast Company, December 8, 2024.

David Brooks is a prominent American journalist, political commentator, and author who writes for The New York Times, where he has been an op-ed columnist since 2003. Known for his thoughtful analysis of American politics, culture, and society, Brooks often takes a moderate conservative perspective while focusing on themes like community, character, and moral development. He's written several influential books including "The Social Animal," which explores human behaviour and decision-making, "The Road to Character," which examines the difference between résumé virtues and eulogy virtues, and "The Second Mountain," about finding deeper meaning and purpose in life. Before joining the Times, Brooks worked at publications like The Wall Street Journal, The Weekly Standard, and The Atlantic. He's also a regular commentator on PBS NewsHour and NPR, and teaches at Yale University. Brooks is known for his ability to bridge political divides and his interest in how psychology, sociology, and moral philosophy intersect with public policy and everyday life.

MAY 18

"Do you have any opinions that you would be reluctant to express in front of a group of your peers?"
- Paul Graham[141]

---

[141] Graham calls this question "The Conformist Test", explaining, "If the answer is no, you might want to stop and think about that. If everything you believe is something you're supposed to believe, could that possibly be a coincidence? Odds are it isn't. Odds are you just think whatever you're told." Graham concludes by writing, "How can you see the wave, when you're the water? Always be questioning. That's the only defence. What can't you say? And why?"

What You Can't Say, Paul Graham, paulgraham.com, January 2024.

Paul Graham is a computer scientist, entrepreneur, essayist, and venture capitalist who co-founded Y Combinator, the world's most influential startup accelerator. A programmer by training, he co-created Viaweb in the 1990s, one of the first web-based software applications, which was sold to Yahoo for $49 million and became Yahoo Store. Y Combinator has funded over 5,000 startups including Airbnb, Dropbox, Stripe, Reddit, and DoorDash, fundamentally changing how early-stage companies get funded and mentored. Beyond his business ventures, Graham is renowned for his essays on startups, programming, and life, published on his website paulgraham.com. His writing covers topics from technical programming concepts to startup advice to broader philosophical observations, and his essays like "Do Things That Don't Scale" and "Maker's Schedule, Manager's Schedule" have become foundational reading in Silicon Valley. Graham is known for his clear, thoughtful writing style and contrarian insights about entrepreneurship, such as emphasising the importance of building something people want rather than focusing on business plans. He stepped back from day-to-day operations at Y Combinator to focus more on his writing and thinking, but remains one of the most respected voices in the startup ecosystem.

MAY 19

*"What is your questions-to-statements ratio?
And can you double it?"
- Jim Collins*[142]

---

[142] Collins recalls how his mentor John W. Gardner brought him into his office and said, 'It occurs to me, Jim, that you spend way too much of your time trying to be interesting. Why don't you channel your time around being interested?' That ten seconds changed my life. Imagine going into every situation, not with how be interesting, but how to be interested, how to ask questions, how to learn from everybody you meet."
Drucker Day Keynote, Jim Collins, May 14, 2010.

Jim Collins is a bestselling author, business researcher, and management consultant who has spent decades studying what makes companies transition from good to great performance. He's best known for his book "Good to Great," which identified key principles that distinguish exceptional companies from merely good ones, including concepts like Level 5 Leadership, the Hedgehog Concept, and getting the right people on the bus. Collins has written several other influential business books including "Built to Last" (co-authored with Jerry Porras), "How the Mighty Fall," and "Great by Choice." His research methodology involves rigorous data analysis and long-term studies of companies, often spanning decades to identify patterns and principles that drive sustained success. Before his writing career, Collins worked as a faculty member at Stanford Graduate School of Business and served as a consultant to corporations and social sector organisations. His work extends beyond the corporate world to nonprofits and educational institutions through books like "Good to Great and the Social Sectors." Collins is known for his disciplined approach to research, his ability to distil complex business concepts into memorable frameworks, and his focus on timeless principles rather than fleeting management fads.

MAY 20

*"A good question to ask yourself today is
"What might I be wrong about?"
This is the only worry worth having."*
- Kevin Kelly[143]

---

[143] "Discovering you were wrong is an update, not a failure," researcher and writer Julia Galef explains, "and your worldview is a living document meant to be revised."

Excellent Advice for Living: Wisdom I Wish I'd Known Earlier, Kevin Kelly, 2023.

Kevin Kelly is an influential author, futurist, and technology philosopher who co-founded Wired magazine in 1993 and served as its executive editor for its first seven years. A prominent voice in tech culture, Kelly has written several acclaimed books exploring technology's impact on society, including "What Technology Wants" and "The Inevitable," where he examines technology as an evolutionary force. Before his tech career, he spent time traveling through Asia and co-founded the Whole Earth Catalog with Stewart Brand, reflecting his lifelong interest in tools, systems, and human potential. Kelly is known for his optimistic yet nuanced view of technology's role in human civilization, coining concepts like "technium" to describe the self-reinforcing system of technology, and he continues to write and speak about emerging technologies, artificial intelligence, and digital culture's future trajectory.

MAY 21

"What evidence would change your mind?"
- Adam Grant[144]

---

[144] "If the answer is 'nothing,'" Grant explains, "then there's no point in continuing the debate. You can lead a horse to water, but you can't make it think."
Think Again: The Power of Knowing What You Don't Know, Adam Grant, 2021.

Adam Grant is an organisational psychologist and bestselling author who serves as a professor at the Wharton School of the University of Pennsylvania. He's known for his research on motivation, generosity, and unconventional thinking, which he's popularised through books like "Give and Take," "Originals," and "Think Again." Grant challenges conventional wisdom about success, arguing that generous people can finish both last and first, and that our greatest strength can become our greatest weakness. He's also a popular speaker and podcast host, known for making psychological research accessible and practical for business leaders and general audiences. His work often focuses on how people can contribute to others while still achieving their own goals, and how organisations can foster innovation and positive change.

MAY 22

"How can I think more clearly?"
- Shane Parrish[145]

---

[145] This question is the central theme of *Clear Thinking: Turning Ordinary Moments Into Extraordinary Results*, Shane Parrish, 2023. The book is a deep dive into the practical application of principles and mental models to improve one's ability to think clearly in various situations. Parrish addresses common barriers to clear thinking including "emotion default," "ego default," "social default," and "inertia default", and offers strategies to overcome them.

Shane Parrish is the founder and leader of Farnam Street (FS), an organisation devoted to helping people develop an understanding of how the world really works, make better decisions, and live a better life by addressing topics such as mental models, decision making, learning, reading, and the art of living. He is the founding partner of Syrus Partners, a holding company that acquires and operates businesses in North America, and previously worked as an executive in the Canadian government, where he led the creation and execution of key cyber-defense initiatives. Parrish also hosts The Knowledge Project podcast. His work is guided by principles instilled by Warren Buffett and Charlie Munger, sharing their wisdom and exploring the mental models they champion to help people develop clarity of thought and breadth of understanding.

MAY 23

"Which of my current views would change if my incentives were different?"
- Morgan Housel[146]

---

[146] Housel echoes investor Charlie Munger who warned of incentive caused bias. "You must have the confidence to override people with more credentials than you" Munger cautioned, "whose cognition is impaired by incentive-caused bias or some similar psychological force that is obviously present." Whilst Munger's advice was aimed at "experts", you also have to guard against this tendency in yourself.
I Have A Few Questions, Morgan Housel, collabfund.com, December 16, 2024.
Morgan Housel is a financial writer, investor, and author best known for his bestselling book "The Psychology of Money," which explores how emotions, behaviour, and psychology drive financial decisions more than technical knowledge or intelligence. A former columnist for The Motley Fool and The Wall Street Journal, Housel has become one of the most influential voices in behavioural finance and investment psychology. His writing focuses on the intersection of psychology and money, emphasizing that financial success depends more on how you behave than what you know. "The Psychology of Money" became a massive bestseller by making complex financial concepts accessible through storytelling and real-world examples, showing how factors like luck, risk, time, and human nature affect wealth building. Housel is a partner at The Collaborative Fund, a venture capital firm, and continues to write about finance, economics, and human behaviour through his blog and various publications. His work emphasises long-term thinking, the power of compounding, the importance of saving, and understanding that everyone's financial situation and goals are different. He's known for his ability to distil complex financial wisdom into memorable, practical insights that resonate with both novice and experienced investors.

MAY 24

"What important truth do very few people agree with you on?"
- Peter Thiel[147]

---

147 "This question sounds easy because it's straightforward." Thiel explains. "Actually, it's very hard to answer. It's intellectually difficult because the knowledge that everyone is taught in school is by definition agreed upon. And it's psychologically difficult because anyone trying to answer must say something she knows to be unpopular. Brilliant thinking is rare, but courage is in even shorter supply than genius."

Zero to One: Notes on Startups, or How to Build the Future, Peter Thiel and Blake Masters, 2014.

Peter Thiel is a German-American entrepreneur, venture capitalist, and author who co-founded PayPal and became one of Silicon Valley's most influential and controversial figures. Born in Germany and raised in California, Thiel studied philosophy at Stanford before earning a law degree and working briefly as a securities lawyer and derivatives trader. In 1998, he co-founded PayPal with Max Levchin, which was sold to eBay for $1.5 billion in 2002, establishing him as part of the legendary "PayPal Mafia" of entrepreneurs. Thiel was Facebook's first major outside investor, putting $500,000 into the company in 2004 for a stake that eventually became worth over $1 billion. He founded Palantir Technologies, a data analytics company that works with government agencies, and established Founders Fund, a venture capital firm that has invested in companies like SpaceX, Airbnb, and Stripe. Known for his contrarian thinking, Thiel wrote "Zero to One," a bestselling book about startups and innovation, and has been a vocal advocate for technological progress while critiquing higher education and promoting alternative institutions.

MAY 25

"What are the best tools to quiet the nervous system and ego and see reality clearly?"
- Graham Duncan[148]

---

[148] Economist and co-author of "Freakonomics" Steven Levitt observed, "emotion is the enemy of rational argument." Research shows that anger can increase susceptibility to misinformation, and when emotions are high, intelligence is usually low. Intense emotions can cloud minds and lead to misguided decision making. George Marshall, Chief of Staff of the US Army during WWII, was lauded as a paragon of leadership, but even Marshall had to work at mastering his emotions. Forrest Pogue noted, "A man of strong emotions, capable of burning or freezing anger, he fought to keep himself under strict control. In his last speech to the cadets at the Virginia Military Institute, his text "Don't be a deep feeler and a poor thinker" stressed the conviction that the mind and not the emotions should be the master".

Current questions I find interesting, Graham Duncan, grahamduncan.blog.

Graham Duncan is a successful investor and talent spotter who co-founded East Rock Capital, a multi-family office investment firm that manages $2 billion for a small number of families and their charitable foundations. Before starting East Rock, Duncan worked at two other investment firms and started his career by co-founding an independent Wall Street research firm. A Yale graduate with a degree in ethics, politics, and economics, Duncan has become known as a "talent whisperer" for his unique ability to identify and nurture emerging investment talent. Duncan's unusual ability to wait out the moment is one of his defining characteristics as an investor, with colleagues noting that he's "not susceptible to impatience the way most people are" when it comes to seeding new investment managers. He also co-chairs The Sohn Investment Conference, which raises money for paediatric cancer research. Duncan maintains an active presence as a thoughtful writer and commentator on investment philosophy, human development, and talent identification, sharing insights through his blog and social media about the intersection of psychology and investing. His approach emphasises patience, deep understanding of human potential, and the importance of allowing talent to develop naturally rather than forcing growth.

MAY 26

"Is this the only story?
Is this the only interpretation that fits here? No?
What are my other options?
What are some of the other stories I could make up
about what happened here?"
- Lisa Barrett[149]

---

149 *Is This The Only Story?*, The Daily Stoic.

Lisa Feldman Barrett is a distinguished psychologist and neuroscientist whose groundbreaking research has fundamentally challenged traditional views of emotion, establishing her as one of the most influential emotion researchers of her generation. A professor at Northeastern University and a researcher at Massachusetts General Hospital, Barrett has revolutionised the field through her "theory of constructed emotion," which argues that emotion is constructed in the moment, by core systems that interact across the whole brain, aided by a lifetime of learning. This theory contradicts the classical view that emotions are universal, hardwired responses, instead proposing that emotions "are not triggered; you create them. They emerge as a combination of the physical properties of your body, a flexible brain that wires itself to whatever environment it develops in, and your culture and upbringing." Her bestselling book "How Emotions Are Made: The Secret Life of the Brain" has brought these scientific insights to a general audience, demonstrating that the emotions we experience arise as a response to our predictions about the world, not as a response to the actual external stimuli that we experience. Feldman Barrett's work has profound implications for psychology, neuroscience, law, and medicine, suggesting that humans have far more agency in their emotional lives than previously understood.

MAY 27

"Are you open to multiple points of view or [do] you demand compliance and uniformity?"
- Seth Godin[150]

---

[150] General Motors President Alfred P. Sloan, described by Peter Drucker as "the most effective executive I have ever known", encouraged dissent. Sloan once said, "Gentlemen, I take it we are all in complete agreement on the subject here." Heads nodded around the table. "Then," continued Sloan, "I propose we postpone further discussion of this matter until our next meeting, to give ourselves time to develop disagreement and perhaps gain some understanding of what the decision is all about." Reed Hastings went even further when he was CEO of Netflix, actively "farming for dissent". Employees would run their ideas past colleagues who tell them candidly what's wrong with it using a Google Doc that's open to everyone.

Seven questions for leaders, Seth Godin, seths.blog, March 13, 2011.

Seth Godin is a bestselling author, entrepreneur, and marketing guru who has fundamentally changed how people think about marketing, leadership, and the spread of ideas. He's written over 20 books, including influential titles like "Purple Cow," which popularised the concept that businesses must be remarkable to succeed, "The Tipping Point" predecessor "Unleashing the Ideavirus," and "Linchpin," which argues that indispensable employees are those who bring creativity and humanity to their work. Godin founded several companies, including Yoyodyne (one of the first internet marketing companies, sold to Yahoo!) and Squidoo, and the altMBA, an intensive online leadership workshop. His daily blog, which he's maintained for decades, reaches millions of readers with insights on marketing, culture, and human behaviour. Godin is known for coining terms like "permission marketing" (marketing to people who want to be marketed to) and advocating for authentic, story-driven approaches over traditional advertising. His philosophy emphasises that in the modern economy, playing it safe is actually the riskiest strategy, and that success comes from being different, generous, and willing to make a difference. He's also a sought-after speaker who challenges conventional business wisdom and encourages people to embrace change and lead rather than follow.

MAY 28

"Which of my strongest beliefs are formed on second-hand information vs. first-hand experience?"
- Morgan Housel[151]

---

[151] *A Few Questions*, Morgan Housel, collabfund.com, May 8, 2025.

Morgan Housel is a financial writer, investor, and author best known for his bestselling book "The Psychology of Money," which explores how emotions, behaviour, and psychology drive financial decisions more than technical knowledge or intelligence. A former columnist for The Motley Fool and The Wall Street Journal, Housel has become one of the most influential voices in behavioural finance and investment psychology. His writing focuses on the intersection of psychology and money, emphasizing that financial success depends more on how you behave than what you know. "The Psychology of Money" became a massive bestseller by making complex financial concepts accessible through storytelling and real-world examples, showing how factors like luck, risk, time, and human nature affect wealth building. Housel is a partner at The Collaborative Fund, a venture capital firm, and continues to write about finance, economics, and human behaviour through his blog and various publications. His work emphasises long-term thinking, the power of compounding, the importance of saving, and understanding that everyone's financial situation and goals are different. He's known for his ability to distil complex financial wisdom into memorable, practical insights that resonate with both novice and experienced investors.

MAY 29

"Wait ... what?"
- James Ryan[152]

---

[152] Ryan says this is one of five truly essential questions that you should regularly ask yourself and others. If you get in the habit of asking these questions Ryan believes you will have a very good chance of being successful and happy. "Wait what" is actually a very effective way of asking for clarification, which is crucial to understanding." Ryan says. "It's the question you should ask before drawing conclusions or before making a decision. The Dean of Harvard College, Rakesh Khurana, gave a great master class this year, where he emphasized the importance of inquiry before advocacy. It's important to understand an idea before you advocate for or against it. The wait, which precedes the what, is also a good reminder that it pays to slow down to make sure you truly understand."

Harvard Graduate School of Education Commencement Address, James E. Ryan, May 28, 2016.

James E. Ryan is a legal scholar who was the President of the University of Virginia from 2018 to 2025, having previously served as dean of Harvard Graduate School of Education and formerly the Matheson and Morgenthau Distinguished Professor at the University of Virginia School of Law. A leading expert on law and education, James Ryan has written extensively about how law structures educational opportunity. He is the author of several influential books, including "Wait, What?: And Life's Other Essential Questions" and "Five Miles Away, A World Apart: One City, Two Schools, and the Story of Educational Opportunity in Modern America". His book "Wait, What?" became a New York Times self-help best-seller, and describes the art of asking good questions, distilling them to five "essential" ones, and how they lead to better answers. Ryan is known for his thoughtful approach to leadership and education policy, emphasising the importance of asking the right questions to strengthen connections and deepen understanding.

MAY 30

"Are you exposing yourself to new inputs and new situations, and challenging yourself to find more interesting ideas?
Are you pushing the ideas you have further, making them more complete, turning them from hunches to notions to ideas to theories?
Are you publishing your theories, sharing your reasoning and having your ideas collide with the real world in service of making things better?"
- Seth Godin[153]

---

[153] *That might not be the right question*, Seth Godin, seths.blog, February 22, 2021.

Seth Godin is a bestselling author, entrepreneur, and marketing guru who has fundamentally changed how people think about marketing, leadership, and the spread of ideas. He's written over 20 books, including influential titles like "Purple Cow," which popularised the concept that businesses must be remarkable to succeed, "The Tipping Point" predecessor "Unleashing the Ideavirus," and "Linchpin," which argues that indispensable employees are those who bring creativity and humanity to their work. Godin founded several companies, including Yoyodyne (one of the first internet marketing companies, sold to Yahoo!) and Squidoo, and the altMBA, an intensive online leadership workshop. His daily blog, which he's maintained for decades, reaches millions of readers with insights on marketing, culture, and human behaviour. Godin is known for coining terms like "permission marketing" (marketing to people who want to be marketed to) and advocating for authentic, story-driven approaches over traditional advertising. His philosophy emphasises that in the modern economy, playing it safe is actually the riskiest strategy, and that success comes from being different, generous, and willing to make a difference. He's also a sought-after speaker who challenges conventional business wisdom and encourages people to embrace change and lead rather than follow.

MAY 31

"What are we missing?
Who has a different perspective?"
- Amy Edmonson[154]

---

[154] You need to hear from everyone in the room, particularly the quieter voices. To do this the nine Justices of the US Supreme Court adopted a rule: "Nobody speaks twice until everybody speaks once".
Amy Edmondson: Fearless - Creating Psychological Safety for Learning, Innovation, and Growth, April 30, 2020.
Amy Edmondson is the Novartis Professor of Leadership and Management at Harvard Business School and a leading expert on psychological safety, team dynamics, and organisational learning. She's best known for coining and researching the concept of "psychological safety", the belief that one can speak up without risk of punishment or humiliation, which she identified as crucial for team performance and innovation. Her book "The Fearless Organization" explores how leaders can create psychologically safe environments where people feel comfortable taking risks, making mistakes, and sharing ideas openly. Edmondson has also written "Teaming: How Organizations Learn, Innovate, and Compete in the Knowledge Economy" and "Right Kind of Wrong: The Science of Failing Well." Her research spans healthcare, technology, and various industries, examining how teams can learn from failures and improve performance through open communication and continuous learning. She's received numerous awards for her teaching and research, and her work has influenced how organisations think about building cultures that encourage innovation, learning, and high performance. Edmondson's insights are particularly valuable in high-stakes environments where mistakes can have serious consequences but learning from them is essential for improvement.

JUNE

COMMUNICATE WITH IMPACT

JUNE 1

"What do your words say you are?"
- Jefferson Fisher[155]

---

[155] Frances Hesselbein rose from volunteer Scout troop leader to CEO of the Girl Scouts organisation in the US. During her thirteen-year tenure, the Girl Scouts tripled minority membership, added 250,000 members to attain a membership of 2.25 million and grew the largely volunteer workforce by over 130,000 volunteers. Hesselbein authored or co-edited 27 books, was awarded the Presidential Medal of Freedom and lived to the age of 107. "For me, "leadership is a matter of how to be, not how to do.'" Hesselbein explained. "A great leader does not preach about their values; they live them. In the end, it is the quality and character of a leader that determines their performance and results. It is all about ethics, collaboration and transformation. Great leaders are consistent with their actions and values. We don't voice a wonderful sentiment and then behave in an opposite way. That's when morale, motivation and productivity go down in an organization, company or movement. A great leader is the living embodiment of their values." Hesselbein said, "You should be a living practicing example of what you are preaching".

The Next Conversation: Argue Less, Talk More, Jefferson Fisher, 2025.

Jefferson Fisher is a lawyer, podcast host, and author who hosts The Jefferson Fisher Podcast. Fisher has become a trial lawyer, speaker, and best-selling author with millions around the world following him for his practical communication advice. In 2022 he began making videos of practical communication tips to help people argue less and talk more. His approach combines his courtroom experience with accessible advice for everyday conversations. Fisher's book "The Next Conversation: Argue Less, Talk More" became a New York Times best seller. The book gives actionable strategies and phrases that will make you a more direct, confident, and productive communicator, offering a tried-and-true framework to transform your life and relationships by improving your next conversation. He's a sought-after speaker at Fortune 500 companies and governmental agencies, and hundreds of thousands of people subscribe to his actionable email newsletter and podcast. His mission is to help people build deeper connections, gain confidence, and take control of their voice.

JUNE 2

"How do others experience you?"
- Nina Ahuja[156]

---

[156] Every interaction you have will affect others in some way. Editor and writer William George Jordan explains that we are "radiating character" and this is constantly weaking or strengthening others. Jordan believed that we can "select the qualities ... to be radiated". Leaders must be conscious of what they are radiating and how it is affecting others.
The Ripple Effect: How Leadership Begins Within, Psychology Today, January 12, 2025.

Dr. Nina Ahuja is a surgeon, award-winning medical educator, senior academic leader, founder of Docs in Leadership & author of bestselling book "Stress in Medicine". She graduated from medical school at McMaster University then completed her residency in ophthalmology at University of Ottawa and began her surgical practice in Hamilton in 2003. She currently serves as Academic Division Head for Ophthalmology at McMaster and President for the Association of Canadian University of Professors of Ophthalmology (ACUPO). Her book "Stress in Medicine: Lessons Learned Through My Years As a Surgeon, From Med School to Residency, and Beyond" was selected as a Recommend Read by the National Business Book Award Panel in 2021. Drawing from her experiences as a frontline healthcare provider, private practice owner, educator, and physician leader, in 2019 Dr. Ahuja founded Docs in Leadership to promote and deliver physician developed leadership education. She is also a certified emotional intelligence instructor and EQ-i 2.0® Certified Practitioner who focuses on empowering M.D. trainees and healthcare providers with emotionally intelligent leadership skills to positively impact patients & systems while maintaining one's own wellness. Her work addresses the unique stresses physicians face and helps create healthier work cultures in healthcare environments.

JUNE 3

"I suggest that, before speaking or taking some other action, you first ask yourself these questions: Is it necessary? Is it true? Is it nonharming? If you can answer yes to all these questions, it may be okay to proceed. If not, you must weigh what is the right action in the situation."
- Judith Hanson Lasater[157]

---

[157] A version of this question has also been misattributed to the 13th century Persian poet, theologian and mystic Jalaluddin Rumi. Irrespective of the source, these are challenging questions to answer before speaking.

Living Your Yoga: Finding the Spiritual in Everyday Life, Judith Hanson Lasater, 2016.

Judith Hanson Lasater is a prominent yoga teacher, author, and physical therapist who has been influential in bringing yoga to the Western world since the 1970s. She is one of the founding members of Yoga Journal magazine and has written numerous books on yoga practice, including "Relax and Renew," "Living Your Yoga," and "Restore and Rebalance." Lasater is particularly known for her expertise in restorative yoga and has been instrumental in developing and popularising this gentle, therapeutic approach to practice. She holds a doctorate in East-West psychology and has taught yoga for over four decades, combining her background in physical therapy with traditional yoga teachings. Lasater has trained thousands of yoga teachers worldwide and continues to lead workshops, retreats, and teacher training programs, emphasizing the integration of yoga philosophy into daily life and the importance of relaxation and stress reduction in modern wellness practices.

JUNE 4

*"What would happen if I only said things
I deeply believed to be true?"*
- Jordan Peterson[158]

---

[158] Peterson echoes author Don Miguel Ruiz who writes, "Be impeccable with your word. Speak with integrity. Say only what you mean. Avoid using the word to speak against yourself or to gossip about others. Use the power of your word in the direction of truth and love." *The Four Agreements: A Practical Guide to Personal freedom*, Don Miguel Ruiz and Janet Mills, 1997.

What are some deep, profound, thought-provoking questions to ponder over?, Jordan B. Peterson, Quora, 2014.

Jordan B. Peterson is a clinical psychologist, professor, and author who gained international prominence for his views on free speech, political correctness, and personal responsibility. He taught at Harvard University and the University of Toronto, specialising in personality psychology, psychopathology, and the psychology of religious and ideological belief. His bestselling book "12 Rules for Life: An Antidote to Chaos" combines psychology, philosophy, and personal anecdotes to offer practical advice for living a meaningful life, emphasizing individual responsibility, self-improvement, and traditional values. His second book, "Beyond Order: 12 More Rules for Life," continues these themes. Peterson's lectures and online content focus on topics like mythology, religion, personal development, and the psychological significance of stories and archetypes.

JUNE 5

*"... for your next conversation, try asking yourself questions like these:
If I had to choose, what's the one thing that I'd need them to understand? What small step can I take to show them that I heard them? What assumptions am I making? How can I show gratitude for this opportunity to talk?
Is there a part of this that I'm trying"*
- Jefferson Fisher[159]

---

159 *The Next Conversation: Argue Less, Talk More*, Jefferson Fisher, 2025.

Jefferson Fisher is a lawyer, podcast host, and author who hosts The Jefferson Fisher Podcast. Fisher has become a trial lawyer, speaker, and best-selling author with millions around the world following him for his practical communication advice. In 2022 he began making videos of practical communication tips to help people argue less and talk more. His approach combines his courtroom experience with accessible advice for everyday conversations. Fisher's book "The Next Conversation: Argue Less, Talk More" became a New York Times best seller. The book gives actionable strategies and phrases that will make you a more direct, confident, and productive communicator, offering a tried-and-true framework to transform your life and relationships by improving your next conversation. He's a sought-after speaker at Fortune 500 companies and governmental agencies, and hundreds of thousands of people subscribe to his actionable email newsletter and podcast. His mission is to help people build deeper connections, gain confidence, and take control of their voice.

JUNE 6

*"Whose voices do you think might need to be heard?
How might you engage with them?"*
- Ronald Heifitz[160]

---

[160] Effective leadership requires what author Glennon Doyle describes as "curating conversations". "It isn't how much you know that matters." Liz Wiseman notes. "What matters is how much access you have to what other people know. It isn't just how intelligent your team members are; it is how much of that intelligence you can draw out and put to use." *Multipliers: How the Best Leaders Make Everyone Smarter,* Elizabeth Wiseman, 2010.

Using Heifetz's principles of adaptive leadership to diagnose and take action in your system, Leadership for change, materials originally adapted from the works of Ronald Heifetz, Alexander Grashow & Marty Linsky by Chris Lawrence☐Pietroni & Mari Davis, dcsleadership.co.uk.

Ronald Heifetz is a pioneering leadership scholar and practitioner who serves as the King Hussein bin Talal Senior Lecturer in Public Leadership and Founding Director of the Center for Public Leadership at Harvard Kennedy School. Formerly a clinical instructor in psychiatry at Harvard Medical School, Heifetz works with leaders in government, nonprofits, and business. He is best known for developing the theory of adaptive leadership, which distinguishes between technical problems that can be solved with existing knowledge and adaptive challenges that require new learning, experimentation, and changes in values or behavior. Heifetz defines adaptive leadership as the act of mobilising a group of individuals to handle tough challenges and emerge triumphant in the end. His influential works include "Leadership Without Easy Answers," "Leadership on the Line," and "The Practice of Adaptive Leadership," which provide frameworks for leading through complex change by taking people outside their comfort zones and addressing the toughest organisational and societal challenges.

JUNE 7

"Who has the right answers but I ignore because they're not articulate?"
- Morgan Housel[161]

---

[161] In "What Makes an Effective Executive", Peter Drucker laid out eight practises of effective executives. Drucker added a final practise which he explained is so important that it is elevated to a rule. That practise is *"Listen first, speak last"*. Irrespective of how articulate someone is. Drucker echoes oil magnate and world's richest man John D. Rockefeller who was renowned for listening to others and speaking infrequently. Rockefeller was quoted as saying, "success comes from keeping the ears open and the mouth closed". Later in life, he was also known to recite the following rhyme –

A wise old owl lived in an oak

The more he saw, the less he spoke

The less he spoke, the more he heard

A Few Questions, Morgan Housel, collabfund.com, May 8, 2025.

Morgan Housel is a financial writer, investor, and author best known for his bestselling book "The Psychology of Money," which explores how emotions, behaviour, and psychology drive financial decisions more than technical knowledge or intelligence. A former columnist for The Motley Fool and The Wall Street Journal, Housel has become one of the most influential voices in behavioural finance and investment psychology. His writing focuses on the intersection of psychology and money, emphasizing that financial success depends more on how you behave than what you know. "The Psychology of Money" became a massive bestseller by making complex financial concepts accessible through storytelling and real-world examples, showing how factors like luck, risk, time, and human nature affect wealth building. Housel is a partner at The Collaborative Fund, a venture capital firm, and continues to write about finance, economics, and human behaviour through his blog and various publications. His work emphasises long-term thinking, the power of compounding, the importance of saving, and understanding that everyone's financial situation and goals are different. He's known for his ability to distil complex financial wisdom into memorable, practical insights that resonate with both novice and experienced investors.

JUNE 8

"If you are trying to develop a good relationship and feel the conversation starting to go in the wrong direction, you can humbly ask some version of "Are we OK?" 'Is this working?' or 'What is happening here?' to explore what might be going wrong and how it might be improved."
- Edgar Schein[162]

---

[162] *Humble Inquiry: The Gentle Art of Asking Instead of Telling,* Edgar H. Schein, 2018.

Edgar H. Schein (1928 - 2023) was a pioneering organisational psychologist and management theorist who fundamentally shaped our understanding of organisational culture and leadership. Schein spent most of his distinguished academic career at MIT Sloan School of Management, where he was a professor emeritus until his death in 2023. He is best known for developing the influential three-level model of organisational culture, which describes culture as consisting of artifacts (visible structures and processes), espoused beliefs and values, and underlying assumptions that truly drive behaviour. His seminal work "Organizational Culture and Leadership" became one of the most cited texts in management literature and established him as the foremost expert on corporate culture. Schein also made significant contributions to the field of career development, coining the concept of "career anchors" - the self-perceived talents, motives, and values that guide career decisions. His approach to organisational consulting emphasised process consultation, where consultants help organisations solve their own problems rather than providing direct solutions. Throughout his career, Schein worked with numerous Fortune 500 companies and government agencies, helping them navigate cultural change and leadership challenges. His humanistic approach to management, which emphasised the importance of psychological safety and authentic relationships in the workplace, influenced generations of leaders and consultants. Schein authored over 30 books and countless articles, leaving an enduring legacy in organisational psychology and management theory.

JUNE 9

*"What is it that leads you to that position? ...
Can you illustrate your point for me?"*
- Peter Senge[163]

---

[163] To get a better appreciation of reality requires triangulation, engaging others to provide multiple vantage points. The scientist Antoine Lavoisier noted, "The human mind adjusts itself to a certain point of view, and those who have regarded nature from one angle, during a portion of their life, can adopt new ideas only with difficulty."

The Fifth Discipline: The Art & Practice of The Learning Organization, Peter Senge, 1990.

Peter Senge is a systems scientist, organisational learning expert, and senior lecturer at MIT Sloan School of Management who revolutionised how organisations think about learning and change. He is best known for his groundbreaking book "The Fifth Discipline: The Art and Practice of the Learning Organization," which introduced the concept of learning organisations, companies that continually expand their capacity to create their future rather than just react to events. Senge's work integrates systems thinking, personal mastery, mental models, shared vision, and team learning into a comprehensive framework for organisational transformation. Through his research at MIT and his work with the Society for Organizational Learning, he has helped countless companies move from traditional hierarchical structures to more adaptive, learning-focused organisations. His systems thinking approach emphasises understanding the interconnectedness of organisational elements rather than focusing on isolated problems, making him one of the most influential management thinkers of the past several decades and a pioneer in applying complexity science to business challenges.

JUNE 10

*"A scrupulous writer, in every sentence that he writes, will ask himself at least four questions, thus:
1. What am I trying to say?
2. What words will express it?
3. What image or idiom will make it clearer?
4. Is this image fresh enough to have an effect?"*
- George Orwell[164]

---

164 Clear communication–written and verbal–is essential to effective leadership. Orwell's questions are reflected in the advice of minister, author and rhetorician Hugh Blair: "To speak or to write perspicuously and agreeably with purity, with grace and strength, are attainments of the utmost consequence to all who purpose, either by speech or writing, to address the Public."

Politics and the English Language, George Orwell, 1948.

George Orwell was the pen name of Eric Arthur Blair (1903-1950), an author and journalist who became one of the most influential writers of the 20th century. Orwell is best known for his dystopian novels "1984" and "Animal Farm," which serve as powerful critiques of totalitarianism and political corruption. His experiences as a colonial policeman in Burma, fighting in the Spanish Civil War, and witnessing the rise of fascism and Stalinism deeply shaped his political consciousness and literary work. Orwell's writing is characterised by clear, direct prose and a commitment to democratic socialism, while warning against the dangers of authoritarianism from both the left and right. His concepts like "Big Brother," "doublethink," and "thoughtcrime" from "1984" have become part of common vocabulary, and his work continues to resonate in discussions about surveillance, propaganda, and political freedom. Beyond his novels, Orwell wrote influential essays including "Politics and the English Language" and "Shooting an Elephant," establishing him as both a masterful fiction writer and incisive social critic.

JUNE 11

*"Do I listen with the intent to understand,
or with the intent to reply?"*
- Stephen Covey[165]

---

[165] Frances Hesselbein said, "When people are speaking, they require our undivided attention. We focus on them; we listen very carefully. We listen to the spoken words and the unspoken messages. This means looking directly at the person, eyes connected; we forget we have a watch, just focusing for that moment on that person." Hesselbein echoed Ernest Hemingway who wrote, "When people talk listen completely. Don't be thinking what you're going to say. Most people never listen. Nor do they observe. You should be able to go into a room and when you come out know everything that you saw there and not only that. If that room gave you any feeling you should know exactly what it was that gave you that feeling."
The 7 Habits of Highly Effective People, Stephen R. Covey, 1989.
Stephen R. Covey (1932-2012) was an educator, author, and businessman who became one of the most influential voices in personal development and leadership through his bestselling book "The 7 Habits of Highly Effective People". His approach emphasised character-based leadership and principle-centred living, arguing that lasting success comes from aligning one's actions with timeless principles like integrity, fairness, and human dignity rather than quick-fix techniques. The seven habits became widely adopted in both corporate and personal settings. Covey founded the Covey Leadership Center (later Franklin Covey) to teach these principles to organisations worldwide and wrote numerous other books, including "First Things First" and "The Leader in Me." His work stood out in the self-help genre for its emphasis on character development over personality techniques, and his concepts like the "Circle of Influence" and "Quadrant II" time management continue to be taught in business schools and leadership programs globally.

JUNE 12

"Do they trust me enough to believe my promises?"
- Seth Godin[166]

---

[166] Trust has been referred to as "the currency of leadership". Robert K. Greenleaf, the founder of servant leadership, put it this way: "The one who states the goal must elicit trust, especially if it is a high risk or visionary goal, because those who follow are asked to accept the risk along with the leader. Leaders do not elicit trust unless one has confidence in their values and competence (including judgment) and unless they have a sustaining spirit (entheos) that will support the tenacious pursuit of a goal."

The most important question, Seth Godin, seths.blog, February 23, 2014.

Seth Godin is a bestselling author, entrepreneur, and marketing guru who has fundamentally changed how people think about marketing, leadership, and the spread of ideas. He's written over 20 books, including influential titles like "Purple Cow," which popularised the concept that businesses must be remarkable to succeed, "The Tipping Point" predecessor "Unleashing the Ideavirus," and "Linchpin," which argues that indispensable employees are those who bring creativity and humanity to their work. Godin founded several companies, including Yoyodyne (one of the first internet marketing companies, sold to Yahoo!) and Squidoo, and the altMBA, an intensive online leadership workshop. His daily blog, which he's maintained for decades, reaches millions of readers with insights on marketing, culture, and human behaviour. Godin is known for coining terms like "permission marketing" (marketing to people who want to be marketed to) and advocating for authentic, story-driven approaches over traditional advertising. His philosophy emphasises that in the modern economy, playing it safe is actually the riskiest strategy, and that success comes from being different, generous, and willing to make a difference. He's also a sought-after speaker who challenges conventional business wisdom and encourages people to embrace change and lead rather than follow.

JUNE 13

"Whose silence do I mistake for agreement?"
- Morgan Housel[167]

---

[167] To access the collective wisdom of a team, the best leaders actively engage everyone in the conversation. Harvard professor Amy Edmondson explains, "For knowledge work to flourish, the workplace must be one where people feel able to share their knowledge! This means sharing concerns, questions, mistakes, and half-formed ideas." Edmonson gives a simple but powerful way to think about the leader's role. Imagine everyone in the team has a thought bubble, like in the comics, extending from their mind. Your role is to find out what is in each bubble. Edmonson says, "In real life you can't see the thought bubbles – but you ought to know they're there!". *The Fearless Organization*, keynote by Amy Edmondson at The HR Congress World Summit, 3 September 2019.

A Few Questions, Morgan Housel, collabfund.com, May 8, 2025.

Morgan Housel is a financial writer, investor, and author best known for his bestselling book "The Psychology of Money," which explores how emotions, behaviour, and psychology drive financial decisions more than technical knowledge or intelligence. A former columnist for The Motley Fool and The Wall Street Journal, Housel has become one of the most influential voices in behavioural finance and investment psychology. His writing focuses on the intersection of psychology and money, emphasizing that financial success depends more on how you behave than what you know. "The Psychology of Money" became a massive bestseller by making complex financial concepts accessible through storytelling and real-world examples, showing how factors like luck, risk, time, and human nature affect wealth building. Housel is a partner at The Collaborative Fund, a venture capital firm, and continues to write about finance, economics, and human behaviour through his blog and various publications. His work emphasises long-term thinking, the power of compounding, the importance of saving, and understanding that everyone's financial situation and goals are different. He's known for his ability to distil complex financial wisdom into memorable, practical insights that resonate with both novice and experienced investors.

JUNE 14

"What do I know?
Who needs to know?
Have I told them?"
- Jim Mattis[168]

---

[168] Mattis explained that having clear intent and sharing context was a key part of USMC leadership culture. "The Marine Corps demanded that, as young officers, we learn how to convey our intent so that it passed intact through the layers of intermediate leadership to our youngest Marines. For instance, you may say, 'We will attack that bridge in order to cut off the enemy's escape.' The critical information is your intent, summed up in the phrase 'in order to.' If a platoon seizes the bridge and cuts off the enemy, the mission is a success. But if the bridge is seized while the enemy continues to escape, the platoon commander will not sit idly on the bridge. Without asking for further orders, he will move to cut off the enemy's escape. Such aligned independence is based upon a shared understanding of the 'why' for the mission. This is key to unleashing audacity". "Once your team knows how to improvise, don't guide them too closely." Mattis writes. "Make clear your intention but let them plan and execute it themselves." Mattis emphasised context rather than control. "Business management books often stress 'centralized planning and decentralized execution.'" he explains. "That is too top-down for my taste. I believe in a centralized vision, coupled with decentralized planning and execution".

Call Sign Chaos: Learning to Lead, Jim Mattis, 2019.

General James Mattis is a retired four-star Marine Corps general and former U.S. Secretary of Defense who is widely regarded as one of the most influential military leaders of his generation. Known for his intellectual approach to warfare and voracious reading habits, Mattis led transformational change throughout his military career, including commanding United States Joint Forces Command and serving as NATO's Supreme Allied Commander Transformation from 2007 to 2010. His leadership philosophy emphasises that "a leader's number one responsibility is to define reality" and the importance of "adapting to new realities while staying true to core values and strategic necessities." Mattis is known for his warrior-scholar approach, combining tactical excellence with strategic thinking, and for developing leaders who could operate in complex, rapidly changing environments. His memoir "Call Sign Chaos: Learning to Lead" reflects his belief that effective leadership requires continuous learning, clear communication of vision, and the ability to navigate uncertainty while maintaining organisational cohesion and purpose.

JUNE 15

"How can I show appreciation for this feedback by listening carefully, considering the message with an open mind, and becoming neither defensive nor angry?"
- Reed Hastings[169]

---

[169] The complete quote from which this question was taken is: "Natural human inclination is to provide a defense or excuse when receiving criticism; we all reflexively seek to protect our egos and reputation. When you receive feedback, you need to fight this natural reaction and instead ask yourself, "How can I show appreciation for this feedback by listening carefully, considering the message with an open mind, and becoming neither defensive nor angry?" Our self-awareness, and capacity for improvement, is correlated with the amount of discomfort we can tolerate. In the words of Bob Proctor's mentor Leland Val Van De Wall, "The degree to which a person can grow is directly proportional to the amount of truth he can accept about himself without running away."

No Rules Rules: Netflix and the Culture of Reinvention, Reed Hastings, 2020.

Reed Hastings is an entrepreneur and technology executive best known as the co-founder and former CEO of Netflix, where he transformed the company from a DVD-by-mail service into the world's leading streaming entertainment platform. Under his leadership from 1997 to 2023, Netflix pioneered the subscription-based streaming model and became a major producer of original content, fundamentally disrupting the traditional television and film industries. Prior to Netflix, Hastings founded Pure Software, a debugging tools company that he sold in the 1990s. He's recognised for his data-driven approach to business decisions and his willingness to cannibalise Netflix's own DVD business to focus on streaming. Hastings has also been active in education reform, serving on various boards and advocating for charter schools, and he stepped down as Netflix CEO in 2023 to focus on philanthropy while remaining executive chairman of the company.

JUNE 16

"What valuable insights or discoveries do you have to share with others? Ultimately, what is the contribution you want to make to the audience?"
- Simon Sinek[170]

---

[170] "When asked to distil his most powerful tip for public speaking—the one that rises above all the rest—his answer is simple." Priddy explains. "'I have one very important rule in public speaking, and that's that you have to show up to give,' he says. 'Very often, before I walk out on stage, I will say to myself out loud, 'You're here to give.''" "According to Simon, it's important to step back and consider what you hope to achieve with your presentation. Take a moment to ask yourself: Why are you here? What valuable insights or discoveries do you have to share with others? Ultimately, what is the contribution you want to make to the audience?"
Simon's #1 Rule of Public Speaking, Emily Priddy, simonsinek.com, December 15, 2023.

Simon Sinek is an author, motivational speaker, and organisational consultant best known for popularizing the concept of "Start With Why" through his famous 2009 TED Talk, which has become one of the most-watched TED presentations of all time. The central idea is that great leaders and organisations inspire action by communicating their purpose and beliefs (the "why") before explaining what they do or how they do it. Sinek has written several bestselling books including "Start With Why," "Leaders Eat Last," and "The Infinite Game," which explore leadership, organisational culture, and sustainable success. He argues that the best leaders create environments of trust and safety where people feel valued and motivated to contribute their best work. Sinek works with organisations ranging from startups to Fortune 500 companies and government agencies, helping them clarify their purpose and build stronger, more inspiring cultures. His approach combines insights from anthropology, psychology, and biology to explain human behaviour in organisational settings, emphasising that people don't buy what you do, they buy why you do it.

JUNE 17

"To help diagnose whether you're clamming up when you should be speaking up, ask the following four questions:
Am I acting out my concerns?
Is my conscience nagging me?
Am I choosing the certainty of silence over the risk of speaking up?
Am I telling myself that I'm helpless?"
- Kerry Patterson[171]

---

171 Patterson's questions echo Martin Luther King Jr. "On some positions," King said, "Cowardice asks the question, 'Is it safe?' Expediency asks the question, 'Is it politic?' And Vanity comes along and asks the question, 'Is it popular?' But Conscience asks the question, 'Is it right?' ... The ultimate measure of a man is not where he stands in moments of convenience, but where he stands in moments of challenge, moments of great crisis and controversy."

Crucial Accountability: Tools for Resolving Violated Expectations, Broken Commitments, and Bad Behavior, Kerry Patterson, 2004.

Kerry Patterson is a co-founder of VitalSmarts (now Crucial Learning) and co-author of several influential New York Times bestselling books on communication and organisational change. Patterson co-authored "Crucial Conversations: Tools for Talking When Stakes Are High" with Joseph Grenny, Ron McMillan, and Al Switzler, a book that has sold more than 2 million copies and has been translated into 28 languages. He is also co-author of other bestsellers including "Change Anything," "Crucial Confrontations," and "Influencer," and has completed doctoral work at Stanford University. Patterson is a recipient of the Mentor of the Year Award and the 2004 William G. Dyer Distinguished Alumni Award. His work focuses on helping individuals and organisations navigate high-stakes conversations and drive behavioural change. As an international corporate consultant and leader at Crucial Learning, he offers courses in the areas of communication, leadership and performance. Patterson's expertise lies in providing practical tools for managing difficult conversations, creating accountability, and achieving positive outcomes when emotions and stakes are high.

JUNE 18

"Is this something we have to agree on?"
- Jefferson Fisher[172]

---

[172] *The Next Conversation: Argue Less, Talk More,* Jefferson Fisher, 2025.

Jefferson Fisher is a lawyer, podcast host, and author who hosts The Jefferson Fisher Podcast. Fisher has become a trial lawyer, speaker, and best-selling author with millions around the world following him for his practical communication advice. In 2022 he began making videos of practical communication tips to help people argue less and talk more. His approach combines his courtroom experience with accessible advice for everyday conversations. Fisher's book "The Next Conversation: Argue Less, Talk More" became a New York Times best seller. The book gives actionable strategies and phrases that will make you a more direct, confident, and productive communicator, offering a tried-and-true framework to transform your life and relationships by improving your next conversation. He's a sought-after speaker at Fortune 500 companies and governmental agencies, and hundreds of thousands of people subscribe to his actionable email newsletter and podcast. His mission is to help people build deeper connections, gain confidence, and take control of their voice.

JUNE 19

"If, instead of seeking approval, you ask, 'What's wrong with it? How can I make it better?', you are more likely to get a truthful, critical answer."
- Paul Arden[173]

---

[173] *It's Not How Good You Are, It's How Good You Want to Be: The world's best-selling book by Paul Arden*, Paul Arden, June 2003.

Paul Arden (1940 - 2008) was a legendary advertising creative director and author who transformed British advertising during his tenure at Saatchi & Saatchi. He served as creative director at Saatchi and Saatchi and authored several influential books on advertising and motivation, including "Whatever You Think, Think The Opposite" and "It's Not How Good You Are, It's How Good You Want To Be." During his 14 years as Executive Creative Director at Saatchi & Saatchi, he was responsible for some of the UK's most successful advertising campaigns including British Airways, Silk Cut, Anchor Butter, InterCity and Fuji. Known for his maverick approach and perfectionism, Arden's unconventional thinking and bold creative vision made him a standout figure in the advertising world of the 1980s and 90s. His books became international bestsellers, distilling his contrarian philosophy and creative insights into accessible wisdom for anyone seeking to break conventional thinking and achieve excellence. Arden left a legacy as both an advertising genius and motivational author who challenged people to think differently about success and creativity.

JUNE 20

"Does the presence you convey authentically reflect the truth of your character?"
- Daryl Conner[174]

---

[174] Conner writes, "When clients experience a practitioner's presence as genuinely reflecting who he/she is, they tend to pay attention. They may or may not agree with what is being said, but projecting the full truth of *who you are* is rare among professional change practitioners, and many clients find it compelling. It draws them in...even if they disagree with the points being made."
It's About The Questions, Daryl Conner, conneracademy.com, 2017.

Daryl Conner is a pioneering change management expert and founder/chairman of Conner Partners, best known for his groundbreaking book "Managing at the Speed of Change". Conner identified that "the single most important factor to managing change successfully is the degree to which people demonstrate resilience: the capacity to absorb high levels of change while displaying minimal dysfunctional behaviour." He introduced influential concepts to the change management field, including the "burning platform" metaphor that has been used for nearly 30 years to describe high urgency regarding change initiatives. For over forty-five years, Conner has educated and advised strategic leaders and veteran change practitioners in many of the world's most successful organisations, helping them understand and navigate transformational change challenges. His work focuses on how organisations and individuals can build resilience to thrive during periods of intense change rather than simply survive them. Conner's approach emphasises that successful change management is less about what to change and more about how to change, making resilience the cornerstone of effective organisational transformation.

JUNE 21

"Is silence killing your company?"
- Leslie A. Perlow and Stephanie Williams[175]

---

[175] Perlow and Williams examine how organisational silence creates destructive cycles in the workplace. The research reveals that while people often decide not to speak up about organisational problems, thinking "it's not worth it," this silence is actually much more damaging than realised. They found that people often remain silent about workplace differences with good intentions, believing it's more productive than airing disagreements, but this creates a vicious cycle of defensiveness and distrust. Perlow and Williams argue that what appears to be a harmless avoidance of conflict actually undermines organisational effectiveness, erodes relationships, and prevents necessary problem-solving. They demonstrate that breaking these patterns of silence requires intentional effort to create psychologically safe environments where people feel empowered to voice concerns and differences constructively.

"Is silence killing your company?", Leslie A. Perlow and Stephanie Williams, Harvard Business Review, May 2003.

Leslie A. Perlow is the Konosuke Matsushita Professor of Leadership at Harvard Business School, renowned for her groundbreaking research on work-life balance and organisational time management. Her goal is to identify ways organisations can alter their work practices to benefit both productivity and employees' well-being. Perlow is best known for her influential studies on "time famine" in the workplace and her work on predictable time off (PTO) policies. She has demonstrated how the 24/7 work culture in professional services creates a vicious cycle where responsiveness breeds the need for more responsiveness. Her research challenges the assumption that long hours are necessary for productivity, showing instead how organisations can achieve better results through structured time management practices. She emphasises that "it doesn't have to be some big, grand organisational initiative. Any team can do it," advocating for grassroots approaches to workplace change that empower employees to collectively transform their work environments.

Stephanie Williams is an experienced leadership consultant and executive coach with over 20 years of experience in organisational development and change management. She partners with leaders to achieve results through people and to embrace transformation, drawing on career experience as a consultant at Booz Allen Hamilton and Watson Wyatt Worldwide, with leadership roles at Chase Manhattan Bank and CH2M HILL, spanning work across Asia, Europe, and North America. Williams holds a Ph.D. in organisational psychology from the University of Michigan and is a certified executive coach who utilises various assessment tools for individual, team, and organisational development. Her work emphasises that "as change is the norm in our world rather than the exception, leading and navigating change effectively is an essential leadership skill."

JUNE 22

*"What am I saying to myself?
What am I saying to my teammates?
What language am I using?
How am I impacting myself?
How am I impacting others?
How am I being my best self every time I step on the field?"*
- Trevor Moawad[176]

---

[176] Moawad highlights the significant impact of verbalising negative thoughts. "[Negative thinking is] a multiple [of] four to seven times more powerful than its equivalent positivity." he explains. "... And then what we started to learn was that if we say things out loud, they're ten times more powerful than if we think [them]. ... So if I'm saying negative things out loud, 'I don't want to be here. I hate ... the heat. What's going on in our world right now?' ... then I'm increasing the probability that what I don't want to happen will happen by 40 to 70 times."

It Takes What It Takes: How to Think Neutrally and Gain Control of Your Life Hardcover, Trevor Moawad with Andy Staples, 2020.

Trevor Moawad (1973-2021) was a pioneering mental conditioning coach who became one of the most respected figures in sports psychology, working with elite athletes, military personnel, and business leaders. He was best known for being the mental conditioning coach to Seattle Seahawks quarterback Russell Wilson for over six years. Moawad worked closely with prestigious NCAA football programs, the US Special Operations community, Major League Baseball, and the NBA. As "the world's best brain trainer" according to Sports Illustrated, he developed battle-tested strategies for managing negativity and achieving peak performance. His approach emphasised "neutral thinking" - focusing on what you can control rather than positive or negative thoughts. Moawad died in 2021 at age 48 after a two-year battle with cancer, leaving behind a legacy of transforming how elite performers approach mental conditioning. His book "It Takes What It Takes" outlines his philosophy of mental toughness and performance optimisation that influenced countless athletes and coaches across professional sports.

JUNE 23

"To make our communications more effective, we need to shift our thinking from 'What information do I need to convey?' to 'What questions do I want my audience to ask?'"
- Chip Heath[177]

---

[177] *Made to Stick: Why Some Ideas Survive and Others Die*, Chip Heath, 2007.

Chip Heath is the Thrive Foundation for Youth Professor of Organizational Behavior at Stanford Graduate School of Business. He graduated from Texas A&M University with a Bachelor of Science degree in industrial engineering and subsequently earned a PhD in psychology from Stanford University before teaching at the University of Chicago Graduate School of Business and Duke University's Fuqua School of Business. His research examines why certain ideas — ranging from urban legends to folk medical cures, from Chicken Soup for the Soul stories to business strategy myths — survive and prosper in the social marketplace of ideas. Heath is best known for co-authoring three New York Times bestselling books with his brother Dan Heath: "Made to Stick: Why Some Ideas Survive and Others Die", which explores the anatomy of memorable ideas, "Switch: How to Change Things When Change is Hard", and "Decisive: How to Make Better Decisions in Life and Work". His work focuses on understanding how to make ideas more effective in organisational and social contexts.

JUNE 24

"What are your mantras?"
- Michael Lombardi & George Raveling[178]

---

[178] Communication repetition theory posits that repeating key messages enhances understanding, recall, and persuasion. Lombardi and Raveling explain, "While long-winded talks of wins, earnings and strategies are undoubtedly necessary at points, our teams are far more likely to remember our catchphrases."
The Daily Coach, April 15, 2021.

Michael Lombardi is a three-time Super Bowl champion as an executive with over 30 years of experience in NFL front offices who recently joined the North Carolina football program as General Manager in December 2024. He has spent 35 years working for the New England Patriots, San Francisco 49ers, the Oakland Raiders and the Cleveland Browns, and has the distinction of the being the only person to make it to the Super Bowl with both the Patriots and 49ers. Beyond his front office work, Lombardi has been a prominent media personality as an NFL analyst, author, and cofounder with George Raveling of The Daily Coach, a newsletter that shares sports and organisational leadership lessons.

George Raveling is a Basketball Hall of Fame coach and Nike executive who has had an extraordinary impact on both basketball and sports marketing. After a successful college coaching career at schools including Washington State, Iowa, and USC, he joined Nike at the request of Phil Knight, where he played an integral role in signing a reluctant Michael Jordan. Raveling has worked as the Director for International Basketball for Nike since his retirement from USC and is known as "the iconic leader who brought Michael Jordan to Nike". Beyond basketball, he has a unique connection to civil rights history and having a personal connection to Martin Luther King Jr.'s "I Have a Dream" speech. Raveling was present at the March on Washington on August 28, 1963, and after Dr. King delivered his speech, King handed Raveling the original typewritten copy.

The two co-founded The Daily Coach newsletter, sharing leadership wisdom from sports and business.

JUNE 25

"How does the medium through which information is conveyed influence the message itself?"
- Marshall McLuhan[179]

---

[179] McLuhan's question encapsulates the central thesis of his groundbreaking work in media theory, most famously expressed in his phrase "the medium is the message." The concept is that the characteristics of a communication medium fundamentally shape and alter the content it carries, often more profoundly than the content itself. McLuhan observed that different media create different cognitive and social effects regardless of their content. For example, television's visual, immediate nature creates a different relationship with information than print's linear, reflective format. He argued that the printing press didn't just spread information—it restructured how humans think, moving from oral, communal knowledge to individual, sequential reasoning. Similarly, electronic media was creating a "global village" where information moves at the speed of light, collapsing space and time. This insight was revolutionary because it shifted focus from what media says to what media does to us. McLuhan recognized that each medium has its own grammar, biases, and effects on human consciousness and social organisation. A speech delivered on radio creates different psychological and social effects than the same speech delivered on television, in print, or in person, because each medium engages different senses and cognitive processes, fundamentally altering how the message is received, processed, and understood.

The Medium is the Massage, Marshall McLuhan, 1967. Note the title was actually misspelled from "Message" during typesetting, but McLuhan decided to leave it.

Marshall McLuhan (1911-1980) was a visionary communications theorist and media philosopher whose prescient ideas about technology and communication fundamentally changed how we understand media's impact on society. His aphorism "the medium is the message" summarised his view of the potent influence of television, computers, and other electronic disseminators of information in shaping styles of thinking and thought. McLuhan coined the term "global village" to describe the phenomenon of the entire world becoming more interconnected as the result of the propagation of media technologies throughout the world. In 1964, McLuhan announced a vision of a hyper-connected world, long before the advent of "smart-communication" that would allow us to be connected to the whole world 24/7, 365 days a year from our pockets. His concepts of "hot" and "cool" media, along with his understanding of how electronic media would reshape human consciousness and social organisation, made him one of the most influential media theorists of the 20th century. Over 40 years ago McLuhan anticipated the internet, writing prophetically that "The new electronic interdependence recreates the world in the image of a global village."

JUNE 26

"How well do my colleagues understand my point of view?"
- Ed Batista[180]

---

[180] *Compasses and Weathervanes (30 Questions for Leaders)*, Ed Batista, edbatista.com, April 14, 2022.

Ed Batista is an executive coach and former Stanford Graduate School of Business lecturer who has become a prominent voice in leadership development and organisational psychology. He has been an executive coach since 2006, working with senior leaders who are facing challenges or seeking to be more effective or fulfilled in their roles, while spending 15 years as a lecturer and leadership coach at Stanford GSB. Most of his clients are technology company CEOs, though he works with leaders across various fields from investing to healthcare. Batista's approach emphasises self-awareness, emotional intelligence, and the transition from technical expertise to effective leadership. His work addresses complex leadership challenges including managing key relationships, improving team dynamics, and navigating the shift from individual contributor to organisational leader. Known for his thoughtful, research-based approach to coaching, Batista has contributed significantly to discussions about executive development, feedback culture, and the psychological aspects of leadership in high-pressure environments.

JUNE 27

*"At the end of a conversation -
'Is there anything I should be asking?'"*
- Dan Rockwell[181]

---

[181] "If you're interested in building relationships, start asking questions." Rockwell writes. "If you're interested in enhancing your opportunities and reaching higher, start asking questions. If you want to honour someone, ask them a question. *Asking questions is the smartest thing you can do.* Most important, asking a question creates silence and silence is the ultimate opportunity."
10 Best Questions Ever, Dan Rockwell, LeadershipFreak, March 5, 2010.

Dan Rockwell is a prolific and insightful thinker on leadership, a former entrepreneur, consultant, world-renowned speaker and creator of Leadership Freak, a leadership blog that has 450,000 subscribers around the world. Named the #1 Most Socially Shared leadership blog, Rockwell's work focuses on practical, accessible leadership insights delivered in bite-sized format. A farm boy from Central Maine, he had his first leadership position in the non-profit world at age nineteen and has since earned an MBA and undergraduate degrees in Theology, Pastoral Ministry, and Construction and Design. His experience spans over thirty-five years and includes business ownership and fifteen years as a Workforce Development Consultant for a regional Penn State Special Affiliate. In 2014 he made his first appearance on the Inc. list of Top Fifty Leadership and Management Experts. Currently, he coaches leaders, consults with organisations, and delivers corporate and community presentations, having started the Leadership Freak blog in January 2010 because he felt a deep need to make a difference in the world.

JUNE 28

*"What am I not saying that needs to be said?
What am I saying that's not being heard?
What's being said that I'm not hearing?"*
- Jerry Colonna[182]

---

[182] "The true leader in a group is rarely the person who talks the most." author Adam Grant explains. "It's usually the person who listens best. Listening is more than hearing what's said. It's noticing and surfacing what isn't said. Inviting dissenting views and amplifying quiet voices are acts of leadership."
Reboot: Leadership and the Art of Growing Up, Jerry Colonna, 2019.

Jerry Colonna is an executive coach, venture capitalist, and author who has become a prominent voice in bringing mindfulness and emotional intelligence to the world of entrepreneurship and leadership. Known as the "CEO Whisperer," he co-founded Flatiron Partners, one of New York's most successful early-stage venture capital firms, before transitioning to executive coaching and founding Reboot.io, a company focused on helping leaders develop self-awareness and authentic leadership skills. His book "Reboot: Leadership and the Art of Growing Up" combines his business experience with insights from Buddhism and psychology, advocating for a more compassionate and introspective approach to leadership that addresses the emotional and psychological challenges of running companies. Colonna's work emphasises the importance of examining one's own patterns, traumas, and unconscious behaviours as a path to becoming a more effective and fulfilled leader. Through his coaching practice, writing, and speaking, he has helped shift the conversation in Silicon Valley and beyond toward recognizing that sustainable success requires not just business acumen but also personal growth and emotional maturity.

JUNE 29

"Who am I not hearing from?"
- Lolly Daskal[183]

---

[183] "Silent voices often hold crucial insights." Daskal explains. "Ask this during discussions and planning sessions. Your quieter team members may see problems and solutions others miss. This question uncovers overlooked perspectives and creates space for diverse thinking. It transforms group dynamics and prevents costly blind spots. You need to hear from everyone in the room, particularly the quieter voices. To do this the nine Justices of the US Supreme Court have adopted a rule, "Nobody speaks twice until everybody speaks once".

5 Power Questions So Revealing They Will Change Your Leadership, Lolly Daskal, lollydaskal.com.

Lolly Daskal is the president and CEO of Lead From Within, a global consultancy that specialises in leadership and entrepreneurial development. With over three decades of experience, Lolly Daskal is one of the most sought-after executive leadership coaches and business consultants worldwide. Her extensive cross-cultural experience spans 14 countries, six languages and hundreds of companies. She is the author of the national bestseller "The Leadership Gap: What Gets Between You and Your Greatness", which explores how leaders can overcome internal obstacles to achieve their potential. Her philosophy centers on helping "people who lead from within," who "are leaders who want nothing more than to live their lives according to their own truths and on their own terms" and "lead from a core level that resides deep within their heart." Her cross-cultural expertise spans 30 years of coaching and she works with Fortune 500 C-suite executives, helping them enhance performance while making meaningful differences in their organisations and lives through her proprietary leadership development programs.

JUNE 30

"What do I want my team to feel after I've communicated with them?"
- Louise Thompson[184]

---

[184] Entrepreneur and author Brady Wilson explains, "People rarely leave your presence neutral – they will leave your presence engaged or depleted". Restaurateur Danny Meyer says, "Business, like life, is all about how you make people feel." Think about an interaction you had with a leader. Did you walk away feeling better or worse?

20 essential questions to ask if you're a communications leader, Louise Thompson, January 23, 2024.

Louise Thompson a Leadership Coach for emerging and aspiring leaders, former board-level Director of Communications Professional Advisor to Organisations and PR Agencies. She is a qualified leadership coach with the Institute of Leadership & Management, and uses established models when working with clients to deliver coaching that enables them to create solutions and take ownership of the outcomes they want to shape. Her work focuses on helping communications and marketing professionals transition into leadership roles by building their confidence and credibility. Thompson emphasises practical leadership development that helps clients succeed as valued leaders while shaping careers with purpose, drawing from her extensive background in corporate communications and board-level leadership experience.

JULY

WIELD LEVERAGE

JULY 1

"How, then, do we exert influence as a leader?"
- James McGregor Burns[185]

---

[185] The answer, according to Burns, is to have clear answers to the following questions -

Decide on whether we are really trying to lead anyone but ourselves, and what part of ourselves, and where, and for what purposes.

Whom are we seeking to lead?

Where are we seeking to go?

Leadership, James McGregor Burns, 1978.

James MacGregor Burns (1918 - 2014) was a distinguished historian, political scientist, and biographer who made significant contributions to the study of leadership and American politics. He won the Pulitzer Prize for History in 1971 for his biography "Roosevelt: The Soldier of Freedom," and was also awarded the National Book Award. Burns is perhaps best known for developing the concept of "transformational leadership" versus "transactional leadership" in his influential book "Leadership", which became foundational work in leadership studies. He wrote numerous biographies of American political figures, including multi-volume works on Franklin D. Roosevelt and John F. Kennedy. Burns also had a long academic career, serving as a professor at Williams College for many decades. He was considered one of America's preeminent presidential historians and leadership theorists until his death in 2014 at age 95.

JULY 2

"What's the system?"
- Donella Meadows[186]

---

[186] When things go wrong, Meadows writes, "stop looking for who's to blame; instead you'll start asking, "What's the system?" The concept of feedback opens up the idea that a system can cause its own behavior." Meadows explains, "A system is a set of things—people, cells, molecules, or whatever—interconnected in such a way that they produce their own pattern of behavior over time."
Thinking in Systems: A Primer, Donella Meadows, 2008. Also refer *Leverage Points: Places to Intervene in a System*, Donella Meadows, 1997.

Donella Meadows (1941-2001) was a pioneering systems thinker, environmental scientist, and author who profoundly influenced how we understand complex systems and social change. She wrote about "leverage points" - places within complex systems where "a small shift in one thing can produce big changes in everything." Meadows co-authored "The Limits to Growth", a groundbreaking study that challenged assumptions about infinite economic growth on a finite planet. Her later work, including "Thinking in Systems: A Primer," made systems thinking accessible to broader audiences. She identified twelve leverage points for intervening in systems, with paradigms, goals, and mindsets representing the highest-leverage changes that can "radically alter" system behaviour. Meadows emphasised that "the higher the leverage point, the more the system will resist changing it," highlighting why transformational change is often so difficult yet so powerful when achieved. Her work continues to influence fields from organisational development to environmental policy, providing frameworks for understanding how to create meaningful, lasting change in complex systems.

JULY 3

"Six months from now, what you will you wish you had spent time on today?"
- James Clear[187]

---

[187] Clear's question is reflected in Morgan Housel's observation. "At every stage of our lives" Housel writes, "we make decisions that will profoundly influence the lives of the people we're going to become, and then when we become those people, we're not always thrilled with the decisions we made. So young people pay good money to get tattoos removed that teenagers paid good money to get. Middle-aged people rushed to divorce people who young adults rushed to marry. Older adults work hard to lose what middle-aged adults worked hard to gain."
3-2-1 Newsletter, James Clear, August 19, 2021.
James Clear is an author, speaker, and entrepreneur best known for his book "Atomic Habits," which became a bestseller and popularised the concept of making small, incremental changes to build better habits and break bad ones. Clear focuses on the science of habit formation, emphasising how tiny improvements compound over time to create remarkable results. His approach centres on four key principles: making habits obvious, attractive, easy, and satisfying. Before his writing career took off, Clear was a successful entrepreneur and has a background in photography and business. He writes regularly about habits, decision-making, and continuous improvement on his website and newsletter, which has attracted millions of readers. Clear's work draws from psychology, neuroscience, and behavioural economics to provide practical strategies for personal and professional development, making complex research accessible to everyday readers seeking to improve their lives through better systems and habits.

JULY 4

*"Did I spend today chasing mice
or hunting antelope?"*
- Newt Gingrich[188]

---

[188] The authors, both political strategists who worked on Bill Clinton's presidential campaign, recount a story. "Newt Gingrich is one of the most successful political leaders of our time. Yes, we disagreed with virtually everything he did, but this is a book about strategy, not ideology. And we've got to give Newt his due. His strategic ability—his relentless focus on capturing the House of Representatives for the Republicans—led to one of the biggest political landslides in American history. Now that he's in the private sector, Newt uses a brilliant illustration to explain the need to focus on the big things and let the little stuff slide: the analogy of the field mice and the antelope. A lion is fully capable of capturing, killing, and eating a field mouse. But it turns out that the energy required to do so exceeds the caloric content of the mouse itself. So a lion that spent its day hunting and eating field mice would slowly starve to death. A lion can't live on field mice. A lion needs antelope. Antelope are big animals. They take more speed and strength to capture and kill, and once killed, they provide a feast for the lion and her pride. A lion can live a long and happy life on a diet of antelope. The distinction is important. Are you spending all your time and exhausting all your energy catching field mice? In the short term it might give you a nice, rewarding feeling. But in the long run you're going to die. So ask yourself at the end of the day, 'Did I spend today chasing mice or hunting antelope?'"

Buck Up, Suck Up . . . and Come Back When You Foul Up: 12 Winning Secrets from the War Room, James Carville and Paul Begala, 2002.

Newt Gingrich is a politician, author, and political commentator who served as the 50th Speaker of the House of Representatives from 1995 to 1999. He was a key figure in the Republican Party's "Contract with America" and the conservative revolution of the 1990s that led to Republicans gaining control of the House for the first time in 40 years. Gingrich represented Georgia's 6th congressional district from 1979 to 1999 and was known for his combative political style and strategic thinking. After leaving Congress, he remained active in politics as a commentator, author, and consultant, writing numerous books on history, politics, and policy. He ran for the Republican presidential nomination in 2012, briefly leading in some primary polls before ultimately losing to Mitt Romney. Gingrich holds a PhD in history and has written both fiction and non-fiction works, including historical novels and books on American politics and policy. He's been a frequent television commentator and continues to be an influential voice in conservative political circles.

JULY 5

"What do I have to do today to solve — or better, avoid — tomorrow's problem?"
- Andy Grove[189]

---

[189] Leadership is about improving tomorrow and anticipating future challenges. "Remember that as you plan you must answer the question:" Grove writes, "What do I have to do today to solve—or better, avoid—tomorrow's problem? Thus, the true output of the planning process is the set of tasks it causes to be implemented. The output of Intel's annual plan, for instance, is the actions taken and changes prompted as a result of the thinking process that took place throughout the organization. I, for one, hardly ever look at the bound volume finally called the Annual Plan. In other words, the output of the planning process is the decisions made and the actions taken as a result of the process."

High Output Management, Andrew S. Grove, 1995.

Andrew "Andy" Stephen Grove (1936 – 2016) was a Hungarian-American businessman and engineer who became one of the most influential leaders in the technology industry as the longtime CEO of Intel Corporation. Born András Gróf in Budapest in 1936, he fled Hungary during the 1956 revolution and immigrated to the United States, where he earned a PhD in chemical engineering from UC Berkeley. Grove joined Intel in 1968 as one of its first employees and rose through the ranks to become CEO in 1987, leading the company during its transformation from a memory chip manufacturer to the world's dominant microprocessor producer. Known for his rigorous management style and strategic thinking, he pioneered concepts like "constructive confrontation" and "Only the Paranoid Survive," emphasising adaptability and competitive vigilance. Grove authored several influential business books, including "High Output Management," which became a cornerstone text on operational excellence and leadership. His leadership philosophy and management practices influenced countless executives and helped establish Silicon Valley's culture of innovation and performance-driven leadership.

JULY 6

"What is the work that keeps working for us once it's done?"
- James Clear[190]

---

[190] Clear gives an example of how this question caused him to cease doing radio interviews. In the case of radio, any value derived stops once the broadcast is over. In contrast, podcasts can be listened to by anyone at any time after they are recorded.
The Tim Ferriss Show, Episode #648, January 6, 2023.
James Clear is an author, speaker, and entrepreneur best known for his book "Atomic Habits," which became a bestseller and popularised the concept of making small, incremental changes to build better habits and break bad ones. Clear focuses on the science of habit formation, emphasising how tiny improvements compound over time to create remarkable results. His approach centres on four key principles: making habits obvious, attractive, easy, and satisfying. Before his writing career took off, Clear was a successful entrepreneur and has a background in photography and business. He writes regularly about habits, decision-making, and continuous improvement on his website and newsletter, which has attracted millions of readers. Clear's work draws from psychology, neuroscience, and behavioural economics to provide practical strategies for personal and professional development, making complex research accessible to everyday readers seeking to improve their lives through better systems and habits.

JULY 7

"What's the smallest first step you can take to move things forward?"
- Caroline Webb[191]

---

[191] Webb's question reveals the key to breaking free from energy ruts. It doesn't require forcing yourself into massive action, it's harnessing the power of tiny wins. Start embarrassingly small: write one terrible sentence, or make your bed. That small hit of accomplishment isn't just psychological, it's neurochemical. Your brain releases a tiny surge of dopamine that creates momentum. Use that energy to tackle something slightly bigger, then something bigger still. Each completed task becomes fuel for the next, creating an upward spiral that can transform your entire day.

How To Have A Good Day: The Essential Toolkit for a Productive Day at Work and Beyond, Caroline Webb, 2016.

Caroline Webb is CEO of Sevenshift, a firm that shows people how to use insights from behavioural science to improve their working life and a senior adviser to McKinsey, where she was previously a partner. She graduated from the University of Cambridge in economics, and received her MPhil from the University of Oxford in economics. Before McKinsey, Webb spent the 1990s working in public policy as an economist at the UK's central bank, the Bank of England, where her work included working closely with the Monetary Policy Committee as author of the Inflation Report and global economic forecasting. She is best known for her book "How to Have a Good Day," which shows how to use recent findings from behavioural economics, psychology and neuroscience to transform the quality of our everyday lives, at work and beyond. She is a founding fellow of the Harvard-affiliated Institute of Coaching and founded McKinsey's flagship leadership development course for senior female executives.

JULY 8

"What goals hold the utmost importance for me?"
- Michael Lombardi & George Raveling[192]

---

[192] Lombardi and Raveling explain, "For guidance in this introspection, consider these questions:

What goals hold the utmost importance for me? Clarity regarding your primary objectives is essential.

What systems and habits currently contribute to realizing these goals? Identifying your routines and practices is the initial step in evaluation.

Do these systems and habits still yield effectiveness? Honest assessment is crucial to determining whether they generate desired outcomes.

What adaptations are needed to realign my systems and habits with my goals? Conscious adjustments are key to sustained alignment with your objectives."

Harnessing the Power of Systems and Habits: Are your current systems and habits harmoniously aligned with your paramount goals? The Daily Coach, August 24, 2023.

Michael Lombardi is a three-time Super Bowl champion as an executive with over 30 years of experience in NFL front offices who recently joined the North Carolina football program as General Manager in December 2024. He has spent 35 years working for the New England Patriots, San Francisco 49ers, the Oakland Raiders and the Cleveland Browns, and has the distinction of the being the only person to make it to the Super Bowl with both the Patriots and 49ers. Beyond his front office work, Lombardi has been a prominent media personality as an NFL analyst, author, and cofounder with George Raveling of The Daily Coach, a newsletter that shares sports and organisational leadership lessons.

George Raveling is a Basketball Hall of Fame coach and Nike executive who has had an extraordinary impact on both basketball and sports marketing. After a successful college coaching career at schools including Washington State, Iowa, and USC, he joined Nike at the request of Phil Knight, where he played an integral role in signing a reluctant Michael Jordan. Raveling has worked as the Director for International Basketball for Nike since his retirement from USC and is known as "the iconic leader who brought Michael Jordan to Nike". Beyond basketball, he has a unique connection to civil rights history and having a personal connection to Martin Luther King Jr.'s "I Have a Dream" speech. Raveling was present at the March on Washington on August 28, 1963, and after Dr. King delivered his speech, King handed Raveling the original typewritten copy.

The two co-founded The Daily Coach newsletter, sharing leadership wisdom from sports and business.

JULY 9

*"Successful leaders don't start out asking,
'What do I want to do?'
They ask, 'What needs to be done?'
Then they ask,
'Of those things that would make a difference, which
are right for me?'"*
- Peter Drucker[193]

---

[193] To wield leverage a leader must understand what is most important to the organisation, and who is best placed to do it. In *The Effective Executive*, Drucker lists the eight practises that make a leader effective. The first two of these practises are asking 'What needs to be done?' and 'What is right for the enterprise?'"
Peter Drucker On Leadership, Rich Karlgaard, Forbes, November 19, 2004.

Peter Drucker (1909-2005) was a management consultant, educator, and author widely regarded as the founder of modern management theory. Drucker wrote over 30 books and countless articles that fundamentally shaped how we think about business, leadership, and organisational effectiveness. He coined many concepts that are now management staples, including "management by objectives," "knowledge worker," and the idea that the purpose of business is to create customers. His most influential works include "The Practice of Management" and "The Effective Executive". Drucker emphasised that management is both an art and a science, focusing on people rather than just processes, and he predicted many major business trends including the rise of the information economy and the importance of innovation. Beyond business, he was a prolific social commentator who wrote about democracy, society, and the role of institutions. His insights remain remarkably relevant today, and he's remembered for his practical wisdom and his belief that effective management could make organisations more productive while also making work more meaningful for people.

JULY 10

"If someone looked at how you spent your time over the last year, would what they see as your priorities match what you see as your priorities?"
- Shane Parrish[194]

---

[194] Parrish says "don't tell me your priorities, show me your calendar". The question is very similar to the one asked by James Clear: "How much overlap is there between what you say is important to you and how you spent your attention over the last month?" *3-2-1 Newsletter*, James Clear, October 21, 2021. Both questions echo Brene Brown who writes, "Calendars are truth-tellers. When you look at your calendar or schedule, do your commitments reflect what's really important to you? If so, how? If not, what does your calendar say?" *Daring Greatly worksheet*, brenebrown.com.

Brain Food – No. 551, Shane Parrish, November 19, 2023.

Shane Parrish is the founder and leader of Farnam Street (FS), an organisation devoted to helping people develop an understanding of how the world really works, make better decisions, and live a better life by addressing topics such as mental models, decision making, learning, reading, and the art of living. He is the founding partner of Syrus Partners, a holding company that acquires and operates businesses in North America, and previously worked as an executive in the Canadian government, where he led the creation and execution of key cyber-defense initiatives. Parrish also hosts The Knowledge Project podcast. His work is guided by principles instilled by Warren Buffett and Charlie Munger, sharing their wisdom and exploring the mental models they champion to help people develop clarity of thought and breadth of understanding.

JULY 11

"What's the first domino?"
- Michael Bungay Stanier[195]

---

[195] Stanier explains, "The first domino ... is about identifying the thing that, if done, removes or solves or reduces many other downstream efforts."
What's the first domino?, thechangesignal.com, February 27, 2025.
Michael Bungay Stanier is an author, leadership coach, and business consultant best known for his bestselling book "The Coaching Habit: Say Less, Ask More & Change the Way You Lead Forever." He founded Box of Crayons, a learning and development company that helps organisations transform from advice-driven to curiosity-led, and currently leads MBS.works, a place where people find clarity, confidence and community to be a force for change. His work focuses on helping leaders develop better coaching skills through practical, science-backed approaches that emphasise asking powerful questions rather than giving advice. His philosophy is captured in his haiku-like summary: "Tell less and ask more. Your advice is not as good as you think it is." Known as a compelling speaker and facilitator who combines practicality, humour, and high audience engagement, Stanier has become a prominent voice in the leadership development space, helping countless managers and executives shift from being advice-givers to becoming more effective coaches who unlock potential in their teams through curiosity and thoughtful questioning.

JULY 12

"Is this something only I can do?"
- Ryan Holiday[196]

---

[196] "Do what only you can do" is a powerful principle for organisational and personal effectiveness. Theory of Constraints (ToC) teaches that every system has constraints or "bottlenecks", and maximum performance comes from optimising these constraint points rather than trying to improve everything simultaneously. At an organisational level, this means identifying the unique capabilities, resources, or positions that only your company can leverage—your organisational constraints that become competitive advantages when properly managed. Just as TOC teaches us to subordinate non-constraint resources to support the constraint, teams should focus their energy on activities that only they can perform while delegating, automating, or eliminating everything else. For individuals, this principle echoes Eliyahu M. Goldratt's emphasis on focusing improvement efforts where they matter most. Rather than trying to optimise every aspect of your work (which often leads to local optimisations that don't improve overall performance), concentrate on the unique value you bring that cannot be easily replicated or replaced. This might be your specific expertise, relationships, creative insights, or decision-making authority. The beauty of this approach is that it forces the same fundamental question that drives TOC: "What is the real constraint here?" In personal terms, this becomes "What is the highest-leverage contribution only I can make?" By identifying and focusing on these unique contributions, you maximize your impact on the system's overall performance, just as TOC maximizes organizational throughput by focusing on the constraint. Holiday explains, "The wise, whether they're Epictetus or Peter Thiel, know the real race is between mimicry and uniqueness, and most of all: purpose. When setting out on some new endeavour — building a business, producing a creative project — the question has to be: Is this something ONLY I can do?"

What If I Said No? (And Other Questions to Consider Daily), Ryan Holiday, Medium, August 21, 2019.

Ryan Holiday is the bestselling author of "Trust Me, I'm Lying", "The Obstacle Is the Way", "Ego Is the Enemy", "Conspiracy", and other books about marketing, culture, and the human condition. Holiday grew up in Sacramento, California, with his father as a police detective and his mother a high school principal. He dropped out of the University of California, Riverside in his sophomore year to pursue marketing and writing. He has written 12 best-selling books, covering topics including philosophy, marketing, history, and how to live well, with his work particularly focused on making ancient Stoic philosophy accessible to modern readers. His work has been translated into over 30 languages and has appeared everywhere from the New York Times to Fast Company. His company, Brass Check, has advised companies such as Google, TASER, and Complex, as well as multiplatinum musicians and some of the biggest authors in the world. Holiday opened The Painted Porch Bookshop in Bastrop, Texas with his wife during the pandemic, supporting local independent bookstores while continuing his mission to popularise Stoic wisdom.

JULY 13

"If someone could only see my actions and not hear my words, what would they say are my priorities?"
- James Clear[197]

---

[197] Clear's question echoes the great psychiatrist, psychotherapist, and psychologist Carl Jung who put it this way: "You are what you do, not what you say you'll do."

3-2-1 Newsletter, James Clear, May 28, 2020.

James Clear is an author, speaker, and entrepreneur best known for his book "Atomic Habits," which became a bestseller and popularised the concept of making small, incremental changes to build better habits and break bad ones. Clear focuses on the science of habit formation, emphasising how tiny improvements compound over time to create remarkable results. His approach centres on four key principles: making habits obvious, attractive, easy, and satisfying. Before his writing career took off, Clear was a successful entrepreneur and has a background in photography and business. He writes regularly about habits, decision-making, and continuous improvement on his website and newsletter, which has attracted millions of readers. Clear's work draws from psychology, neuroscience, and behavioural economics to provide practical strategies for personal and professional development, making complex research accessible to everyday readers seeking to improve their lives through better systems and habits.

JULY 14

"Will this action make the future easier or harder?"
- Shane Parrish[198]

---

[198] This question echoes author and educator Stephen R. Covey who wrote, "But until a person can say deeply and honestly, 'I am what I am today because of the choices I made yesterday,' that person cannot say, 'I choose otherwise.'"
Clear Thinking: Turning Ordinary Moments Into Extraordinary Results, Shane Parrish, 2023.
Shane Parrish is the founder and leader of Farnam Street (FS), an organisation devoted to helping people develop an understanding of how the world really works, make better decisions, and live a better life by addressing topics such as mental models, decision making, learning, reading, and the art of living. He is the founding partner of Syrus Partners, a holding company that acquires and operates businesses in North America, and previously worked as an executive in the Canadian government, where he led the creation and execution of key cyber-defense initiatives. Parrish also hosts The Knowledge Project podcast. His work is guided by principles instilled by Warren Buffett and Charlie Munger, sharing their wisdom and exploring the mental models they champion to help people develop clarity of thought and breadth of understanding.

JULY 15

"How do you spend your time?"
-Rob Ryles[199]

---

[199] Tech entrepreneur Keith Rabois believes that the best predictor of success is the "innate ability to allocate time properly". Studies have shown that knowledge workers waste several hours each day, and 90% of managers squander their time. Psychiatrist and author M. Scott Peck warned, "Until you value yourself, you won't value your time. Until you value your time, you will not do anything with it."

The Leader Manager Coach Podcast, Rob Ryles, 8th September 2019.

Rob Ryles is a UEFA A Licensed football coach and FA Youth Award Coach with professional game experience at domestic and international levels. He brings a science and medicine background to his coaching work, having operated across Europe, USA and Africa at International, Premiership, League, Non-League and grassroots levels with both World Cup and European Championship experience. Ryles hosts the popular "Leader Manager Coach Podcast," where he examines knowledge, philosophies, wisdom and insight to help people lead, manage and coach in football, sport and life. His approach combines traditional football coaching with broader leadership principles, drawing inspiration from legendary figures like Bill Shankly who sparked his obsession with football management and coaching. Through his podcast, writing, and coaching work, Ryles bridges the gap between tactical football knowledge and transferable leadership skills applicable beyond the sport.

JULY 16

"What is your one absolutely fundamental contribution that would not happen without you?"
- Jim Collins[200]

---

[200] "When a friend of mine became the chairman of the board of trustees of a leading university," Collins recalls, "he posed a question: "How will I know I've done a great job?" I pondered what Drucker would say, and then answered: "Identify one big thing that would most contribute to the future of the university and orchestrate getting it done. If you make one distinctive contribution—a key decision that would not have happened without your leadership (even if no one ever credits you for your catalytic role)—then you will have rendered a great service." Drucker applied this idea to his own consulting. When I asked him what he contributed to his clients, he modestly said, "I have generally learned more from them than they learned from me." Then, pausing for effect, he added, "Of course, in each case there was one absolutely fundamental decision they would not have made without me." What is your one absolutely fundamental contribution that would not happen without you?"

Ten Lessons I Learned from Peter Drucker, Jim Collins, Foreword to the 50th Anniversary Edition of The Effective Executive, May 17, 2016.

Jim Collins is a bestselling author, business researcher, and management consultant who has spent decades studying what makes companies transition from good to great performance. He's best known for his book "Good to Great," which identified key principles that distinguish exceptional companies from merely good ones, including concepts like Level 5 Leadership, the Hedgehog Concept, and getting the right people on the bus. Collins has written several other influential business books including "Built to Last" (co-authored with Jerry Porras), "How the Mighty Fall," and "Great by Choice." His research methodology involves rigorous data analysis and long-term studies of companies, often spanning decades to identify patterns and principles that drive sustained success. Before his writing career, Collins worked as a faculty member at Stanford Graduate School of Business and served as a consultant to corporations and social sector organisations. His work extends beyond the corporate world to nonprofits and educational institutions through books like "Good to Great and the Social Sectors." Collins is known for his disciplined approach to research, his ability to distil complex business concepts into memorable frameworks, and his focus on timeless principles rather than fleeting management fads.

JULY 17

"Where are your best leverage points?"
- Dan Heath[201]

---

[201] "Folks who do systems analysis have a great belief in 'leverage points.'" systems thinker Donella Meadows explains. "These are places within a complex system (a corporation, an economy, a living body, a city, an ecosystem) where a small shift in one thing can produce big changes in everything. This idea is not unique to systems analysis — it's embedded in legend. The silver bullet, the trimtab, the miracle cure, the secret passage, the magic password, the single hero who turns the tide of history. The nearly effortless way to cut through or leap over huge obstacles. We not only want to believe that there are leverage points, we want to know where they are and how to get our hands on them. Leverage points are points of power." From *Leverage Points: Places to Intervene in a System*, Donella Meadows, 1997.

Reset: How To Change What's Not Working, Dan Heath, 2025.

Dan Heath is a bestselling author, speaker and fellow at Duke University's CASE center who has co-authored four New York Times bestsellers with his brother Chip: "Decisive," "Switch," "Made to Stick," and "The Power of Moments," with their books selling over 3 million copies worldwide and being translated into 33 languages. A Senior Fellow at Duke University's CASE center, he holds an M.B.A. from Harvard Business School and a B.A. from the Plan II Honors Program at the University of Texas at Austin. Beyond his collaborative work with Chip, Dan wrote his first solo book, "Upstream: The Quest to Solve Problems Before They Happen," which became an instant Wall Street Journal bestseller. He also hosts the award-winning podcast "What It's Worth" and focuses his work on helping organizations and individuals solve problems more effectively, often emphasising prevention over reaction and the power of creating memorable moments.

JULY 18

*"What really matters most right now?
What really has to happen today, if nothing else?
Project forward to the end of the day.
What will you be most glad or relieved to
have done?"*
- Caroline Webb[202]

---

[202] Although much focus of leadership is the future, it can only be improved by acting in the present. Webb echoes Greek philosopher Aristippus: "... concentrate one's mind on the day, and indeed on that part of the day in which one is acting or thinking. Only the present belongs to us, not the past nor what is anticipated. The former has ceased to exist, and it is uncertain if the latter will exist."

How To Have A Good Day: The Essential Toolkit for a Productive Day at Work and Beyond, Caroline Webb, 2016.

Caroline Webb is CEO of Sevenshift, a firm that shows people how to use insights from behavioural science to improve their working life and a senior adviser to McKinsey, where she was previously a partner. She graduated from the University of Cambridge in economics, and received her MPhil from the University of Oxford in economics. Before McKinsey, Webb spent the 1990s working in public policy as an economist at the UK's central bank, the Bank of England, where her work included working closely with the Monetary Policy Committee as author of the Inflation Report and global economic forecasting. She is best known for her book "How to Have a Good Day," which shows how to use recent findings from behavioural economics, psychology and neuroscience to transform the quality of our everyday lives, at work and beyond. She is a founding fellow of the Harvard-affiliated Institute of Coaching and founded McKinsey's flagship leadership development course for senior female executives.

JULY 19

"Does it make a difference?"
- Frances Hesselbein[203]

---

[203] When asked what defines an exceptional career, Hesselbein answered as follows. "An exceptional career is one that provides an opportunity to serve. It is a satisfying career in which you can't wait to get up in the morning to begin! You have a sense of purpose and mission. You know why you do what you do. It is a response to a call to serve. Once we do that, everything flows positively. When I choose what I do, I ask, *does it make a difference?*"

#ExceptionalCareers Series: Giving You the Edge for Success, Sanyin Siang, HuffPost, November 12, 2014.

Frances Hesselbein (1915 - 2022) was a transformational leader who became one of America's most respected authorities on leadership and management through her groundbreaking work with the Girl Scouts of the USA. She served as CEO of the Girl Scouts from 1976 to 1990, where she revolutionised the organisation by transforming it from a traditional to a modern institution capable of serving girls from all backgrounds. Starting as a volunteer troop leader in 1960 despite having no daughters, Hesselbein rose through the ranks and applied principles she learned from management guru Peter Drucker to create innovative organisational models focused on mission, leadership development, and inclusivity. Hesselbein was awarded the Presidential Medal of Freedom, America's highest civilian honour, by President Clinton in 1998 for her leadership as CEO and her service as "a pioneer for women, volunteerism, diversity". After leaving the Girl Scouts, she became the founding president and CEO of the Peter F. Drucker Foundation for Nonprofit Management (later renamed the Leader to Leader Institute), where she continued her work helping nonprofit organisations achieve excellence. Hesselbein authored several influential books on leadership and was widely regarded as one of the most effective nonprofit executives in American history, demonstrating that principled, mission-driven leadership could create lasting organisational and social change. She passed away in 2022 at age 107, leaving behind a legacy of servant leadership and organisational transformation.

JULY 20

*"What if, rather than fighting our preprogrammed instinct to seek the easiest path, we could embrace it, even use it to our advantage?
What if, instead of asking, "How can I tackle this really hard but essential project?," we simply inverted the question and asked,
"What if this essential project could be made easy?"*
- Greg McKeown[204]

---

[204] This question can serve as an unlock. After grinding through his previous books and in preparing for writing his next book in 2015, Tim Ferriss asked, "What would this look like if it were easy?" "This question and the next both came about in 2015." he writes. "These days, more than any other question, I'm asking, "What would this look like if it were easy?" If I feel stressed, stretched thin, or overwhelmed, it's usually because I'm overcomplicating something or failing to take the simple/easy path because I feel I should be trying "harder" (old habits die hard)." *17 Questions That Changed My Life*, Tim Ferriss, tim.blog.
Effortless: Make It Easier to Do What Matters Most, Greg McKeown, 2021.

Greg McKeown is a business writer, consultant, and bestselling author. McKeown is the author of two New York Times bestsellers, "Essentialism: The Disciplined Pursuit of Less" and "Effortless: Make It Easier to Do What Matters Most," which together have sold 3 million copies and been published in 40 languages. His core philosophy of Essentialism teaches people to focus on what truly matters by eliminating the non-essential from their lives and work. McKeown has become one of the most sought-after public speakers in the world, speaking to hundreds of organisations while traveling to more than 45 countries, with clients including Apple, Amazon, Google, and Microsoft. He also hosts a popular podcast and runs the Essentialism Academy, helping individuals and organisations apply his principles to achieve greater impact through more disciplined choices about where to invest their time and energy.

JULY 21

"Does it make the boat go faster?"
- Peter Blake[205]

---

[205] Blake used this simple yet powerful question as the ultimate decision-making filter for his sailing teams. The philosophy behind the question was ruthlessly practical: every decision, resource allocation, crew selection, equipment choice, and strategic move had to pass this single test. If an activity, expense, or initiative didn't directly contribute to making the boat go faster, it was eliminated, no matter how traditional, comfortable, or politically correct it might be. This laser focus on what truly mattered helped Blake's teams achieve extraordinary success in some of the world's most challenging sailing competitions. The question has since become a widely adopted business principle, representing the discipline of maintaining absolute clarity about your primary objective and refusing to be distracted by activities that don't serve that goal. It embodies the essence of strategic focus: identifying what really moves the needle and having the courage to say no to everything else, even when those other things seem important or urgent.

Making sure the dollars flow Team NZ's way, The New Zealand Herald, 17 January, 2003.

Sir Peter Blake (1948 – 2001) was a legendary yachtsman widely regarded as one of the greatest sailors of the modern era who achieved remarkable success across multiple decades of competitive sailing. Blake won the 1989-1990 Whitbread Round the World Race and held the Jules Verne Trophy from 1994 to 1997 by setting the around-the-world sailing record as co-skipper of ENZA New Zealand. He also won the America's Cup in 1995 and successfully defended it in 2000, along with claiming the 1994 Trophée Jules Verne. Blake was knighted in 1995 for services to yachting and received numerous honors including World Sailor of the Year in 1994. His life was tragically cut short at age 53 when he was shot and killed by pirates in 2001 during an environmental expedition on the Amazon River. Blake's legacy endures as a national icon who inspired generations of sailors and environmental advocates.

JULY 22

"What is the limiting factor?"
- James Clear[206]

---

[206] This question is closely related to the work of Eliyahu M. Goldratt whose work on the Theory of Constraints (TOC) emphasises the importance of identifying system constraints or "bottlenecks", and also former Intel CEO Andrew (Andy) S. Grove, who stressed the importance of finding the limiting (difficult, sensitive, expensive or time consuming) step within a process. Refer *The Goal: A Process of Ongoing Improvement*, Eliyahu M Goldratt and Jeff Cox, 2012, and *High Output Management*, Andrew S. Grove, 1995.

3-2-1 Newsletter, James Clear, June 17, 2021.

James Clear is an author, speaker, and entrepreneur best known for his book "Atomic Habits," which became a bestseller and popularised the concept of making small, incremental changes to build better habits and break bad ones. Clear focuses on the science of habit formation, emphasising how tiny improvements compound over time to create remarkable results. His approach centres on four key principles: making habits obvious, attractive, easy, and satisfying. Before his writing career took off, Clear was a successful entrepreneur and has a background in photography and business. He writes regularly about habits, decision-making, and continuous improvement on his website and newsletter, which has attracted millions of readers. Clear's work draws from psychology, neuroscience, and behavioural economics to provide practical strategies for personal and professional development, making complex research accessible to everyday readers seeking to improve their lives through better systems and habits.

JULY 23

"What should we stop doing?"
- Jack Bergstrand[207]

---

[207] The question stems from a practise Peter Drucker called "planned abandonment". Drucker's test for whether a business activity should be abandoned was to ask whether, if you were starting from scratch, you would still be doing the activity.

What Should You Stop Doing?, Rick Wartzman, Forbes Magazine, February 19, 2013.

Jack Bergstrand is a business transformation consultant and author who founded Brand Velocity Inc. and Consequent Consulting, and serves on the board of the Drucker Institute. A former senior executive at Coca-Cola, he works with a broad range of companies from Fortune 500 to startups as an expert in enterprise reinvention. Consequent was born of a 35-year journey by Bergstrand to help organizations win in a rapidly changing marketplace. He is the author of several books including "The Velocity Advantage" and "Reinvent Your Enterprise," which focus on cross-functional alignment and knowledge work productivity management systems. Bergstrand's work centers on managing knowledge-based work to achieve faster and better results, and he has built his consultancy into one of the largest independent strategic communications and advisory firms by combining senior-level capital markets experience with deep sector knowledge.

JULY 24

"Are you the bottleneck?"
- Brad Feld[208]

---

[208] "I spent some time with a CEO yesterday." Feld explains. "He was frustrated. As we talked, it became clear that he was the bottleneck in a number of key processes in his company. At some point I just asked "Are you the bottleneck?" He paused, thought for a moment, and then said "Yes." I asked a few more questions. "Why?" "What can you change?" "Who can you delegate to?" "What's holding you back?" These questions are easy to ask, but often hard to answer. If you are a CEO, VP, manager, or anyone that others depend on for input, decisions, or approval, ask yourself regularly: "Am I the bottleneck?" If the answer is yes, then get to work on fixing it. Now."

Are You The Bottleneck, Brad Feld, March 21, 2007.

Brad Feld is a venture capitalist, entrepreneur, and author based in Boulder, Colorado. He's a partner at Foundry Group, which he co-founded with Seth Levine, Ryan McIntyre, and Jason Mendelson, and has been an early-stage investor and entrepreneur for over 30 years. Feld was an early investor in successful companies like Harmonix, Zynga, MakerBot, and Fitbit. He's perhaps best known for co-authoring "Venture Deals: Be Smarter Than Your Lawyer and Venture Capitalist" with Jason Mendelson, which has become a definitive guide for entrepreneurs navigating venture capital funding. Feld is also a prolific blogger at "Feld Thoughts," an active speaker on entrepreneurship and venture capital topics, and has written several other books including "Startup Boards" and "Startup Opportunities." He's been instrumental in building the Boulder startup ecosystem and is known for his "give first" philosophy in the entrepreneurial community.

JULY 25

"What's the ONE Thing I can do such that by doing it everything else will be easier or unnecessary?"
- Gary Keller[209]

---

[209] Keller argues that extraordinary results come from focusing on a single priority rather than trying to multitask or balance everything equally.

The One Thing: The Surprisingly Simple Truth Behind Extraordinary Results, Gary Keller with Jay Papasan.

Gary Keller is the founder and chairman of Keller Williams Realty, one of the largest real estate companies in the world. Keller started his real estate career in the 1970s and founded Keller Williams in 1983 in Austin, Texas, building it into a global franchise with hundreds of thousands of agents. His book "The ONE Thing," co-written with Jay Papasan, popularises the concept of focusing on the single most important task that will make everything else easier or unnecessary, emphasising the power of concentrated effort over multitasking. Keller has also written other business and real estate books including "The Millionaire Real Estate Agent" and "The Millionaire Real Estate Investor." Known for his systems-oriented approach to business and productivity, he advocates for creating models and frameworks that can be replicated and scaled, principles that have guided both his real estate empire and his writing on achieving extraordinary results through focused action.

JULY 26

*"What positive impact can I have
here and now on this day?"
- Ted Gioia*[210]

---

[210] "I think about this all the time nowadays." Gioia writes, "That wasn't always the case, but here is another example where a negative (aging) can lead to positive things. Some people have an easier time answering this question. If you're a social worker or medical professional or counsellor or in some other similar situation, you help people every day as part of your job. But for the rest of us, it's not so easy." He continues. "I've learned that if I think about this problem on a daily basis—what positive impact can I have here and now on this day?—I start making better decisions. I begin doing better things. Even the smallest matters of daily life provide an opportunity for this. That's reassuring—because those are constantly at hand and don't require changing the whole world."

My 12 Favorite Problems: A dozen things that drive my writing, research, thinking & actions, Ted Gioia, The Honest Broker, October 14, 2023.

Ted Gioia is a cultural critic, music historian, record producer, and jazz pianist who has published 12 books, translated into 9 languages. He's best known for his comprehensive work "The History of Jazz," which has been universally hailed as a classic and is among the most authoritative and thorough books of its kind. Gioia has authored several other influential music books including "Music: A Subversive History", "West Coast Jazz", "The Jazz Standards: A Guide to the Repertoire", and "The Birth (and Death) of the Cool". Beyond his book writing, he is author of the popular Substack newsletter The Honest Broker, where he provides cultural commentary and music criticism. As both a practicing jazz pianist and scholar, Gioia brings a unique dual perspective to his writing, combining deep musical knowledge with accessible historical narrative and cultural analysis.

JULY 27

"Does this help us achieve our mission?"
- Brian Armstrong[211]

---

[211] "When you narrow focus, you are increasing the resourcing on the remaining priority." businessman and author Frank Slootman explains. "It doesn't have to time-slice and compete any more with a bunch of other stuff. And then things begin to move, stuff is getting done, and we move to the next thing. Many people and organizations are focused a mile wide and an inch deep. It can't be a surprise when they progress at snail's pace. Log jams get broken when you sift through the reams of activities and you create fewer and clearer objectives. Do less, at a time. I've often felt that providence moves, too, when you un-clutter priorities. Like an Invisible Hand, all of a sudden things are on the move." Momentum is the fuel for motivation.

Our Mission, Strategy and Culture, Brian Armstrong, Medium, July 3, 2021.

Brian Armstrong is the co-founder and CEO of Coinbase, one of the largest cryptocurrency exchanges in the United States. He founded the company in 2012 alongside Fred Ehrsam, with the vision of making cryptocurrency accessible to mainstream users through a user-friendly platform. Under his leadership, Coinbase went public in 2021 through a direct listing on NASDAQ, becoming one of the most high-profile crypto companies to enter traditional markets. Armstrong has been a prominent advocate for cryptocurrency adoption and regulatory clarity in the digital asset space, frequently engaging with policymakers and regulators to shape the industry's future. He's known for his focus on building compliant, regulated cryptocurrency infrastructure and has positioned Coinbase as a bridge between traditional finance and the emerging crypto economy.

JULY 28

"What is the best I can do under the given circumstances?"
- Stephen Covey[212]

---

[212] "When we say that leadership is a choice, "Covey explains, "it basically means you can choose the level of initiative you want to exercise in response to the question, 'What is the best I can do under the given circumstances?'".
The 8th Habit: From Effectiveness To Greatness, Stephen R. Covey, 2005.

Stephen R. Covey (1932-2012) was an educator, author, and businessman who became one of the most influential voices in personal development and leadership through his bestselling book "The 7 Habits of Highly Effective People". His approach emphasised character-based leadership and principle-centred living, arguing that lasting success comes from aligning one's actions with timeless principles like integrity, fairness, and human dignity rather than quick-fix techniques. The seven habits became widely adopted in both corporate and personal settings. Covey founded the Covey Leadership Center (later Franklin Covey) to teach these principles to organisations worldwide and wrote numerous other books, including "First Things First" and "The Leader in Me." His work stood out in the self-help genre for its emphasis on character development over personality techniques, and his concepts like the "Circle of Influence" and "Quadrant II" time management continue to be taught in business schools and leadership programs globally.

JULY 29

"How can I add value here?"
-Ria Tagulinao[213]

---

[213] The question echoes Peter Drucker who suggests that the effective executive must continually ask, "What is the most important contribution I can make to the performance of this organization?" *The Effective Executive*, Peter Drucker, 1967.

3 Key Mindset Shifts That Made Me a Significantly Happier Person, Ria Tagulinao, Medium, May 25, 2021.

Ria Tagulinao is a writer who works professionally as a Senior Strategist at Ogilvy. Her articles have been featured in publications like Forge and Illumination on Medium, and she has also contributed to The Good Men Project. Her writing focuses on topics related to productivity, writing advice, and personal development.

JULY 30

"Is it necessary?
Can it be simplified?"
- Harvey Firestone[214]

---

[214] Harvey Firestone's questions reflect the core philosophy that made him one of America's great industrial leaders and founder of the Firestone Tire and Rubber Company. These questions emerged from hard-won experience during the company's near-collapse in 1920, when Firestone faced a debt crisis that forced him to fundamentally rethink how business should operate. During the boom years, Firestone had developed elaborate hierarchies, headcount ballooned, multiple management layers generated endless memos, and they even published a million-circulation magazine. The crisis taught him that complexity kills companies—what he called "fancy fails" while "simple scales." These two questions became his diagnostic tools for cutting through organisational bloat and focusing on what truly mattered. The philosophy represents Firestone's belief that most business problems stem from unnecessary complexity rather than insufficient sophistication. By constantly asking whether something was necessary and whether it could be simplified, he stripped away the bureaucratic layers and processes that didn't directly contribute to serving customers or generating value. This approach helped him rebuild the company into a more resilient, focused enterprise and became a cornerstone of his management philosophy that emphasised clear purpose and operational simplicity.

Men and Rubber: The Story of Business, Harvey S. Firestone, 1926.

Harvey S. Firestone (1868 – 1938) was an entrepreneur and tire industry pioneer who transformed the automotive landscape in the early 20th century. Born in Columbiana, Ohio, and raised on a farm built by his grandfather, Firestone's entrepreneurial journey began when he moved to Detroit as a district manager for a buggy company. After working in the rubber industry creating bicycle tires, Firestone founded the Firestone Tire & Rubber Company in 1900 to develop tires for automobiles. He pioneered the manufacture of pneumatic tires for the Ford Model T automobile, and a sale of thousands of tires to Ford in 1906 propelled Firestone to the top of the American tire industry. He saw the advantages of the pneumatic tire, as compared to the solid tire, and made several improvements. By 1926 Firestone's company was producing more than 10 million tires, establishing him as one of America's most successful industrialists and a close friend of fellow innovators Henry Ford and Thomas Edison.

JULY 31

"How do you invest in developing leadership but not in creating dependency of that leadership upon you?"
- Marshall Ganz[215]

---

[215] The supreme form of leadership leverage is the creation of more leaders. In the words of Max De Pree, "Leaders are also responsible for future leadership. They need to identify, develop, and nurture future leaders." If done well, those leaders will do the same, generating a self-perpetuating leadership pipeline. A test comes from author Noel Tichy who says, "The ultimate test for a leader is not whether he or she makes smart decisions and takes decisive action, but whether he or she teaches others to be leaders and builds an organization that can sustain its success even when he or she is not around."
Interview with Marshall Ganz by Paul VanDeCarr, narrativearts.org, 2012.

Marshall Ganz is the Rita E. Hauser Senior Lecturer in Leadership, Organizing, and Civil Society at Harvard Kennedy School, where he teaches, researches, and writes on leadership, narrative, strategy, and organisation in social movements and civic associations. He left Harvard College in 1964, a year before graduating, to volunteer as a civil rights organiser in Mississippi and then joined Cesar Chavez and the United Farm Workers in 1965, where he spent 16 years gaining experience in union, community, and political organising and eventually became director of organising. During the 1980s, he worked with grassroots groups to develop effective organising programs and designed innovative voter mobilisation strategies for electoral campaigns. After returning to complete his Harvard degree in 1991, he has become a leading authority on community organising and public narrative, coaching and advising social, civic, educational, and political groups worldwide on organising, training, and leadership development.

AUGUST

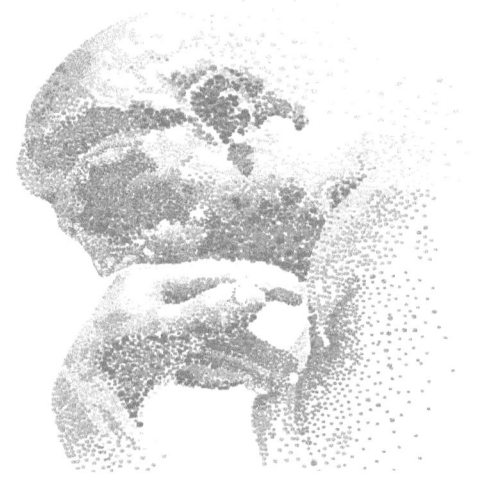

SHAPE THE CULTURE

AUGUST 1

"If I could get a sense of the way your culture works by meeting just one person, who would that person be?"
- Daniel Coyle[216]

---

[216] Another question to describe culture which author and speaker Simon Sinek asks is, "How do people feel when they walk in the door here?"

The Culture Code: The Secrets of Highly Successful Groups, Daniel Coyle, 2018.

Daniel Coyle is a New York Times bestselling author known for books including "The Culture Code," "The Talent Code," "The Little Book of Talent," and "The Secret Race." He works as a contributing editor for Outside magazine and serves as a special advisor to the Cleveland Guardians baseball team. Coyle specializes in studying high-performing teams and talent development, spending years observing elite groups around the world to understand how they build culture, develop skills, and achieve success. Winner of the 2012 William Hill Sports Book of the Year Prize (with Tyler Hamilton), he splits his time between Cleveland, Ohio during the school year and Homer, Alaska in the summer with his wife Jen and their four children. His work focuses on translating the science of skill acquisition and team dynamics into practical insights for coaches, leaders, and organizations seeking to unlock human potential and build stronger cultures.

AUGUST 2

"Is this a place where they will let me do my best?"
- Max De Pree[217]

---

[217] "To make a commitment," De Pree writes, "any employee should be able to answer "yes" to the following question: Is this a place where they will let me do my best?"
Leadership is an Art, Max De Pree, 1987.
Max De Pree (1924 – 2017) was an American businessman and leadership author who transformed Herman Miller from a furniture manufacturer into one of the most innovative and profitable companies of the 20th century while pioneering human-centered management philosophy. De Pree was the son of Herman Miller founder D.J. De Pree and assumed leadership of the company in the early 1960s alongside his brother Hugh. During his tenure as CEO, Herman Miller became one of the most profitable Fortune 500 companies and revolutionised office workspaces with its modern designs. De Pree codified the company's values in a series of books on leadership that have sold more than a million copies in over 20 languages. His most famous work, "Leadership is an Art", along with follow-up books "Leadership Jazz" and "Leading Without Power," established him as a bestselling leadership author who emphasised creativity, human dignity, and servant leadership. Known for his philosophy that "leadership is a serious meddling in other people's lives," De Pree believed leaders had a responsibility to help others reach their potential and created a corporate culture that valued both design excellence and human flourishing until his death in 2017.

AUGUST 3

"'How can I set up a situation that brings out the good in these people?'"
- Chip Heath[218]

---

[218] Heath prefaces this question with, "A good change leader never thinks, 'Why are these people acting so badly? They must be bad people.' A change leader thinks, 'How can I set up a situation that brings out the good in these people?'".
Switch: How to Change Things When Change Is Hard, Chip Heath, 2010.
Chip Heath is the Thrive Foundation for Youth Professor of Organizational Behavior at Stanford Graduate School of Business. He graduated from Texas A&M University with a Bachelor of Science degree in industrial engineering and subsequently earned a PhD in psychology from Stanford University before teaching at the University of Chicago Graduate School of Business and Duke University's Fuqua School of Business. His research examines why certain ideas — ranging from urban legends to folk medical cures, from Chicken Soup for the Soul stories to business strategy myths — survive and prosper in the social marketplace of ideas. Heath is best known for co-authoring three New York Times bestselling books with his brother Dan Heath: "Made to Stick: Why Some Ideas Survive and Others Die", which explores the anatomy of memorable ideas, "Switch: How to Change Things When Change is Hard", and "Decisive: How to Make Better Decisions in Life and Work". His work focuses on understanding how to make ideas more effective in organisational and social contexts.

AUGUST 4

"How would you feel at work if ...
You had the right to design your own job?
Your team was free to set its own goals and define its own methods? You were encouraged to grow your skills and take on new challenges? Your workmates felt more like family than colleagues? You never felt encumbered by pointless rules and red tape? You felt trusted in every situation to use your best judgment? You were accountable to your colleagues rather than a boss? You didn't have to waste time sucking up or playing political games? You had the chance to help shape the strategy and direction of your organization? Your influence and compensation depended on your abilities and not your rank?"
- Gary Hamel[219]

---

[219] "Humanocracy" is a management philosophy and organisational model that emphasises purpose-driven work, continuous learning, and creating environments where people can use their full range of human capabilities rather than being reduced to mere cogs in a machine.

Humanocracy: Creating Organizations as Amazing as the People Inside Them, Gary Hamel, 2020.

Gary Hamel is a renowned management theorist, business strategist, and author who has significantly influenced modern corporate thinking. He's best known for his work on strategic innovation, core competencies, and organisational transformation, having coined influential concepts like "strategic intent" and "core competence" alongside C.K. Prahalad. Hamel has authored several influential business books including "Competing for the Future" and "The Future of Management," and is a visiting professor at London Business School. He founded the Management Innovation eXchange (MIX) and Strategos consulting firm, and is widely regarded as one of the world's most influential business thinkers, frequently appearing on lists of top management gurus for his forward-thinking ideas about corporate strategy and organisational change.

AUGUST 5

"How, then, do you make failure into something people can face without fear?"
- Ed Catmull[220]

---

[220] "Part of the answer is simple:" Catmull explains. "If we as leaders can talk about our mistakes and our part in them, then we make it safe for others. You don't run from it or pretend it doesn't exist. That is why I make a point of being open about our meltdowns inside Pixar, because I believe they teach us something important: Being open about problems is the first step toward learning from them. My goal is not to drive fear out completely, because fear is inevitable in high-stakes situations. What I want to do is loosen its grip on us. While we don't want too many failures, we must think of the cost of failure as an investment in the future."

Creativity, Inc.: Overcoming the Unseen Forces That Stand in the Way of True Inspiration, Ed Catmull, 2014.

Ed Catmull is a computer graphics pioneer and co-founder of Pixar Animation Studios who revolutionised both technology and creative management. With a PhD in computer science, he developed foundational 3D rendering techniques before co-founding Pixar with Steve Jobs in 1986, where they created "Toy Story" and numerous acclaimed films. After Disney's 2006 acquisition of Pixar, Catmull became president of both studios, helping revitalize Disney Animation. His book "Creativity, Inc." details his innovative management philosophy, including "Braintrust" feedback meetings and psychological safety practices that fostered creativity while managing complex projects, making him a respected leader in both Silicon Valley and Hollywood.

AUGUST 6

"What would you suggest?
What would it take for you to agree?
Can you live with it?"
- Steven Gaffney[221]

---

221 Gaffney explains the context of the questions –

"1. "What would you suggest?" - Use this question to pivot from a culture of complaints or criticism to one of solution-oriented thinking. It reframes the conversation from dwelling on problems to brainstorming potential solutions.

2. "What would it take for you to agree?" - This question uncovers the conditions or criteria that need fulfillment for a change in viewpoint or a consensus. It facilitates the conversation's journey towards agreement and collaborative action.

3. "Can you live with it?" - This question is a thermometer for assessing someone's level of concern or objection towards a decision or scenario. It spurs them to evaluate their disagreement, considering whether it necessitates continued discussion, or if it's something they can accept."

Unconditional Power: Thriving in Any Situation, No Matter How Frustrating, Complex, or Unpredictable, Steven Gaffney, 2023.

Steven Gaffney is a communication expert and author who specialises in honest, authentic workplace communication and leadership development. He is the author of three books including, "Just Be Honest" "Honesty Works" and "Honesty Sells," and an expert on getting the unsaid said. His work focuses on helping individuals and organisations overcome communication barriers and build more effective relationships through transparency and directness. His latest book, "Unconditional Power: A Formula for Thriving in Any Situation, No Matter How Frustrating, Complex, and Unpredictable," is based on his work with organisations operating in an array of sectors and establishes a blueprint to overcome any obstacles. Gaffney's approach centres on the concept that power comes from your mindset and internal resources, and helps people navigate challenging situations through practical communication strategies and mental frameworks for resilience.

AUGUST 7

"How do we keep our culture intact as we scale?"
- Reed Hastings[222]

---

[222] In 2009 the leadership at Netflix knew they were staring into a period of incredible growth, and that talent density often shrinks with high growth. This can lead to increasing process, attrition of talent, and ultimately chaos, echoing Admiral Hyman Rickover's warning, "More than ambition, more than ability, it is rules that limit contribution; rules are the lowest common denominator of human behaviour. They are a substitute for rational thought." They believed for an organisation to grow and succeed, talent density needs to outstrip organisational demand. The Netflix Culture Deck created by Patty McCord, Reed Hastings and colleagues laid out how Netflix planned for talent density to outstrip business complexity as the organisation grew. Netflix choice was to grow, but with "ever more high performance people". Under Hastings' leadership, Netflix focused on hiring top talent (increasing "talent density"), fostering freedom and responsibility, and prioritising context over controls.

No Rules Rules: Netflix and the Culture of Reinvention, Reed Hastings, 2020.

Reed Hastings is an entrepreneur and technology executive best known as the co-founder and former CEO of Netflix, where he transformed the company from a DVD-by-mail service into the world's leading streaming entertainment platform. Under his leadership from 1997 to 2023, Netflix pioneered the subscription-based streaming model and became a major producer of original content, fundamentally disrupting the traditional television and film industries. Prior to Netflix, Hastings founded Pure Software, a debugging tools company that he sold in the 1990s. He's recognised for his data-driven approach to business decisions and his willingness to cannibalise Netflix's own DVD business to focus on streaming. Hastings has also been active in education reform, serving on various boards and advocating for charter schools, and he stepped down as Netflix CEO in 2023 to focus on philanthropy while remaining executive chairman of the company.

AUGUST 8

"How can I best help you now?"
- Derek Sivers[223]

---

223 Siver explains, "Never forget that absolutely everything you do is for your customers. Make every decision - even decisions about whether to expand the business, raise money, or promote someone - according to what's best for your customers. If you're ever unsure what to prioritize, just ask your customers the open-ended question, "How can I best help you now?" Then focus on satisfying those requests... It's counterintuitive, but the way to grow your business is to focus entirely on your existing customers. Just thrill them, and they'll tell everyone."
Anything You Want: 40 Lessons for a New Kind of Entrepreneur, Derek Sivers, 2011.

Derek Sivers is an entrepreneur, author, and philosopher best known for founding CD Baby, which became the largest seller of independent music online before he sold it for $22 million and gave the proceeds to charity. Born a musician himself, Sivers created CD Baby in 1998 to help independent artists sell their music online when few platforms existed for that purpose. His book "Anything You Want" chronicles the unconventional business lessons he learned while building CD Baby, emphasizing customer service, simplicity, and purpose over profit maximisation. Sivers is known for his minimalist lifestyle, contrarian thinking, and practical philosophy about business and life, which he shares through his popular blog, TED talks, and books. After selling CD Baby, he moved to Singapore and later New Zealand, focusing on writing, programming, and sharing insights about entrepreneurship, decision-making, and living deliberately. His approach often challenges conventional wisdom, advocating for doing what feels right rather than what's expected, and he's become a respected voice in the startup and creative communities for his thoughtful, experience-based advice on building businesses that serve both customers and personal values.

AUGUST 9

"Why not instead assume that everyone is inherently talented, and then spur them to live up to those expectations?"
- D. Michael Abrashoff[224]

---

224 Abrashoff adds, "Too idealistic? On the contrary, that's exactly how Benfold became the best damn ship in the U.S. Navy."

It's Your Ship: Management Techniques from the Best Damn Ship in the Navy, D. Michael Abrashoff, 2012.

Michael Abrashoff is a former U.S. Navy captain who gained recognition for his leadership philosophy and transformation of the USS Benfold, a guided-missile destroyer. During his command from 1997 to 1999, he implemented innovative leadership practices that dramatically improved the ship's performance, retention rates, and crew morale while reducing costs. His approach emphasised empowering subordinates, eliminating bureaucratic obstacles, and focusing on results rather than rigid procedures. After leaving the Navy, Abrashoff became a popular leadership consultant and speaker, sharing his insights on effective leadership in both military and corporate settings. He authored the book "It's Your Ship" which became a bestseller and outlined his principles for creating high-performing organizations through engaged leadership and empowered teams.

AUGUST 10

"How we can put the customer at the center of what we do so we earn customers for life?"
- Mary Barra[225]

---

[225] Barra's question mirrors Peter Drucker who said, "The purpose of business is to create and keep a customer."
Mary Barra Opens Up About GM's $500 Million Bet On Lyft, Emily Jane Fox, Vanity Fair, January 11, 2016.

Mary Barra is an American businesswoman who has served as CEO of General Motors since 2014, making her the first woman to lead a major global automaker. She began her career at GM as an 18-year-old co-op student in 1980 and worked her way up through various engineering and executive roles over more than three decades. Under her leadership, GM has undergone a significant transformation, including a major push into electric vehicles with the goal of phasing out gasoline-powered cars by 2035, and substantial investments in autonomous vehicle technology through its Cruise division. Barra led the company through major challenges including a recall crisis early in her tenure and the COVID-19 pandemic, while positioning GM as a leader in the automotive industry's shift toward electrification and sustainability. She's been recognised as one of the most powerful women in business and has advocated for diversity and inclusion in the automotive industry and corporate America more broadly.

AUGUST 11

"How are we going to be when we gather together?"
- Peter Block[226]

---

[226] "The key to creating or transforming community, then, is to see the power in the small but important elements of being with others." Block explains. "The shift we seek needs to be embodied in each invitation we make, each relationship we encounter, and each meeting we attend. For at the most operational and practical level, after all the thinking about policy, strategy, mission, and milestones, it gets down to this: How are we going to be when we gather together?"
Community: The Structure of Belonging, Peter Block, 2008.

Peter Block is an organisational development consultant, author, and speaker known for his work on empowerment, community building, and transformational change in organisations. He's written several influential books including "Flawless Consulting," "The Empowered Manager," and "Community: The Structure of Belonging." Block focuses on shifting organisational cultures from dependency and control toward accountability and partnership, emphasizing the importance of engaging people's commitment rather than just their compliance. His approach centres on the belief that sustainable change happens when individuals take personal responsibility and when organisations create conditions for authentic engagement and shared ownership of outcomes.

AUGUST 12

"Are we changing as fast as the world around us?"
- Gary Hamel[227]

---

[227] Hamel's question relates to one asked by former Intel CEO Andy Grove: "Are you trying new ideas, new techniques, and new technologies, and I mean personally trying them, not just reading about them? Or are you waiting for others to figure out how they can re-engineer your workplace—and you out of that workplace?"

Humanocracy: Creating Organizations as Amazing as the People Inside Them, Gary Hamel, 2020.

Gary Hamel is a renowned management theorist, business strategist, and author who has significantly influenced modern corporate thinking. He's best known for his work on strategic innovation, core competencies, and organisational transformation, having coined influential concepts like "strategic intent" and "core competence" alongside C.K. Prahalad. Hamel has authored several influential business books including "Competing for the Future" and "The Future of Management," and is a visiting professor at London Business School. He founded the Management Innovation eXchange (MIX) and Strategos consulting firm, and is widely regarded as one of the world's most influential business thinkers, frequently appearing on lists of top management gurus for his forward-thinking ideas about corporate strategy and organisational change.

AUGUST 13

"How is this organization different from all other organizations?"
- Adam Grant[228]

---

[228] "But how do you figure out the culture of a company you've never worked for?" Grant asks. "As Nicole tried to evaluate company cultures, she kept asking the Passover question: "How is this organization different from all other organizations?" And, as with Passover, I told Nicole, the answer should come in the form of a story. Ask people to tell you a story about something that happened at their organization but wouldn't elsewhere."

The One Question You Should Ask About Every New Job, Adam Grant, New York Times, December 19, 2015.

Adam Grant is an organisational psychologist and bestselling author who serves as a professor at the Wharton School of the University of Pennsylvania. He's known for his research on motivation, generosity, and unconventional thinking, which he's popularised through books like "Give and Take", "Originals", and "Think Again". Grant challenges conventional wisdom about success, arguing that generous people can finish both last and first, and that our greatest strength can become our greatest weakness. He's also a popular speaker and podcast host, known for making psychological research accessible and practical for business leaders and general audiences. His work often focuses on how people can contribute to others while still achieving their own goals, and how organisations can foster innovation and positive change.

AUGUST 14

"What would it mean to be done for the day?"
- David Maloney[229]

---

[229] Maloney's question echoes the P/PC Balance from Stephen Covey's "The 7 Habits of Highly Effective People". The idea is that there is a critical equilibrium between Production (P) - the results you want - and Production Capability (PC) - the resources that produce those results. Using Aesop's fable of the goose and golden eggs, Covey explains how focusing solely on short-term results destroys long-term capacity, while neglecting results for capability-building leads to stagnation. Effective individuals and organisations simultaneously achieve desired outcomes while maintaining and developing their underlying assets, whether skills, health, relationships, or equipment, to ensure sustainable success rather than temporary gains that compromise future performance.

The Importance of Reaching a Point in Your Day when You Feel Finished, Dr David Maloney Psychotherapy. Also refer to Oliver Burkeman who references this video on his blog *The Imperfectionist*.

Dr. David Maloney is a psychologist and therapist who specialises in helping people overcome procrastination, build motivation, and discover their life purpose. His work helps people to end self-sabotage and conflicted limiting beliefs, offering both individual therapy sessions and online courses. What makes his approach unique is that it comes from personal experience - he had a chronic procrastination habit up until about 8 years ago when he hit an all-time low while he was in graduate school, describing it as "a repeating nightmare" and "a perpetual guilt cycle". Dr. Maloney has authored several books on procrastination, including "Procrastination Decoded: How to Overcome Procrastination by Ending the Guilt Cycle, Building Self-Respect and Adopting The 'Now or Never' Philosophy" and "The Study Virus: How to Completely Eliminate Academic Procrastination and Unleash Your Full Potential." His approach is described as "entirely counter-intuitive" compared to traditional productivity advice, rather than emphasizing the usual mantras of working harder or grinding, he focuses on accessing "a powerful, deliberate, compassionate and encouraging aspect of your own consciousness". His courses promise to help people go "step by step from experiencing chronic procrastination to easily and happily getting things done, drama free" while experiencing "life guilt-free" and dramatically increasing "self-esteem, self-respect and self-trust."

AUGUST 15

"If people are like plants, what are the conditions we need to flourish?"
- Jonathan Haidt[230]

---

[230] The leader's role is to create the optimal conditions for success. "The temptation to lead as a chess master," author and general Stanley McChrystal writes, "controlling each move of the organization ... must give way to an approach as a gardener, enabling rather than directing." As a leader this responsibility, to create the optimal environment, extends to yourself. *The Happiness Hypothesis: Finding Modern Truth in Ancient Wisdom*, Jonathan Haidt, 2006.

Jonathan Haidt is a prominent social psychologist and author who serves as the Thomas Cooley Professor of Ethical Leadership at NYU Stern School of Business. His main areas of study are the psychology of morality and moral emotions, with his principal scientific contributions coming from moral foundations theory, which attempts to explain the evolutionary origins of human moral reasoning based on innate, gut feelings rather than logic and reason. His mission is to use research on moral psychology to help people understand each other and to help important social institutions work better. Haidt is best known for his influential books "The Righteous Mind" and "The Coddling of the American Mind", as well as his recent work "The Anxious Generation" examining social media's impact on adolescent mental health. His work has been instrumental in explaining political polarisation and moral differences across cultures, making complex psychological research accessible to broad audiences seeking to understand social change and human behaviour.

AUGUST 16

"How can I help you deliver excellent service?"
- Daniel Cable[231]

---

[231] Cable explains, "PwC started with a small, wise intervention: take the standard fifteen-minute format for the weekly meeting and have managers start the meeting with a basic servant leadership question: How can I help you deliver excellent service?"

Alive at Work: The Neuroscience of Helping Your People Love What They Do, Daniel M. Cable, 2018.

Daniel M. Cable is Professor of Organisational Behaviour at London Business School, where he focuses on employee engagement, organisational culture, and transforming workplaces from compliance-driven to commitment-based environments. His research and teaching focus on organisational culture, activating positive emotions, and getting employees into commitment instead of just compliance. Previously a professor at Georgia Tech and the University of North Carolina, Cable has won London Business School's Excellence in Teaching Award and has been twice honoured by the Academy of Management with Best Article awards. He was selected for the 2018 Thinkers50 Radar List and is recognised for his work on leadership mindset, change management, and the connection between organisational brands and employee behaviours. His research particularly emphasises how leaders can create conditions that allow people to express their authentic selves at work, leading to higher performance and engagement.

AUGUST 17

*"When one of your people does something dumb don't blame them.
Instead ask yourself what context you failed to set.
Are you articulate and inspiring enough in expressing your goals and strategy?
Have you clearly explained all the assumptions and risks that will help your team to make good decisions?
Are you and your employees highly aligned on vision and objectives?"*
- Reed Hastings[232]

---

[232] "Just culture" refers to an organisational approach that balances accountability with learning, particularly in high-risk industries like healthcare, aviation, and nuclear power. The concept recognises that most errors stem from systemic issues rather than individual failings. The approach requires strong leadership commitment and clear policies that help managers respond consistently and fairly to different types of safety events. It is about being "just", neither blame-free nor punitive, but appropriately balanced based on the nature of the behavior and circumstances involved.

No Rules Rules: Netflix and the Culture of Reinvention, Reed Hastings, 2020.

Reed Hastings is an entrepreneur and technology executive best known as the co-founder and former CEO of Netflix, where he transformed the company from a DVD-by-mail service into the world's leading streaming entertainment platform. Under his leadership from 1997 to 2023, Netflix pioneered the subscription-based streaming model and became a major producer of original content, fundamentally disrupting the traditional television and film industries. Prior to Netflix, Hastings founded Pure Software, a debugging tools company that he sold in the 1990s. He's recognised for his data-driven approach to business decisions and his willingness to cannibalise Netflix's own DVD business to focus on streaming. Hastings has also been active in education reform, serving on various boards and advocating for charter schools, and he stepped down as Netflix CEO in 2023 to focus on philanthropy while remaining executive chairman of the company.

AUGUST 18

"The question at the core of bureaucracy is, 'How do we get human beings to better serve the organization?'
The question at the heart of humanocracy is, 'What sort of organization elicits and merits the best that human beings can give?'"
- Gary Hamel[233]

---

[233] Humanocracy is a philosophy that replaces traditional bureaucratic hierarchies with decentralised, human-centered structures. It emphasises empowering employees at all levels to make decisions, prioritising creativity and initiative over rigid rules and management layers. The approach aims to unlock human potential by treating workers as creative partners rather than managed resources, creating more agile and innovative organisations.
Humanocracy: Creating Organizations as Amazing as the People Inside Them, Gary Hamel, 2020.

Gary Hamel is a renowned management theorist, business strategist, and author who has significantly influenced modern corporate thinking. He's best known for his work on strategic innovation, core competencies, and organisational transformation, having coined influential concepts like "strategic intent" and "core competence" alongside C.K. Prahalad. Hamel has authored several influential business books including "Competing for the Future" and "The Future of Management," and is a visiting professor at London Business School. He founded the Management Innovation eXchange (MIX) and Strategos consulting firm, and is widely regarded as one of the world's most influential business thinkers, frequently appearing on lists of top management gurus for his forward-thinking ideas about corporate strategy and organisational change.

AUGUST 19

"What is most likely to be the cause of your next accident or serious incident? How do you know that? What are you doing about it? Is it working?"
- William Voss[234]

---

[234] Voss explains, "If you want to go deeper, let me give you four simple audit questions that are really easy to answer if you have an effective [Safety Management System] SMS, and impossible to answer if you don't." A SMS (Safety Management System) is a systematic approach to managing safety in organisations, particularly in high-risk industries like aviation, healthcare, and manufacturing. It's a structured framework that includes policies, procedures, and practices designed to identify hazards, assess risks, implement controls, and continuously monitor and improve safety performance. The system emphasises proactive risk management rather than just reactive responses to incidents, integrating safety considerations into all organisational decision-making processes.

SMS Reconsidered, William R. Voss, Flight Safety Foundation, May 17, 2012.

William R. Voss is a distinguished aviation safety leader who has played pivotal roles in global aviation safety organisations throughout his career. He served as President and CEO of the Flight Safety Foundation, an independent international non-profit organisation dedicated to advancing aviation safety, and previously held positions at the International Civil Aviation Organization (ICAO) since 2004, where he oversaw development of major international safety initiatives. He has served as a Special Adviser to the Director of the Air Navigation Bureau at ICAO and was one of 19 independent experts on the ICAO Air Navigation Commission appointed by countries from around the world. Voss began his aviation career with the Federal Aviation Administration (FAA) as an air traffic controller and held various operational and staff positions before transitioning to international aviation safety leadership. His work has focused on developing global safety standards, promoting safety culture across the aviation industry, and fostering international collaboration to reduce aviation risks worldwide. Through his leadership roles, Voss has been instrumental in shaping modern aviation safety practices and policies that have contributed to making commercial aviation one of the safest forms of transportation.

AUGUST 20

"How can organizations cultivate a culture that encourages giving without leading to burnout?"
- Adam Grant[235]

---

[235] Robert Greenleaf explains that enduring resilience is "a set of choices to give one the best performance over a lifespan". If an average human lifespan is 4000 weeks, we can expect our working lives to extend over 2000 weeks or so. Doing something for this long requires pacing, working sustainably and building reserve capacity instead of redlining. To paraphrase bestselling author Morgan Housel, whether it is relationships, investing, career, education or exercise, we shouldn't be interested in anything unsustainable. Always trying to extract 100% will lead to burnout and the inability to sustain wellness.
Give and Take: Why Helping Others Drives Our Success, Adam Grant, 2014.
Adam Grant is an organisational psychologist and bestselling author who serves as a professor at the Wharton School of the University of Pennsylvania. He's known for his research on motivation, generosity, and unconventional thinking, which he's popularised through books like "Give and Take," "Originals," and "Think Again." Grant challenges conventional wisdom about success, arguing that generous people can finish both last and first, and that our greatest strength can become our greatest weakness. He's also a popular speaker and podcast host, known for making psychological research accessible and practical for business leaders and general audiences. His work often focuses on how people can contribute to others while still achieving their own goals, and how organisations can foster innovation and positive change.

AUGUST 21

"Do you care enough to do great work? How could we create a system where great work is easier to do?"
- Seth Godin[236]

---

[236] *Direct questions worth answering*, Seth Godin, seths.blog, January 24, 2024.

Seth Godin is a bestselling author, entrepreneur, and marketing guru who has fundamentally changed how people think about marketing, leadership, and the spread of ideas. He's written over 20 books, including influential titles like "Purple Cow," which popularised the concept that businesses must be remarkable to succeed, "The Tipping Point" predecessor "Unleashing the Ideavirus," and "Linchpin," which argues that indispensable employees are those who bring creativity and humanity to their work. Godin founded several companies, including Yoyodyne (one of the first internet marketing companies, sold to Yahoo!) and Squidoo, and the altMBA, an intensive online leadership workshop. His daily blog, which he's maintained for decades, reaches millions of readers with insights on marketing, culture, and human behaviour. Godin is known for coining terms like "permission marketing" (marketing to people who want to be marketed to) and advocating for authentic, story-driven approaches over traditional advertising. His philosophy emphasises that in the modern economy, playing it safe is actually the riskiest strategy, and that success comes from being different, generous, and willing to make a difference. He's also a sought-after speaker who challenges conventional business wisdom and encourages people to embrace change and lead rather than follow.

AUGUST 22

"What if a company did everything within its power to create the conditions for individuals to overcome their own internal barriers to change, to take stock of and transcend their own blind spots, and to see errors and weaknesses as prime opportunities for personal growth?"
- Robert Kegan[237]

---

[237] A common leadership mistake is working within the system. The temptation is high - you feel needed, revert to what is familiar, and can have an immediate impact. An effective leader resists being drawn in, and remains focussed on the system. Their energies are directed to changing the future conditions their team will be operating in, and creating the circumstances in which their people can perform at their best. Paraphrasing author Tom DeMarco, a leader's function is not to make people work, but to make it possible for people to work. The leader's role is to create the optimal conditions for success.

An Everyone Culture: Becoming a Deliberately Developmental Organization, Robert Kegan, 2016.

Robert Kegan is a renowned developmental psychologist who served as the William and Miriam Meehan Professor in Adult Learning and Professional Development at Harvard Graduate School of Education for forty years until his retirement in 2016. As a neo-Piagetian constructive-developmental psychologist, he expanded Jean Piaget's cognitive development stages of childhood to adulthood, bringing together constructivism and developmentalism. Kegan is best known for championing the idea that there is life after adolescence; that adult mental development need not end at age twenty; that adults may, indeed must, continue to develop throughout adulthood. A licensed clinical psychologist and practicing therapist, he lectures widely to professional and lay audiences and consults in the area of professional development. His groundbreaking work on adult development theory has influenced fields ranging from education and leadership development to organisational psychology, helping people understand how individuals continue to grow and transform their meaning-making systems throughout their lives.

AUGUST 23

"Do you ever walk around your facility listening solely for what is being communicated through informal language? How can you create an environment in which men and women freely express their uncertainties and fears as well as their innovative ideas and hopes?"
- L. David Marquet[238]

---

[238] Marquet advocates moving from the traditional command-and-control culture toward a leaderleader model. He challenges leaders to –

1. Listen for informal cues, what people are really saying beneath formal reports.
2. Encourage authenticity, including doubts and intuitive insights.
3. Model vulnerability, showing that it's okay to be uncertain.
4. Build trust, enabling candid dialogue across all levels.

Marquet is guiding leaders to create psychologically safe environments where creativity and honesty thrive, transforming institutional culture from compliance to engagement.

Turn The Ship Around!: A True Story of Turning Followers into Leaders, L. David Marquet, 2016.

L. David Marquet is a former U.S. Navy submarine captain who became a prominent leadership author and speaker after transforming the USS Santa Fe from one of the worst-performing submarines in the fleet to one of the best. His leadership philosophy, detailed in his bestselling book "Turn the Ship Around!", centers on moving from a "leader-follower" model to a "leader-leader" model, where he empowered his crew to think and act like leaders rather than simply following orders. Marquet's approach emphasises giving control rather than taking control, and his methods have been widely adopted in corporate settings. He retired from the Navy as a Captain in 2009 and now works as a leadership consultant, helping organisations develop more effective leadership structures.

AUGUST 24

"Do we sense that we are meant to journey together?"
- Frederic Laloux[239]

---

[239] Laloux discusses the onboarding and sense of belonging in organisations, particularly those embracing the "Teal" paradigm. "Teal" is a term coined by Laloux to describe the next evolutionary stage of organisational development, building upon earlier models (Red, Amber, Orange, Green). Teal organizations are distinguished by three breakthrough characteristics -

1. Selfmanagement – no traditional hierarchy; decision-making is distributed, teams steer themselves.

2. Wholeness – people are invited to bring their entire selves to work, blending emotional, creative, and rational aspects.

3. Evolutionary purpose – organisations are seen as living systems; strategy emerges organically in service of a deeper mission.

When assessing whether someone truly belongs in a Teal organisation, or whether a given team or partnership is viable, the question isn't just about skills or experience. It's about shared vision, and a sense that "we're meant to journey together", that there's a deeper, purposeful alignment between individuals and the organisation's mission. The question encapsulates Laloux's conviction that the success of organisations depends not only on structures or processes but on a sense of shared purpose and belonging.

Reinventing Organizations: A Guide to Creating Organizations Inspired by the Next Stage of Human Consciousness, Frederic Laloux, 2014.

Frederic Laloux is an organisational theorist and former business coach who has sparked a global movement of organisations adopting radically more powerful – and soulful – management practices. A former Associate Partner with McKinsey & Company, he holds an MBA from INSEAD and a degree in coaching from Newfield Network in Boulder, Colorado. He moved from Brussels with his young family to join an ecovillage in upstate New York. Laloux has travelled widely and speaks five languages. His groundbreaking 2014 book "Reinventing Organizations" describes the emergence of a new management paradigm, a radically more soulful, purposeful and powerful ways to structure and run businesses and non-profits, schools and hospitals based on three pillars related to wholeness, self-management, and evolutionary purpose. The book has influenced thousands of organisations worldwide to move beyond traditional hierarchical structures toward what he calls "Teal" organisations.

AUGUST 25

"Whom must we fearlessly become?"
- Keith Yamashita[240]

---

240 Berger quotes entrepreneur and author Keith Yamashita. "... Yamashita points out, it's just as important to look forward when asking big questions about purpose. He urges clients to work on Whom must we fearlessly become? That can be a difficult challenge, he says, because it requires 'envisioning a version of the company that does not exist yet.'" From *Unstuck: A Tool for Yourself, Your Team, and Your World*, Keith Yamashita, 2004.

A More Beautiful Question: The Power of Inquiry to Spark Breakthrough Ideas, Warren Berger, 2014.

Keith Yamashita is dedicated to using creativity as a powerful catalyst for change in the world and for the past two decades at SYPartners, has worked with leaders at major companies including Activision Blizzard, Apple, eBay, Emerson Collective, Facebook, IBM, General Electric, Johnson & Johnson, and Oprah Winfrey Network. He is the cofounder and principal of Stone Yamashita Partners (SYP), which was founded in 1994 and began life as a traditional design firm but slowly evolved to resemble a management consultancy as much as a graphic design firm. As a consultant, author and speaker, Yamashita helps companies turn their struggling businesses around and rebrand themselves, encouraging organisations to become stronger by helping their members seek greatness at the individual level, as duos and as members of society. He and his team at SY Partners have spent nearly a quarter century helping individuals and companies transform, working with major brands like Starbucks, IBM, and Target to become better versions of themselves.

AUGUST 26

"How can we have meetings that are productive and uplifting, where we speak from our hearts and not from our egos?"
- Frederic Laloux[241]

---

[241] "The hierarchical pyramid feels outdated, but what other structure could replace it? How about decision-making?" Laloux writes. "Everybody should make meaningful decisions, not just a few higher-ups, but isn't that just a recipe for chaos? How about promotions and salary increases? Can we find ways to handle such matters without bringing politics to the table? How can we have meetings that are productive and uplifting, where we speak from our hearts and not from our egos? How can we make purpose central to everything we do, and avoid the cynicism that lofty-sounding mission statements often inspire? What we need is not merely some grand vision of a new type of organization. We need concrete answers to dozens of practical questions like these."

Reinventing Organizations: A Guide to Creating Organizations Inspired by the Next Stage of Human Consciousness, Frederic Laloux, 2014.

Frederic Laloux is an organisational theorist and former business coach who has sparked a global movement of organisations adopting radically more powerful – and soulful – management practices. A former Associate Partner with McKinsey & Company, he holds an MBA from INSEAD and a degree in coaching from Newfield Network in Boulder, Colorado. He moved from Brussels with his young family to join an ecovillage in upstate New York. Laloux has travelled widely and speaks five languages. His groundbreaking 2014 book "Reinventing Organizations" describes the emergence of a new management paradigm, a radically more soulful, purposeful and powerful ways to structure and run businesses and non-profits, schools and hospitals based on three pillars related to wholeness, self-management, and evolutionary purpose. The book has influenced thousands of organisations worldwide to move beyond traditional hierarchical structures toward what he calls "Teal" organisations.

AUGUST 27

"How do we create a culture where people bring their whole selves to work?"
- Martin Webster[242]

---

[242] The amount of discretionary energy which is dormant in many organisations is significant. This energy is effectively withheld. If a leader learns how to access this energy, it can be transformative. US Secretary of Health, Education and Welfare John W. Gardner observed, "The reservoir of unused human talent and energy is vast, and learning to tap that reservoir more effectively is one of the exciting tasks ahead for humankind." Vast amounts of latent energy can be called forth by a leader under the right conditions.

Leading With Heart webinar series, Martin Webster, 2022.

Martin Webster is a leadership development expert and founder of "The Lazy Leader," an independent publication he created for everyone starting their leadership journey, where he shares experiences and promotes leadership development alongside the pursuit of "productive laziness." Webster founded The Lazy Leader building on the success of his previous Leadership Thoughts blog, with the platform focusing on encouraging leadership development, leadership teams, business transformation, and project management through weekly articles and content. His philosophy centres around the counterintuitive concept that "lazy" leaders can be highly effective by finding efficient ways to accomplish difficult tasks, drawing inspiration from the idea that choosing a lazy person for a hard job often results in finding the easiest solution. The Lazy Leader operates as an independent publication designed to help new managers and leaders reach their full potential.

AUGUST 28

"Are we making decisions based on context rather than control?"
- Reed Hastings[243]

---

[243] In the Netflix Culture Deck (August 2009), Reed Hastings and Patty McCord, then Netflix Chief Talent Officer state, "Our model is to increase employee freedom as we grow, rather than limit it, to continue to attract and nourish innovative people, so we have better chance of sustained success." Netflix took the view that high performance people do better work if they understand the context.

No Rules Rules: Netflix and the Culture of Reinvention, Reed Hastings, 2020. Also refer *How Netflix Reinvented HR: Trust people, not policies. Reward candor. And throw away the standard playbook*, Patty McCord, Harvard Business Review, January-February 2014.

Reed Hastings is an entrepreneur and technology executive best known as the co-founder and former CEO of Netflix, where he transformed the company from a DVD-by-mail service into the world's leading streaming entertainment platform. Under his leadership from 1997 to 2023, Netflix pioneered the subscription-based streaming model and became a major producer of original content, fundamentally disrupting the traditional television and film industries. Prior to Netflix, Hastings founded Pure Software, a debugging tools company that he sold in the 1990s. He's recognised for his data-driven approach to business decisions and his willingness to cannibalise Netflix's own DVD business to focus on streaming. Hastings has also been active in education reform, serving on various boards and advocating for charter schools, and he stepped down as Netflix CEO in 2023 to focus on philanthropy while remaining executive chairman of the company.

AUGUST 29

"Am I in the right place?"
- Howard Stevenson[244]

---

[244] "There are places that are toxic." Stevenson explains, "There are places that are good for other people, bad for us. How do you evaluate the culture in which you're embedded? I know for me, Harvard Business School has been a great benefit in my life. I was embedded in a place that gave me freedom to do what I wanted to do. It gave me insight and access. But there are a lot of places that I think I would have failed. So I had to choose the right culture."

Building a Life, Howard H. Stevenson, Harvard Business School, 2013.

Howard Stevenson is a prominent figure in entrepreneurship education and research, best known for his long tenure at Harvard Business School where he served as the Sarofim-Rock Baker Foundation Professor of Business Administration. He's often referred to as the "godfather of entrepreneurship studies" at Harvard and played a pivotal role in establishing entrepreneurship as a legitimate academic discipline. Stevenson developed influential frameworks for understanding entrepreneurship, including his widely-cited definition of entrepreneurship as "the pursuit of opportunity beyond resources controlled." He has authored numerous books and articles on entrepreneurship, venture capital, and business strategy, and has been instrumental in shaping how entrepreneurship is taught in business schools worldwide. Throughout his career, he has also been involved with various entrepreneurial ventures and has served on numerous boards, bridging the gap between academic theory and practical business application.

AUGUST 30

"How can we make society both more productive and more humane?"
- Peter Drucker[245]

---

[245] Collins explains that this was *the* central question that Drucker had dedicated himself to during his working life. As a leader it is a question that demands we consider not just efficiency and output, but also the well-being and dignity of individuals. To achieve this balance, Drucker advocated for an approach that prioritises self-knowledge, wisdom, and leadership, focusing on making human strengths productive and aligning activities with clear goals and a shared vision.
Ten Lessons I Learned from Peter Drucker, Jim Collins, Foreword to the 50th Anniversary Edition of The Effective Executive, May 17, 2016.

Peter Drucker (1909-2005) was a management consultant, educator, and author widely regarded as the founder of modern management theory. Drucker wrote over 30 books and countless articles that fundamentally shaped how we think about business, leadership, and organisational effectiveness. He coined many concepts that are now management staples, including "management by objectives," "knowledge worker," and the idea that the purpose of business is to create customers. His most influential works include "The Practice of Management" and "The Effective Executive". Drucker emphasised that management is both an art and a science, focusing on people rather than just processes, and he predicted many major business trends including the rise of the information economy and the importance of innovation. Beyond business, he was a prolific social commentator who wrote about democracy, society, and the role of institutions. His insights remain remarkably relevant today, and he's remembered for his practical wisdom and his belief that effective management could make organisations more productive while also making work more meaningful for people.

AUGUST 31

"What is life like for those I'm leading?"
- Jeff Harmon[246]

---

[246] "Nothing can animate the future quite like a question." Harmon writes. "What does life resemble or is similar to for those you lead? What's the experience they are having?" Harmon's advice is "Establish a routine to ask this question: What is life like for those I'm leading? Ask it every day, do something about it, and watch your future be powerfully animated."

The Most Powerful Leadership Question, Jeff Harmon, leadchangegroup.com, November 25, 2014.

Jeff Harmon is a leadership consultant and coach who runs Brilliance Within Coaching & Consulting, specialising in working with leaders in the pharmaceutical, biotech, and technology sectors in the New York City metro area, where he is called upon by CEOs and senior leaders tasked with growing their businesses 3-5x. Over the past 20 years, Jeff has led or supported the delivery of over 200,000 hours of strategy across financial services, information technology, pharmaceutical, and non-profit industries. As a thought leader in leadership and culture development, he is the author of "The Anatomy of a Principled Leader" and "Become a Better Leader," and has built his career on two core principles: how you lead matters and it's not about me. Jeff has helped hundreds of leaders execute business strategy while developing their leadership capacity.

SEPTEMBER

SHARPEN THE SAW

SEPTEMBER 1

*"Was yesterday better than the day before?
How can you make today better?"*
- Chad Fowler[247]

---

[247] "You might not be able to see a noticeable difference in the whole with each incremental change, though." Fowler writes. "When you're trying to become more respected in your workplace or be healthier, the individual improvements you make each day often won't lead directly to tangible results. This is, as we saw before, the reason big goals like these become so demotivating. So, for most of the big, difficult goals you're striving for, it's important to think not about getting closer each day to the goal, but rather, to think about doing better in your efforts toward that goal than yesterday. I can't, for example, guarantee that I'll be less fat today than yesterday, but I can control whether I do more today to lose weight. And if I do, I have a right to feel good about what I've done. This consistent, measurable improvement in my actions frees me from the cycle of guilt and procrastination that most of us are ultimately defeated by when we try to do Big Important Things."

The Big Question: Are You Better Than Yesterday?, Tim Ferriss, tim.blog, July 28, 2009.

Chad Fowler is a prominent figure in the software development and technology community, known for his work as a programmer, author, and speaker. He's written several influential books on software development, including "The Passionate Programmer" (originally titled "My Job Went to India") and co-authored "Rails Recipes." Fowler has been involved in organizing major technology conferences, particularly serving as an organiser for RubyConf, one of the key conferences for the Ruby programming language community. He's also worked as a CTO and technology leader at various companies, and has been recognised for his contributions to agile software development practices and his insights on career development for programmers. Fowler is known for his practical approach to both technical and professional development in the tech industry.

SEPTEMBER 2

"If we could be truly excellent at only one thing, what would it be?"
- Greg McKeown[248]

---

[248] To avoid the trap of trying to do it all, and not improving at anything, McKeown asks this question, prefacing it with, "Instead, ask the more essential question that will inform every future decision you will ever make". This question forces you to move beyond the trap of trying to be good at everything and instead identify your singular point of excellence - whether as an individual, team, or organisation. It's designed to eliminate the noise of competing priorities and reveal what truly matters most. The question assumes that excellence requires concentrated effort and that spreading yourself too thin across multiple areas prevents you from achieving true mastery in any one area. "Essentialists see trade-offs as an inherent part of life, not as an inherently negative part of life." he explains. "Instead of asking, 'What do I have to give up?' they ask, 'What do I want to go big on?'"

Essentialism: The Disciplined Pursuit of Less, Greg McKeown, 2014.

Greg McKeown is a business writer, consultant, and bestselling author. McKeown is the author of two New York Times bestsellers, "Essentialism: The Disciplined Pursuit of Less" and "Effortless: Make It Easier to Do What Matters Most," which together have sold 3 million copies and been published in 40 languages. His core philosophy of Essentialism teaches people to focus on what truly matters by eliminating the non-essential from their lives and work. McKeown has become one of the most sought-after public speakers in the world, speaking to hundreds of organisations while traveling to more than 45 countries, with clients including Apple, Amazon, Google, and Microsoft. He also hosts a popular podcast and runs the Essentialism Academy, helping individuals and organisations apply his principles to achieve greater impact through more disciplined choices about where to invest their time and energy.

SEPTEMBER 3

"How long will you put off what you are capable of doing just to continue what you are comfortable doing?"
- James Clear[249]

---

[249] As the saying goes, there is no growth without struggle and discomfort. Author and ultramarathon runner Dean Karnazes believes, "Struggling and suffering are the essence of a life worth living. If you're not pushing yourself beyond the comfort zone, if you're not demanding more from yourself - expanding and learning as you go – you're choosing a numb existence. You're denying yourself an extraordinary trip."
3-2-1 Newsletter, James Clear, August 8, 2019.
James Clear is an author, speaker, and entrepreneur best known for his book "Atomic Habits," which became a bestseller and popularised the concept of making small, incremental changes to build better habits and break bad ones. Clear focuses on the science of habit formation, emphasising how tiny improvements compound over time to create remarkable results. His approach centres on four key principles: making habits obvious, attractive, easy, and satisfying. Before his writing career took off, Clear was a successful entrepreneur and has a background in photography and business. He writes regularly about habits, decision-making, and continuous improvement on his website and newsletter, which has attracted millions of readers. Clear's work draws from psychology, neuroscience, and behavioural economics to provide practical strategies for personal and professional development, making complex research accessible to everyday readers seeking to improve their lives through better systems and habits.

SEPTEMBER 4

"You must help a child become a virtuous, responsible, awake being capable of full reciprocity, able to take care of himself, and others, and to thrive while doing so.
Why would you think of it acceptable and do anything less for yourself? ...
You need to consider the future and think what might my life look like if I'm caring for myself properly? What should I be doing when I have some freedom to improve my health, expand my knowledge and strength to my body?"
- Jordan Peterson[250]

---

[250] Speaker and author Jim Rohn said, "The day you graduate from childhood to adulthood is the day you take full responsibility for your life." Your wellbeing and longevity requires complete self-responsibility. It is realising, as David Goggins puts it, that "No one is going to come help you. No one's coming to save you."
12 Rules for Life: An Antidote to Chaos, Jordan B Peterson, 2018.
Jordan B. Peterson is a clinical psychologist, professor, and author who gained international prominence for his views on free speech, political correctness, and personal responsibility. He taught at Harvard University and the University of Toronto, specialising in personality psychology, psychopathology, and the psychology of religious and ideological belief. His bestselling book "12 Rules for Life: An Antidote to Chaos" combines psychology, philosophy, and personal anecdotes to offer practical advice for living a meaningful life, emphasizing individual responsibility, self-improvement, and traditional values. His second book, "Beyond Order: 12 More Rules for Life," continues these themes. Peterson's lectures and online content focus on topics like mythology, religion, personal development, and the psychological significance of stories and archetypes.

SEPTEMBER 5

*"What are the most likely sources of pain in my life over the next year?
How can I prepare for or prevent them?"*
- James Clear[251]

---

[251] *3-2-1 Newsletter,* James Clear, August 5, 2019.

James Clear is an author, speaker, and entrepreneur best known for his book "Atomic Habits," which became a bestseller and popularised the concept of making small, incremental changes to build better habits and break bad ones. Clear focuses on the science of habit formation, emphasising how tiny improvements compound over time to create remarkable results. His approach centres on four key principles: making habits obvious, attractive, easy, and satisfying. Before his writing career took off, Clear was a successful entrepreneur and has a background in photography and business. He writes regularly about habits, decision-making, and continuous improvement on his website and newsletter, which has attracted millions of readers. Clear's work draws from psychology, neuroscience, and behavioural economics to provide practical strategies for personal and professional development, making complex research accessible to everyday readers seeking to improve their lives through better systems and habits.

SEPTEMBER 6

"Are you courageous enough to abandon a practice that has made you successful in the past?"
- Roselinde Torres[252]

---

[252] "Great leaders dare to be different." Torres explains. "They don't just talk about risk-taking, they actually do it."
What it takes to be a great leader, Roselinde Torres, TED@BCG San Francisco, October 2013.
Roselinde Torres is a leadership expert, author, and senior partner at Boston Consulting Group (BCG), where she leads the firm's leadership development work globally. She's known for her research on what makes leaders effective in today's rapidly changing business environment and has developed frameworks for understanding 21st-century leadership challenges. Torres is perhaps best known for her popular TED Talk "What It Takes to Be a Great Leader," where she presents three key questions that distinguish great leaders. Her work focuses on helping leaders adapt to increasing complexity, uncertainty, and rapid change in the modern business world. She has extensive experience working with C-suite executives and boards across various industries to develop leadership capabilities. Torres emphasises the importance of leaders being able to navigate ambiguity, build diverse networks, and continuously evolve their approaches rather than relying solely on traditional leadership models.

SEPTEMBER 7

"How long are you going to wait before you demand the best for yourself and in no instance bypass the discriminations of reason?

...

What kind of teacher, then, are you still waiting for in order to refer your self-improvement to him?"
- Epictetus[253]

---

[253] Epictetus challenges readers to stop delaying their commitment to philosophical wisdom and virtuous living, asking why continue to postpone demanding excellence from themselves when they already know what they should do.

The Manual [Enchiridion] of Epictetus, Section 51, circa 125 CE.

Epictetus (c. 50-135 CE) was a Greek Stoic philosopher who, despite being born into slavery, became one of the most influential teachers of ancient philosophy through his profound insights on freedom, virtue, and human agency. After gaining his freedom, he established a school of philosophy in Nicopolis where he taught that true liberty comes not from external circumstances but from understanding what is within our control versus what is not - the fundamental principle of his philosophy. His teachings, recorded by his student Arrian in works like the "Discourses" and the "Enchiridion" (Handbook), emphasised that we cannot control external events but can always control our responses, judgments, and attitudes toward them. Epictetus taught that suffering comes from our opinions about events rather than the events themselves, and that by focusing solely on our choices, actions, and character, we can achieve genuine tranquillity and freedom regardless of our external situation. His philosophy of practical Stoicism, forged through personal experience of both literal and philosophical liberation, continues to influence cognitive behavioural therapy and modern approaches to resilience and mental well-being.

SEPTEMBER 8

"What kind of person will you have to become to get all you want?"
- Jim Rohn[254]

---

[254] "Write down the kinds of skills you'll need to develop and the knowledge you'll need to gain." Rohn suggests. "The answers will give you some new goals for personal development. Remember this rule: Income Rarely Exceeds Personal Development."
7 Strategies For Wealth And Happiness: Power Ideas from America's Foremost Business Philosopher, Jim Rohn, 1996.

Jim Rohn (1930-2009) was an entrepreneur, author and motivational speaker who became one of the most influential figures in the personal development industry. His parents owned and worked a farm in Caldwell, Idaho, where Rohn grew up as an only child. A successful entrepreneur, author, and motivational speaker, he achieved his first million by 31, thanks to his dedication, resilience, and keen insights. His rags to riches story played a large part in his work, which influenced others in the personal development industry, and he was the recipient of the 1985 National Speakers Association CPAE Award for excellence in speaking. He frequently stressed the notion that in order to attain success an individual must continually strive to improve themselves, firmly believing that investing in self-education, self-reflection, skill development is the gateway to unleashing a person's capabilities. Rohn is remembered for his philosophy of personal responsibility and his famous quote: "Formal education will make you a living; self-education will make you a fortune."

SEPTEMBER 9

"How are you developing yourself as a leader?"
- Bill George[255]

---

[255] In the same vein as self-care, the responsibility for your ongoing education is yours alone. Does this development need to be a rigid, structured endeavour? Not if you don't want it to be. It is whatever works for you. Nobel prize winning physicist Richard Feynman's advice was to "Study hard what interests you the most in the most undisciplined, irreverent and original manner possible."

True North, Bill George, Talks at Google, October 23, 2008.

Bill George is a prominent business leader, author, and Harvard Business School professor who is widely recognised as one of the foremost authorities on authentic leadership. He was the CEO of Medtronic from 1991 to 2001 where he achieved remarkable success. George is the author of best-selling books including "Authentic Leadership" and "True North" which have become foundational texts in leadership development. His concept of authentic leadership emphasises that effective leaders must be true to themselves, understand their values and purpose, and lead from a place of genuine conviction rather than trying to emulate others. His speeches convey powerful principles: organisations can only achieve their full potential by developing authentic leaders inside them; each individual must cultivate True North, a moral compass to successfully navigate the challenges of leadership. After leaving Medtronic, George became a professor at Harvard Business School where he teaches leadership courses and continues his research on authentic leadership development. He has served on the boards of Goldman Sachs, Novartis, Target, ExxonMobil, and Mayo Clinic. His work focuses on helping leaders discover their authentic selves, develop their moral compass, and create organisations where people can find meaning and purpose in their work. George's influence extends beyond academia, as he's sought after as a speaker and advisor for his insights on leadership in an era where trust and authenticity are increasingly valued in business.

SEPTEMBER 10

"What is the diversity measure of your personal and professional stakeholder network?"
- Roselinde Torres[256]

---

[256] Torres explains, "Great leaders understand that having a more diverse network is a source of pattern identification at greater levels and also of solutions, because you have people that are thinking differently than you are."
What it takes to be a great leader, Roselinde Torres, TED@BCG San Francisco, October 2013.

Roselinde Torres is a leadership expert, author, and senior partner at Boston Consulting Group (BCG), where she leads the firm's leadership development work globally. She's known for her research on what makes leaders effective in today's rapidly changing business environment and has developed frameworks for understanding 21st-century leadership challenges. Torres is perhaps best known for her popular TED Talk "What It Takes to Be a Great Leader," where she presents three key questions that distinguish great leaders. Her work focuses on helping leaders adapt to increasing complexity, uncertainty, and rapid change in the modern business world. She has extensive experience working with C-suite executives and boards across various industries to develop leadership capabilities. Torres emphasises the importance of leaders being able to navigate ambiguity, build diverse networks, and continuously evolve their approaches rather than relying solely on traditional leadership models.

SEPTEMBER 11

"What will the people who don't hold you in highest regard say about you?"
- Stanley McChrystal[257]

---

[257] How we are perceived, the external image presented to the world, differs from our self-perception. The image of the person you think you are does not exist outside of your mind. This realisation can be surprising, like the moment don't recognise yourself in a photo. A different version of you exists in the mind of everyone you have ever met.

Technology CEO Mike Zani uses the analogy of a T-shirt to describe the problem. You can see what is on the front of your shirt—it is all your positive qualities that people tell you about, and which have led to your success. But you cannot see what is on the back, those things which people might be reluctant to say to your face. If we are to improve, we will need to encourage people to tell us what is on the back of our T-shirts.

Tools of Titans: The Tactics, Routines, and Habits of Billionaires, Icons, and World-Class Performers, Timothy Ferriss, 2016.

Stanley McChrystal is a retired U.S. Army four-star general who became one of America's most respected military leaders and organisational transformation experts. McChrystal spent 34 years in the Army, rising to become the commander of U.S. and International Security Assistance Forces in Afghanistan from 2009 to 2010. He is perhaps best known for leading Joint Special Operations Command (JSOC) from 2003 to 2008, where he revolutionised counterterrorism operations in Iraq and Afghanistan by transforming traditional military hierarchies into agile, networked organisations capable of rapid decision-making and execution. McChrystal's leadership philosophy centres on what he calls "Team of Teams" - the idea that in complex, rapidly changing environments, organisations must become networks of small, empowered teams rather than traditional command-and-control structures. This approach, detailed in his bestselling book "Team of Teams: New Rules of Engagement for a Complex World," has been widely adopted by businesses and organisations seeking to become more adaptive and responsive. After retiring from the military, McChrystal founded the McChrystal Group, a leadership consulting firm that helps organisations apply military-tested leadership principles to business challenges. He has also written several other influential books, including "Leaders: Myth and Reality," which examines different leadership styles throughout history, and "My Share of the Task," a memoir of his military service. McChrystal currently teaches at Yale University and serves on various boards, continuing to share insights about leadership, teamwork, and organisational change.

SEPTEMBER 12

"How is your environment design impacting your choices? And what will you do to improve it?"
- James Clear[258]

---

[258] "You may think that you control most of your choices, but the truth is that a large portion of your actions every day are simply a response to the environment design around you." Clear explains. "But you can take control. "By changing your surroundings," he writes, "you can place a hurdle in the way of bad behaviours and remove the barriers to good ones. I like to refer to this strategy as environment design."
How to Improve Your Health and Productivity Without Thinking, James Clear, jamesclear.com.

James Clear is an author, speaker, and entrepreneur best known for his book "Atomic Habits," which became a bestseller and popularised the concept of making small, incremental changes to build better habits and break bad ones. Clear focuses on the science of habit formation, emphasising how tiny improvements compound over time to create remarkable results. His approach centres on four key principles: making habits obvious, attractive, easy, and satisfying. Before his writing career took off, Clear was a successful entrepreneur and has a background in photography and business. He writes regularly about habits, decision-making, and continuous improvement on his website and newsletter, which has attracted millions of readers. Clear's work draws from psychology, neuroscience, and behavioural economics to provide practical strategies for personal and professional development, making complex research accessible to everyday readers seeking to improve their lives through better systems and habits.

SEPTEMBER 13

"Did I win? Did I lose? Those are the wrong questions. The correct question is: Did I make my best effort? That's what matters. The rest of it just gets in the way."
- John Wooden[259]

---

[259] Wooden's question echoes the philosopher Epictetus who writes: "The chief task in life is simply this: to identify and separate matters so that I can say clearly to myself which are externals not under my control, and which have to do with the choices I actually control."

Wooden: A Lifetime of Observations and Reflections On and Off the Court, John Wooden, 1997.

John Wooden (1910-2010) was an American basketball coach and teacher who became a legendary figure in college sports, known as much for his character and wisdom as for his unprecedented success. As head coach at UCLA from 1948 to 1975, he led the Bruins to an extraordinary 10 NCAA championships in 12 years, including seven consecutive titles from 1967 to 1973—a feat unmatched in college basketball. Beyond his coaching achievements, Wooden was revered for his "Pyramid of Success," a philosophical framework emphasizing character traits like industriousness, friendship, and self-control as the foundation for achievement. His famous "Woodenisms"—pithy sayings like "Be quick, but don't hurry" and "Success is peace of mind in knowing you did your best"—became widely quoted principles that transcended sports. Even after retiring from coaching, Wooden continued to inspire through his books and speaking, embodying the ideal of the teacher-coach who viewed developing young people's character as more important than winning games.

SEPTEMBER 14

*"How is my current network serving me?
Are there any holes?
Is there anyone in my network with whom I want to
develop stronger relationships?"
- Kathleen Kram*[260]

---

[260] Kram suggests developing a network or "team of mentors", and that you should check your mentoring team annually, even if there haven't been significant changes in your life. Kram suggests asking yourself -
- How is my current network serving me? Are there any holes?
- Is there anyone in my network with whom I want to develop stronger relationships?
- Is there anything in front of me that would benefit from greater assistance?
This Is What The Best Mentors Do, Dr. Ruth Gotian, Forbes, Feb 23, 2021.
Kathleen (Kathy) E. Kram is the Shipley Professor in Management at the Boston University School of Management and a pioneering researcher in the field of mentoring and organisational development. She is best known for her seminal work "Mentoring at Work: Developmental Relationships in Organizational Life," which has become a foundational text in understanding workplace mentoring relationships. Her primary interests are in the areas of adult development, relational learning, mentoring, diversity issues in executive development, leadership, and organisational change processes. With thousands of citations of her work, Kram has significantly shaped how organisations understand and implement mentoring programs. She is currently exploring the nature of peer coaching, mentoring circles, and developmental networks as part of her ongoing program of research on relational learning, and leadership development.

SEPTEMBER 15

"What am I working to get better at?"
- Ryan Holiday[261]

---

[261] The aim, as writer George Leonard wrote, is "to go on learning prodigiously from birth to death". "Pick up a book on a topic you know next to nothing about." Holiday writes. "Put yourself in rooms where you're the least knowledgeable person. Technology has eliminated the barriers to learning. The information available to us has never been easier to access. There is no excuse for ever ending the process of improving."

What If I Said No? (And Other Questions to Consider Daily), Ryan Holiday, Medium, August 21, 2019.

Ryan Holiday is the bestselling author of "Trust Me, I'm Lying", "The Obstacle Is the Way", "Ego Is the Enemy", "Conspiracy", and other books about marketing, culture, and the human condition. Holiday grew up in Sacramento, California, with his father as a police detective and his mother a high school principal. He dropped out of the University of California, Riverside in his sophomore year to pursue marketing and writing. He has written 12 best-selling books, covering topics including philosophy, marketing, history, and how to live well, with his work particularly focused on making ancient Stoic philosophy accessible to modern readers. His work has been translated into over 30 languages and has appeared everywhere from the New York Times to Fast Company. His company, Brass Check, has advised companies such as Google, TASER, and Complex, as well as multiplatinum musicians and some of the biggest authors in the world. Holiday opened The Painted Porch Bookshop in Bastrop, Texas with his wife during the pandemic, supporting local independent bookstores while continuing his mission to popularise Stoic wisdom.

SEPTEMBER 16

"How do we continually find inspiration so that we can inspire others?"
- Warren Berger[262]

---

[262] This question expands on an idea from polymath Albert Schweitzer. "In everyone's life, at some time," Schweitzer writes, "our inner fire goes out. It is then burst into flame by an encounter with another human being. We should all be thankful for those people who rekindle the inner spirit."
A More Beautiful Question: The Power of Inquiry to Spark Breakthrough Ideas, Warren Berger, 2014.

Warren Berger is an innovation expert and "questionologist" who has dedicated his career to exploring the transformative power of inquiry. He is the author or co-author of more than 12 books on innovation, including the bestseller "A More Beautiful Question: The Power of Inquiry to Spark Breakthrough Ideas" and the internationally acclaimed "Glimmer," which was named one of Business Week's Best Innovation and Design Books of the Year. Berger has studied hundreds of the world's foremost innovators, entrepreneurs, and creative thinkers to learn how they ask questions, generate original ideas, and solve problems. His work appears in prestigious publications including Fast Company, Harvard Business Review, Psychology Today, and The New York Times, and he has keynoted conferences for major organisations while serving as a guest lecturer at universities across the country. At the core of his philosophy is the belief that "questions are more important than answers," positioning questioning as a fundamental skill for breakthrough thinking and problem-solving in both business and personal contexts.

SEPTEMBER 17

*"Healthy striving is self-focused:
'How can I improve?'
Perfectionism is other-focused:
'What will they think?'"*
- Brené Brown[263]

---

[263] Artist, teacher and writer Julia Cameron puts it this way: "The perfectionist is never satisfied. The perfectionist never says, 'This is pretty good. I think I'll just keep going.' To the perfectionist, there is always room for improvement. The perfectionist calls this humility. In reality, it is egotism. It is pride that makes us want to write a perfect script, paint a perfect painting, perform a perfect audition monologue. Perfectionism is not a quest for the best. It is a pursuit of the worst in ourselves, the part that tells us that nothing we do will ever be good enough - that we should try again."
The Gifts of Imperfection, Brené Brown, 2010.

Brené Brown is a research professor, author, and public speaker who has become one of the most influential voices on vulnerability, shame, courage, and leadership. Brown spent over two decades studying courage, vulnerability, shame, and empathy as a researcher at the University of Houston Graduate College of Social Work. Her 2010 TED Talk "The Power of Vulnerability" became one of the most-viewed TED Talks of all time, catapulting her from academia into mainstream recognition and sparking a global conversation about the importance of embracing vulnerability as a source of strength rather than weakness. She has written several bestselling books including "Daring Greatly," "Rising Strong," and "Dare to Lead," which translate her research into practical insights for personal and professional development. Brown's work challenges cultural norms that equate vulnerability with weakness, instead arguing that vulnerability is essential for creativity, innovation, and meaningful connection. She has consulted with major organisations and leaders worldwide, helping to reshape how businesses approach leadership, team dynamics, and organisational culture. Her blend of rigorous research, personal storytelling, and practical application has made her a sought-after speaker and thought leader who continues to influence how people understand courage, authenticity, and human connection.

SEPTEMBER 18

"Does it still serve me?
Does it make me happier?
Does it make me healthier?
Does it make me accomplish whatever I set out to
accomplish?"
- Naval Ravikant[264]

---

[264] "It's really important to be able to uncondition yourself," Ravikant writes, " to be able to take your habits apart and say, "Okay, this is a habit I probably picked up when I was a toddler trying to get my parent's attention. Now I've reinforced it and reinforced it, and I call it a part of my identity. Does it still serve me? Does it make me happier? Does it make me healthier? Does it make me accomplish whatever I set out to accomplish?"

The Almanack of Naval Ravikant: A Guide to Wealth and Happiness, Eric Jorgenson, 2020.

Naval Ravikant is a Silicon Valley entrepreneur, angel investor, and philosopher who has become one of the most influential voices on wealth creation, happiness, and decision-making. He's the co-founder and former CEO of AngelList, the platform that democratised startup investing and job matching in tech. As an angel investor, Naval has backed numerous successful companies including Twitter, Uber, Yammer, and Postmates, establishing himself as one of the most successful early-stage investors in Silicon Valley. Beyond his business success, he's gained a massive following for his philosophical insights on wealth, happiness, and life, often shared through Twitter threads, podcasts, and interviews. His thoughts were compiled into the popular book "The Almanack of Naval Ravikant," compiled by Eric Jorgenson. Naval is known for his aphoristic wisdom and his emphasis on building specific knowledge, taking accountability, and leveraging technology to create value. He advocates for principles like reading voraciously, thinking independently, and focusing on long-term compounding in both wealth and knowledge. His blend of practical business acumen with Eastern philosophy and rational thinking has made him a guru figure for entrepreneurs and investors seeking financial success and personal fulfillment.

SEPTEMBER 19

"How quickly can you learn from your mistakes?"
- James Clear[265]

---

[265] The ability to learn rapidly, including from your mistakes, is the key to growth. Clear echoes legendary investor Charlie Munger who observed, "I constantly see people rise in life who are not the smartest, sometimes not even the most diligent, but they are learning machines. They go to bed every night a little wiser than they were when they got up and boy does that help, particularly when you have a long run ahead of you." Become a perpetual learning machine.

3-2-1 Newsletter, James Clear, August 24, 2023.

James Clear is an author, speaker, and entrepreneur best known for his book "Atomic Habits," which became a bestseller and popularised the concept of making small, incremental changes to build better habits and break bad ones. Clear focuses on the science of habit formation, emphasising how tiny improvements compound over time to create remarkable results. His approach centres on four key principles: making habits obvious, attractive, easy, and satisfying. Before his writing career took off, Clear was a successful entrepreneur and has a background in photography and business. He writes regularly about habits, decision-making, and continuous improvement on his website and newsletter, which has attracted millions of readers. Clear's work draws from psychology, neuroscience, and behavioural economics to provide practical strategies for personal and professional development, making complex research accessible to everyday readers seeking to improve their lives through better systems and habits.

SEPTEMBER 20

*"The question isn't 'How do I feel confident?'
The question is 'What can I do to create experiences
that build my confidence?' Confidence is
found in the doing."*
- Jefferson Fisher[266]

---

[266] *The Next Conversation: Argue Less, Talk More*, Jefferson Fisher, 2025.

Jefferson Fisher is an American lawyer, podcast host, and author who hosts The Jefferson Fisher Podcast. Fisher has become a trial lawyer, speaker, and best-selling author with millions around the world following him for his practical communication advice. In 2022 he began making videos of practical communication tips to help people argue less and talk more. His approach combines his courtroom experience with accessible advice for everyday conversations. Fisher's book "The Next Conversation: Argue Less, Talk More" became a New York Times best seller. The book gives actionable strategies and phrases that will make you a more direct, confident, and productive communicator, offering a tried-and-true framework to transform your life and relationships by improving your next conversation. He's a sought-after speaker at Fortune 500 companies and governmental agencies, and hundreds of thousands of people subscribe to his actionable email newsletter and podcast. His mission is to help people build deeper connections, gain confidence, and take control of their voice.

SEPTEMBER 21

"And how's that working out for you?"
- Oliver Burkeman[267]

---

[267] Burkeman explains, "What makes AHTWOFY? so powerful is that it drills down to the question of what motivates our counterproductive behaviours - the secret emotional payoffs we get from procrastinating, or holding ourselves to perfectionistic standards, or living an overly cautious life, or working to the point of burnout, etcetera."

The Imperfectionist, Oliver Burkeman, June 27, 2023.

Oliver Burkeman is an author and journalist known for his thoughtful, often contrarian approach to productivity and happiness. He wrote the popular "This Column Will Change Your Life" for The Guardian for over a decade, where he explored psychology, productivity culture, and the pursuit of well-being with a healthy dose of scepticism toward self-help orthodoxies. His most acclaimed book, "Four Thousand Weeks: Time Management for Mortals", challenges conventional productivity advice by arguing that our limited time on earth—roughly 4,000 weeks for the average human lifespan—should lead us to embrace our constraints rather than constantly seek optimisation. Burkeman's work stands out in the self-improvement space for its philosophical depth, dry humour, and willingness to question whether the relentless pursuit of efficiency and happiness might actually be counterproductive, offering instead a more realistic and accepting approach to human limitations.

SEPTEMBER 22

*"The next time you hear yourself saying,
"I'm just no good at ...,"
ask yourself, "Why not?"*
- Marshall Goldsmith[268]

---

[268] "Believing that your qualities are carved in stone - the fixed mindset - creates an urgency to prove yourself over and over." Carol Dweck writes. "If you have only a certain amount of intelligence, a certain personality, and a certain moral character - well, then you'd better prove that you have a healthy dose of them. It simply wouldn't do to look or feel deficient in these most basic characteristics. ... There's another mindset in which these traits are not simply a hand you're dealt and have to live with, always trying to convince yourself and others that you have a royal flush when you're secretly worried it's a pair of tens. In this mindset, the hand you're dealt is just the starting point for development. This growth mindset is based on the belief that your basic qualities are things you can cultivate through your efforts. Although people may differ in every which way - in their initial talents and aptitudes, interests, or temperaments - everyone can change and grow through application and experience. ... Do people with this mindset believe that anyone can be anything, that anyone with proper motivation or education can become Einstein or Beethoven? No, but they believe that a person's true potential is unknown (and unknowable); that it's impossible to foresee what can be accomplished with years of passion, toil, and training." *Mindset: The New Psychology of Success*, Carol S Dweck, 2008.
What Got You Here, Won't Get You There, Marshall Goldsmith, 2007.

Marshall Goldsmith is a renowned executive coach and leadership expert, best known for his work with Fortune 500 CEOs and senior executives. He's the author of several influential books, including the bestseller "What Got You Here Won't Get You There," which explores how the behaviours of leaders that create success at one level may actually hinder advancement to higher positions. Goldsmith pioneered the concept of "feedforward" (focusing on future possibilities rather than past mistakes) and developed systematic approaches to behavioural change in leadership. He's consistently ranked among the top leadership thinkers globally and has coached hundreds of major corporate leaders.

SEPTEMBER 23

"If you were going to invest now in your future best self, where would you put your time and your energy?"
- Robert Waldinger[269]

---

[269] *What makes a good life? Lessons from the longest study on happiness*, Robert Waldinger, TEDxBeaconStreet, November 2015.

Robert Waldinger is a psychiatrist, professor at Harvard Medical School, and the current director of the Harvard Study of Adult Development, one of the longest-running studies of human happiness and well-being ever conducted. The Harvard Study of Adult Development is a longitudinal study that began in 1938 and reveals that the strength of our connections with others can predict the health of both our bodies and our brains as we go through life. Waldinger is co-author of the New York Times bestseller "The Good Life: Lessons from the World's Longest Scientific Study of Happiness," which distils decades of research showing that the level of satisfaction with relationships in midlife is now recognised as a good predictor of healthy aging. His famous TED Talk on what makes a good life has been viewed millions of times, and his work demonstrates that strong relationships are more important for long-term happiness and health than wealth, fame, or career success.

SEPTEMBER 24

"Who do you spend time with?"
- Ryan Holiday[270]

---

[270] "Goethe would say 'Tell me who you spend time with and I will tell you who you are.' Holiday explains. "Who we know and what we do that influences more than any other factor, who we will become. Because what you do puts you around people, and the people you're around affects what you do. Think about your friends and colleagues: do they inspire you, validate you, or drag you down? We seem to understand that a young kid who spends time with kids who don't want to go anywhere in life, probably isn't going to go anywhere in life. What we understand less is that an adult who spends time with other adults who tolerate crappy jobs, or unhappy lifestyles is going to find themselves making similar choices. Same goes for what you read, what you watch, what you think about. Your life comes to resemble its environment (Ben Hardy calls this the proximity effect). So choose your surroundings wisely."

12 Questions That Will Change Your Life, Ryan Holiday, Medium, January 2, 2018.

Ryan Holiday is the bestselling author of "Trust Me, I'm Lying", "The Obstacle Is the Way", "Ego Is the Enemy", "Conspiracy", and other books about marketing, culture, and the human condition. Holiday grew up in Sacramento, California, with his father as a police detective and his mother a high school principal. He dropped out of the University of California, Riverside in his sophomore year to pursue marketing and writing. He has written 12 best-selling books, covering topics including philosophy, marketing, history, and how to live well, with his work particularly focused on making ancient Stoic philosophy accessible to modern readers. His work has been translated into over 30 languages and has appeared everywhere from the New York Times to Fast Company. His company, Brass Check, has advised companies such as Google, TASER, and Complex, as well as multiplatinum musicians and some of the biggest authors in the world. Holiday opened The Painted Porch Bookshop in Bastrop, Texas with his wife during the pandemic, supporting local independent bookstores while continuing his mission to popularise Stoic wisdom.

SEPTEMBER 25

"What do I currently do that adds the most quality and meaning to my life? How can I do more of that (and less of what detracts from that quality)?"
- Jordan Peterson[271]

---

[271] *What are some deep, profound, thought-provoking questions to ponder over?*, Jordan B. Peterson, Quora, 2014.

Jordan B. Peterson is a clinical psychologist, professor, and author who gained international prominence for his views on free speech, political correctness, and personal responsibility. He taught at Harvard University and the University of Toronto, specialising in personality psychology, psychopathology, and the psychology of religious and ideological belief. His bestselling book "12 Rules for Life: An Antidote to Chaos" combines psychology, philosophy, and personal anecdotes to offer practical advice for living a meaningful life, emphasizing individual responsibility, self-improvement, and traditional values. His second book, "Beyond Order: 12 More Rules for Life," continues these themes. Peterson's lectures and online content focus on topics like mythology, religion, personal development, and the psychological significance of stories and archetypes.

SEPTEMBER 26

"Question yourself every day.
Ask yourself:
Who am I?
What have I learned?
What have I created?
What forward progress have I made?
Who have I helped?
What am I doing to improve myself - today -
to get better, faster, stronger, healthier, smarter?"
- Jocko Willink[272]

---

[272] *Discipline Equals Freedom: Field Manual*, Jocko Willink, 2017.

Jocko Willink is a retired U.S. Navy SEAL officer, author, and leadership consultant who has become one of the most recognised voices on discipline, leadership, and mental toughness. Willink served 20 years in the Navy SEALs, including leading SEAL Team Three's Task Unit Bruiser during the Battle of Ramadi in Iraq, one of the most decorated special operations units of the Iraq War. After retiring from the military, he co-authored the bestselling book "Extreme Ownership: How U.S. Navy SEALs Lead and Win" with fellow SEAL Leif Babin, which translates battlefield leadership principles into business and personal contexts. The book's central philosophy—that leaders must take complete responsibility for everything in their sphere of influence—has influenced countless executives and organisations. Willink hosts the popular "Jocko Podcast," where he discusses leadership, discipline, and mental fortitude, and emphasising his philosophy that "discipline equals freedom." He has written several other books including "Discipline Equals Freedom" and children's books teaching leadership principles. Through his company Echelon Front, he provides leadership consulting to businesses and organisations. Known for his no-nonsense approach, intense work ethic, and philosophy of taking ownership of problems rather than making excuses, Willink has become a cult figure among those seeking to develop mental toughness and leadership skills.

SEPTEMBER 27

*"Ask yourself:
When was the last time you had three or even four completely uninterrupted hours to yourself and your work?"*
- Jason Fried[273]

---

[273] Peter Drucker revealed, "If there is any one "secret" of effectiveness, it is concentration. Effective executives do first things first and they do one thing at a time." Drucker explained that success stems from quality, uninterrupted time. "This is the "secret" of those people who "do so many things" and apparently so many difficult things." he writes. "They do only one at a time. As a result, they need much less time in the end than the rest of us."
It Doesn't Have to Be Crazy at Work, Jason Fried, 2018.

Jason Fried is the co-founder and CEO of 37signals, the company behind popular products like Basecamp (a project management tool) and HEY (an email service). He's been running 37signals for 23 years, having launched Basecamp in 2004. 37signals operates as an unconventional company with fewer than 80 employees serving over 100,000 customers, generating tens of millions in profit annually without investors or a board. Fried is also a prolific author, having co-written several influential business books including "REWORK," "Remote," and "It Doesn't Have to Be Crazy at Work," and hosts the REWORK podcast. He's known for advocating alternative approaches to business growth, work culture, and company management, often challenging conventional startup wisdom about fundraising and scaling.

SEPTEMBER 28

"How are you spending your time? If we took at look at your calendar, how much time is spent reacting or responding to incoming, how much is under your control, and how much is focused on the hard part?"
- Seth Godin[274]

---

[274] A test comes from former US Secretary of State John Foster Dulles who said, "The measure of success is not whether you have a tough problem to deal with, but whether it is the same problem you had last year". Weaponise your calendar. Writer Annie Dillard says, "A schedule defends from chaos and whim" and "it is a scaffolding on which a worker can stand and labor".
Five useful questions, Seth Godin, seths.blog, June 14, 2021.
Seth Godin is a bestselling author, entrepreneur, and marketing guru who has fundamentally changed how people think about marketing, leadership, and the spread of ideas. He's written over 20 books, including influential titles like "Purple Cow," which popularised the concept that businesses must be remarkable to succeed, "The Tipping Point" predecessor "Unleashing the Ideavirus," and "Linchpin," which argues that indispensable employees are those who bring creativity and humanity to their work. Godin founded several companies, including Yoyodyne (one of the first internet marketing companies, sold to Yahoo!) and Squidoo, and the altMBA, an intensive online leadership workshop. His daily blog, which he's maintained for decades, reaches millions of readers with insights on marketing, culture, and human behaviour. Godin is known for coining terms like "permission marketing" (marketing to people who want to be marketed to) and advocating for authentic, story-driven approaches over traditional advertising. His philosophy emphasises that in the modern economy, playing it safe is actually the riskiest strategy, and that success comes from being different, generous, and willing to make a difference. He's also a sought-after speaker who challenges conventional business wisdom and encourages people to embrace change and lead rather than follow.

SEPTEMBER 29

"Every time you have to make a choice about anything, think 'Does this go toward or away from what I want?' Always choose what goes toward what you want."
- Barbara Sher[275]

---

[275] The question echoes philosopher and psychologist William James. "Seize the very first possible opportunity to act on every resolution you make," he writes, "and on every emotional prompting you may experience in the direction of the habits you aspire to gain."

I Could Do Anything If I Only Knew What It Was: How to Discover What You Really Want and How to Get It Barbara Sher, 1994.

Barbara Sher (1935-2020) was a pioneering career counsellor and bestselling author who is often called "the godmother of life coaching." She is best known for her influential book "Wishcraft: How to Get What You Really Want", which became a groundbreaking guide for helping people identify their dreams and create practical plans to achieve them. Sher was dedicated to showing people how to do what they love, developing Success Teams and providing ideas, information, contacts and a cheering section that wouldn't quit. Her books have sold millions of copies and been translated into many languages. Sher's approach focused on helping people discover their authentic interests and talents, overcome resistance and fear, and create actionable steps toward their goals. Her work emphasised the importance of community support and practical problem-solving rather than just positive thinking. Through her workshops, seminars, and books, she helped countless individuals transform their careers and lives, establishing many of the foundational principles that would later become standard in the life coaching industry.

SEPTEMBER 30

"Are you proud of the choices you are making at home? Are you proud of the choices you are making at work?"
- Connie Podesta[276]

---

[276] Enduring personal and organisational effectiveness requires learning to care of yourself and those you lead. In his commencement speech at Georgia Tech in 1996, former President and CEO of Coca-Cola Enterprises Brian Dyson reminds us why self-care is important: "Imagine life as a game in which you are juggling some five balls in the air. You name them: work, family, health, friends and spirit – and you're keeping all of these in the air. You will soon understand that work is a rubber ball. If you drop it, it will bounce back. But the other four balls – family, health, friends and spirit – are made of glass. If you drop one of these, they will be irrevocably scuffed, marked, nicked, damaged or even shattered. They will never be the same. You must understand that and strive for balance in your life."

Two Questions to Ask Yourself Every Morning, Greg McKeown, gregmckeown.com, October 23, 2014.

Connie Podesta is a keynote speaker, human behavior expert, and award-winning author who specialises in sales, leadership development, and organisational change. Podesta is an expert in the psychology of human behavior as it applies to sales, leadership, change, accountability and engagement. Known for her comedic and entertaining presentation style, she focuses on helping leaders develop the attitudes, mindsets, and strategies necessary to build high-performing teams and drive organisational success through understanding human behavior and motivation.

OCTOBER

LEAD CHANGE

OCTOBER 1

"Why?"
- Daryl Conner[277]

---

[277] Daryl Conner starts with the question: *"Why?"* People will resist change, and that resistance will be articulated as "why?" Conner suggests that senior management need to prepare very thorough answers to the following questions -
- What's wrong with the way we've been doing things?
- Why were we doing them wrong before?
- What will happen to me?
- When?
- What can I do about it?
- What is expected of me?
- What does it mean in my day-to-day job?
- What will management or leadership do about it?
- If I encounter problems, what do I do, to whom do I turn?

Managing at the Speed of Change, Daryl Conner, 1992.

Daryl Conner is a pioneering change management expert and founder/chairman of Conner Partners, best known for his groundbreaking book "Managing at the Speed of Change". Conner identified that "the single most important factor to managing change successfully is the degree to which people demonstrate resilience: the capacity to absorb high levels of change while displaying minimal dysfunctional behaviour." He introduced influential concepts to the change management field, including the "burning platform" metaphor that has been used for nearly 30 years to describe high urgency regarding change initiatives. For over forty-five years, Conner has educated and advised strategic leaders and veteran change practitioners in many of the world's most successful organisations, helping them understand and navigate transformational change challenges. His work focuses on how organisations and individuals can build resilience to thrive during periods of intense change rather than simply survive them. Conner's approach emphasises that successful change management is less about what to change and more about how to change, making resilience the cornerstone of effective organisational transformation.

OCTOBER 2

"What is the change you seek to make?
Are you here to make a contribution?
Or are you here to take something?
Are you here to do what you are told - or are you
here to question and to make things different?"
- Seth Godin[278]

---

[278] *Failing On Our Way To Mastery: Seth Godin on The Knowledge Project*, Shane Parrish, 23 February 2021.

Seth Godin is a bestselling author, entrepreneur, and marketing guru who has fundamentally changed how people think about marketing, leadership, and the spread of ideas. He's written over 20 books, including influential titles like "Purple Cow," which popularised the concept that businesses must be remarkable to succeed, "The Tipping Point" predecessor "Unleashing the Ideavirus," and "Linchpin," which argues that indispensable employees are those who bring creativity and humanity to their work. Godin founded several companies, including Yoyodyne (one of the first internet marketing companies, sold to Yahoo!) and Squidoo, and the altMBA, an intensive online leadership workshop. His daily blog, which he's maintained for decades, reaches millions of readers with insights on marketing, culture, and human behaviour. Godin is known for coining terms like "permission marketing" (marketing to people who want to be marketed to) and advocating for authentic, story-driven approaches over traditional advertising. His philosophy emphasises that in the modern economy, playing it safe is actually the riskiest strategy, and that success comes from being different, generous, and willing to make a difference. He's also a sought-after speaker who challenges conventional business wisdom and encourages people to embrace change and lead rather than follow.

OCTOBER 3

*"What's the *real* reason for change?"*
- Michael Bungay Stanier[279]

---

[279] Quoting Margaret Heffernan, Bungay Stanier writes, "'If you're doing a cost-cutting program. Call it that. You know, let's not pussyfoot around. You fool nobody, and you just make people incredibly cynical.' But put aside the marketing and the spin for a moment that you might be using to influence others. Do you know the real reason for change? Do you know what really matters to your CEO, your change sponsor, the power brokers in the SLT, your boss, and the other figures of influence and power? It's one thing to figure out how to pitch a transformation project to an audience. It's another one to fall for your own PR and not know what's really going on, or why."

*What's the *real* reason for change?*, The Change Signal, thechangesignal.com, March 6, 2025.

Michael Bungay Stanier is an author, leadership coach, and business consultant best known for his bestselling book "The Coaching Habit: Say Less, Ask More & Change the Way You Lead Forever." He founded Box of Crayons, a learning and development company that helps organisations transform from advice-driven to curiosity-led, and currently leads MBS.works, a place where people find clarity, confidence and community to be a force for change. His work focuses on helping leaders develop better coaching skills through practical, science-backed approaches that emphasise asking powerful questions rather than giving advice. His philosophy is captured in his haiku-like summary: "Tell less and ask more. Your advice is not as good as you think it is." Known as a compelling speaker and facilitator who combines practicality, humour, and high audience engagement, Stanier has become a prominent voice in the leadership development space, helping countless managers and executives shift from being advice-givers to becoming more effective coaches who unlock potential in their teams through curiosity and thoughtful questioning.

OCTOBER 4

"Where are you looking to anticipate the next change to your business model or your life?"
- Roselinde Torres[280]

---

[280] "The answer to this question is on your calendar." Torres explains. "Who are you spending time with? On what topics? Where are you traveling? What are you reading? And then how are you distilling this into understanding potential discontinuities, and then making a decision to do something right now so that you're prepared and ready? Great leaders are not head-down. They see around corners, shaping their future, not just reacting to it."

What it takes to be a great leader, Roselinde Torres, TED@BCG San Francisco, October 2013.

Roselinde Torres is a leadership expert, author, and senior partner at Boston Consulting Group (BCG), where she leads the firm's leadership development work globally. She's known for her research on what makes leaders effective in today's rapidly changing business environment and has developed frameworks for understanding 21st-century leadership challenges. Torres is perhaps best known for her popular TED Talk "What It Takes to Be a Great Leader," where she presents three key questions that distinguish great leaders. Her work focuses on helping leaders adapt to increasing complexity, uncertainty, and rapid change in the modern business world. She has extensive experience working with C-suite executives and boards across various industries to develop leadership capabilities. Torres emphasises the importance of leaders being able to navigate ambiguity, build diverse networks, and continuously evolve their approaches rather than relying solely on traditional leadership models.

OCTOBER 5

"If you're actually proposing something thoughtful and practical, perhaps you could answer three questions:
And then what happens? After we take this action, after you shut down that agency, eliminate that division or launch this new project, what will happen after that?
How will that work? What are the mechanics involved, the ones that don't suspend the laws of physics or organizational behavior that will support this new way forward?
Why? Can you explain, beyond your reality-suspending confidence, why the system will respond to your approach?"
- Seth Godin[281]

---

281 *Three more questions*, Seth Godin, seth.blog, January 12, 2023.

Seth Godin is a bestselling author, entrepreneur, and marketing guru who has fundamentally changed how people think about marketing, leadership, and the spread of ideas. He's written over 20 books, including influential titles like "Purple Cow," which popularised the concept that businesses must be remarkable to succeed, "The Tipping Point" predecessor "Unleashing the Ideavirus," and "Linchpin," which argues that indispensable employees are those who bring creativity and humanity to their work. Godin founded several companies, including Yoyodyne (one of the first internet marketing companies, sold to Yahoo!) and Squidoo, and the altMBA, an intensive online leadership workshop. His daily blog, which he's maintained for decades, reaches millions of readers with insights on marketing, culture, and human behaviour. Godin is known for coining terms like "permission marketing" (marketing to people who want to be marketed to) and advocating for authentic, story-driven approaches over traditional advertising. His philosophy emphasises that in the modern economy, playing it safe is actually the riskiest strategy, and that success comes from being different, generous, and willing to make a difference. He's also a sought-after speaker who challenges conventional business wisdom and encourages people to embrace change and lead rather than follow.

OCTOBER 6

*"Is everyone clear on the plan
and their role in it?"*
- Alan Mulally[282]

---

[282] The question is paraphrased from Mulally's "Working Together" philosophy. Consultant Mark Kenny summarises Mulally's approach -

"One, everyone knows the plan for the team (or company) to succeed – everyone. There is absolutely no confusion by anyone on your team or anywhere in your organization. Everyone knows what must be done. Even the part-time receptionist. ... Communicating the plan never stops. Everyone knows.

Two, how people treat each other is crystal clear with zero tolerance. We treat each other with love, respect, listening, helping, appreciation. This means a list of specific behaviors that everyone knows and that you review at the start of EVERY meeting.

Three, you have a clear process and trust the process. Alan created business process reviews where every objective was color coded green/yellow/red. Everyone rated their own objective / initiative and shared the status once a week. More importantly, it was an environment of sharing where people were open about issues. No hidden issues. No secrets. And people have a spirit of helping each other solve problems. This means that you as the leader must create an environment where people can be vulnerable, open with issues, and rewarded for sharing. You must do this. Otherwise you are managing a secret."

Alan Mulally's Working Principles, markkennyspeaks.com, 18 May 2020.

Alan Mulally is a business executive best known for his transformational leadership roles at Boeing and Ford Motor Company. Mulally spent 37 years at Boeing, where he led the development of the Boeing 777 aircraft and eventually became CEO of Boeing Commercial Airplanes. His work at Boeing established him as an innovative leader who could manage complex engineering projects while fostering collaboration across large organisations. Mulally was recruited as CEO of Ford in 2006, just before the global financial crisis. While General Motors and Chrysler required government bailouts, he successfully led Ford through the recession without federal assistance, implementing his "One Ford" strategy that focused the company on a unified global vision. His turnaround of Ford is considered one of the greatest corporate transformations in business history, taking the company from near-bankruptcy to profitability and market leadership. Central to Mulally's leadership philosophy is what he calls the "Working Together Management System," which emphasises transparency, accountability, and collaborative problem-solving. Famous for his weekly Business Plan Review meetings where problems were openly discussed without blame, he created a culture where issues could be identified and resolved quickly. Since retiring from Ford in 2014, Mulally has served on various boards and continues to be sought after for his insights on leadership, organisational transformation, and manufacturing excellence.

OCTOBER 7

"What does powerful sponsorship look like?"
- Daryl Conner[283]

---

[283] Change without sponsorship remains activism, change with sponsorship can become transformation. Management consultant and author Bill Dettmer puts it like this: "When all is said and done, successful change depends at least as much (if not more) on the effectiveness of leadership and behavioural modification than on the technical and economic merits of the solution." The Logical Thinking Process: A Systems Approach to Complex Problem Solving, H. William Dettmer
Leading Successful Change in Disruptive Environments, Change Leaders Conference, September 29, 2020.

Daryl Conner is a pioneering change management expert and founder/chairman of Conner Partners, best known for his groundbreaking book "Managing at the Speed of Change". Conner identified that "the single most important factor to managing change successfully is the degree to which people demonstrate resilience: the capacity to absorb high levels of change while displaying minimal dysfunctional behaviour." He introduced influential concepts to the change management field, including the "burning platform" metaphor that has been used for nearly 30 years to describe high urgency regarding change initiatives. For over forty-five years, Conner has educated and advised strategic leaders and veteran change practitioners in many of the world's most successful organisations, helping them understand and navigate transformational change challenges. His work focuses on how organisations and individuals can build resilience to thrive during periods of intense change rather than simply survive them. Conner's approach emphasises that successful change management is less about what to change and more about how to change, making resilience the cornerstone of effective organisational transformation.

OCTOBER 8

"What change do I seek to make with this project?
What is my strategy to make this change happen?
Can I articulate it clearly?
What resistance should I anticipate?
What can I learn to increase my odds of success?
Am I building the scaffolding people will need to adopt and move forward?
What partnerships, alliances or collaborations could increase the scaffolding around this project?"
- Seth Godin[284]

---

[284] *Direct questions worth answering*, Seth Godin, January 24, 2024, seths.blog.

Seth Godin is a bestselling author, entrepreneur, and marketing guru who has fundamentally changed how people think about marketing, leadership, and the spread of ideas. He's written over 20 books, including influential titles like "Purple Cow," which popularised the concept that businesses must be remarkable to succeed, "The Tipping Point" predecessor "Unleashing the Ideavirus," and "Linchpin," which argues that indispensable employees are those who bring creativity and humanity to their work. Godin founded several companies, including Yoyodyne (one of the first internet marketing companies, sold to Yahoo!) and Squidoo, and the altMBA, an intensive online leadership workshop. His daily blog, which he's maintained for decades, reaches millions of readers with insights on marketing, culture, and human behaviour. Godin is known for coining terms like "permission marketing" (marketing to people who want to be marketed to) and advocating for authentic, story-driven approaches over traditional advertising. His philosophy emphasises that in the modern economy, playing it safe is actually the riskiest strategy, and that success comes from being different, generous, and willing to make a difference. He's also a sought-after speaker who challenges conventional business wisdom and encourages people to embrace change and lead rather than follow.

OCTOBER 9

"Who needs to know about the proposed change in advance? How will they feel about the proposed change?"
- Ed Batista[285]

---

[285] *Who Needs to Know? How Will They Feel? (On Change),* Ed Batista, edbatista.com, May 31, 2021.

Ed Batista is an executive coach and former Stanford Graduate School of Business lecturer who has become a prominent voice in leadership development and organisational psychology. He has been an executive coach since 2006, working with senior leaders who are facing challenges or seeking to be more effective or fulfilled in their roles, while spending 15 years as a lecturer and leadership coach at Stanford GSB. Most of his clients are technology company CEOs, though he works with leaders across various fields from investing to healthcare. Batista's approach emphasises self-awareness, emotional intelligence, and the transition from technical expertise to effective leadership. His work addresses complex leadership challenges including managing key relationships, improving team dynamics, and navigating the shift from individual contributor to organisational leader. Known for his thoughtful, research-based approach to coaching, Batista has contributed significantly to discussions about executive development, feedback culture, and the psychological aspects of leadership in high-pressure environments.

OCTOBER 10

"Is the change I'm making contagious? How can I alter the culture I'm creating to make it more so?"
- Seth Godin[286]

---

[286] *The Strategy Questions*, Seth Godin, seths.blog, October 22, 2024.

Seth Godin is a bestselling author, entrepreneur, and marketing guru who has fundamentally changed how people think about marketing, leadership, and the spread of ideas. He's written over 20 books, including influential titles like "Purple Cow," which popularised the concept that businesses must be remarkable to succeed, "The Tipping Point" predecessor "Unleashing the Ideavirus," and "Linchpin," which argues that indispensable employees are those who bring creativity and humanity to their work. Godin founded several companies, including Yoyodyne (one of the first internet marketing companies, sold to Yahoo!) and Squidoo, and the altMBA, an intensive online leadership workshop. His daily blog, which he's maintained for decades, reaches millions of readers with insights on marketing, culture, and human behaviour. Godin is known for coining terms like "permission marketing" (marketing to people who want to be marketed to) and advocating for authentic, story-driven approaches over traditional advertising. His philosophy emphasises that in the modern economy, playing it safe is actually the riskiest strategy, and that success comes from being different, generous, and willing to make a difference. He's also a sought-after speaker who challenges conventional business wisdom and encourages people to embrace change and lead rather than follow.

OCTOBER 11

"What happens when I encounter resistance from a powerful figure? What happens when I encounter resistance from a crowd? The last time I had to stand alone, what did I do?"
- Ed Batista[287]

---

[287] "Compasses point true north and help us stay on our chosen path, no matter what's happening around us." Batista explains. "They're not disrupted by environmental changes--but they can't tell us anything about those changes, and sometimes that's important information. Weathervanes are buffeted by the wind, turning to and fro and occasionally spinning in circles. They can't guide us to a destination, but they can tell us a lot about how difficult the trip might be, what we might encounter along the way, and if we should be traveling at all. The compass is a popular metaphor for leadership--we value its steadfastness and reliability, and we want our leaders to exhibit those same qualities. The weathervane sometimes symbolizes *bad* leadership--we're sceptical of leaders who are too easily swayed and seem to lack conviction. But the most effective leaders integrate aspects of both: They have a clearly defined perspective, a set of values they strive to uphold, and the courage to make hard choices and unpopular decisions. But they're also aware of prevailing sentiments in their environment, open to alternative points of view, and able to adapt when necessary."

Compasses and Weathervanes (30 Questions for Leaders), Ed Batista, edbatista.com, April 14, 2022.

Ed Batista is an executive coach and former Stanford Graduate School of Business lecturer who has become a prominent voice in leadership development and organisational psychology. He has been an executive coach since 2006, working with senior leaders who are facing challenges or seeking to be more effective or fulfilled in their roles, while spending 15 years as a lecturer and leadership coach at Stanford GSB. Most of his clients are technology company CEOs, though he works with leaders across various fields from investing to healthcare. Batista's approach emphasises self-awareness, emotional intelligence, and the transition from technical expertise to effective leadership. His work addresses complex leadership challenges including managing key relationships, improving team dynamics, and navigating the shift from individual contributor to organisational leader. Known for his thoughtful, research-based approach to coaching, Batista has contributed significantly to discussions about executive development, feedback culture, and the psychological aspects of leadership in high-pressure environments.

OCTOBER 12

"Is there a network of leaders across the organization and at multiple levels suitably equipped to function as sponsors of change?"
- Daryl Conner[288]

---

288 *The Board's Role in Major Change: Mechanics and Mindsets for Successful Change Execution*, Daryl Conner, conneradvisory.com, November 2022.

Daryl Conner is a pioneering change management expert and founder/chairman of Conner Partners, best known for his groundbreaking book "Managing at the Speed of Change". Conner identified that "the single most important factor to managing change successfully is the degree to which people demonstrate resilience: the capacity to absorb high levels of change while displaying minimal dysfunctional behaviour." He introduced influential concepts to the change management field, including the "burning platform" metaphor that has been used for nearly 30 years to describe high urgency regarding change initiatives. For over forty-five years, Conner has educated and advised strategic leaders and veteran change practitioners in many of the world's most successful organisations, helping them understand and navigate transformational change challenges. His work focuses on how organisations and individuals can build resilience to thrive during periods of intense change rather than simply survive them. Conner's approach emphasises that successful change management is less about what to change and more about how to change, making resilience the cornerstone of effective organisational transformation.

OCTOBER 13

*"Are we on the same team?
What's the right path forward?"
- Seth Godin*[289]

---

[289] *Two questions behind every disagreement*, Seth Godin, seths.blog, September 12, 2012.

Seth Godin is a bestselling author, entrepreneur, and marketing guru who has fundamentally changed how people think about marketing, leadership, and the spread of ideas. He's written over 20 books, including influential titles like "Purple Cow," which popularised the concept that businesses must be remarkable to succeed, "The Tipping Point" predecessor "Unleashing the Ideavirus," and "Linchpin," which argues that indispensable employees are those who bring creativity and humanity to their work. Godin founded several companies, including Yoyodyne (one of the first internet marketing companies, sold to Yahoo!) and Squidoo, and the altMBA, an intensive online leadership workshop. His daily blog, which he's maintained for decades, reaches millions of readers with insights on marketing, culture, and human behaviour. Godin is known for coining terms like "permission marketing" (marketing to people who want to be marketed to) and advocating for authentic, story-driven approaches over traditional advertising. His philosophy emphasises that in the modern economy, playing it safe is actually the riskiest strategy, and that success comes from being different, generous, and willing to make a difference. He's also a sought-after speaker who challenges conventional business wisdom and encourages people to embrace change and lead rather than follow.

OCTOBER 14

"What's working, and how can we do more of it?" Sounds simple, doesn't it? Yet, in the real world, this obvious question is almost never asked. Instead, the question we ask is more problem focused: 'What's broken, and how do we fix it?'"
- Chip Heath[290]

---

[290] It is easy to focus on what is not working, particularly during periods of change. This question echoes the approach of David Cooperrider, an organisational theorist and professor at Case Western Reserve University's Weatherhead School of Management, best known for developing Appreciative Inquiry (AI). One of the questions Cooperider likes to ask is "Am I looking for what's broken ... or what's working?"

Switch: How to Change Things When Change Is Hard, Chip Heath, 2010.

Chip Heath is the Thrive Foundation for Youth Professor of Organizational Behavior at Stanford Graduate School of Business. He graduated from Texas A&M University with a Bachelor of Science degree in industrial engineering and subsequently earned a PhD in psychology from Stanford University before teaching at the University of Chicago Graduate School of Business and Duke University's Fuqua School of Business. His research examines why certain ideas — ranging from urban legends to folk medical cures, from Chicken Soup for the Soul stories to business strategy myths — survive and prosper in the social marketplace of ideas. Heath is best known for co-authoring three New York Times bestselling books with his brother Dan Heath: "Made to Stick: Why Some Ideas Survive and Others Die", which explores the anatomy of memorable ideas, "Switch: How to Change Things When Change is Hard", and "Decisive: How to Make Better Decisions in Life and Work". His work focuses on understanding how to make ideas more effective in organisational and social contexts.

OCTOBER 15

*"What are the employees saying about the change?
How do you know?"*
- Karin Hurt[291]

---

[291] *12 Questions To Get Your Team Thinking More Strategically*, Karin Hurt, leadchangegroup.com, February 2, 2015.

Karin Hurt is the CEO and founder of Let's Grow Leaders, an international leadership development firm focused on human-centered leadership. A former Verizon Wireless executive with two decades of corporate experience, she helps leaders find clarity in uncertainty, drive innovation, and achieve breakthrough results without losing their humanity. She is an award-winning author of five books including "Courageous Cultures" and "Powerful Phrases for Dealing with Workplace Conflict," and was named one of Inc. Magazine's Great Leadership Speakers. Since founding Let's Grow Leaders in 2013 with her husband David Dye, she has helped develop tens of thousands of leaders across the globe, providing practical leadership tools and development programs that create lasting change in organisations.

OCTOBER 16

"What is holding us back?"
- Martin Webster[292]

---

[292] *Top 5 Questions Great Leaders Should Ask Their Teams,* Martin Webster, leadingwithquestions.com, March 6, 2014.

Martin Webster is a leadership development expert and founder of "The Lazy Leader," an independent publication he created for everyone starting their leadership journey, where he shares experiences and promotes leadership development alongside the pursuit of "productive laziness." Webster founded The Lazy Leader building on the success of his previous Leadership Thoughts blog, with the platform focusing on encouraging leadership development, leadership teams, business transformation, and project management through weekly articles and content. His philosophy centres around the counterintuitive concept that "lazy" leaders can be highly effective by finding efficient ways to accomplish difficult tasks, drawing inspiration from the idea that choosing a lazy person for a hard job often results in finding the easiest solution. The Lazy Leader operates as an independent publication designed to help new managers and leaders reach their full potential.

OCTOBER 17

"How can I help others embrace change instead of fearing it?"
- John Maxwell[293]

---

[293] *Leader Shift: 11 Essential Changes Every Leader Must Embrace*, John C. Maxwell, 2019.

John C. Maxwell is an author, speaker, and leadership expert widely recognised as one of the world's foremost authorities on leadership development and personal growth. Having written over 100 books, many of which have become New York Times bestsellers, Maxwell has sold more than 31 million copies worldwide, with titles including "The 21 Irrefutable Laws of Leadership," "Developing the Leader Within You," and "The 5 Levels of Leadership" becoming foundational texts in leadership education. A former pastor who transitioned into full-time leadership training, Maxwell founded several organisations including EQUIP and the John Maxwell Team, which have trained millions of leaders across more than 180 countries. His teaching emphasises practical leadership principles, personal development, and the importance of adding value to others, making complex leadership concepts accessible to audiences ranging from corporate executives to community leaders. Maxwell's influence extends globally through his speaking engagements, coaching programs, and mentorship initiatives, establishing him as a pivotal figure in modern leadership development.

OCTOBER 18

"... the big question I think we should all be asking as it relates to systems change is: how do we develop the collective leadership we need? How do we get to the place where we have enough people working at every level of the system, inside and outside the system, who are all on the same mission ...?"
- Wendy Kopp[294]

---

[294] The supreme form of leadership leverage is the creation of more leaders. In the words of Max De Pree, "Leaders are also responsible for future leadership. They need to identify, develop, and nurture future leaders." If done well, those leaders will do the same, generating a self-perpetuating leadership pipeline.

Locally-Led, Globally-Informed: Wendy Kopp's Vision for Education, Nora Marketos, LinkedIn, April 14, 2025.

Wendy Kopp is the CEO and Co-founder of Teach For All, a global network of independent organisations working to ensure all children have the opportunity to fulfill their potential. She conceived of and proposed the idea of Teach For America in her undergraduate thesis at Princeton University in 1989, then founded and led the organisation for 24 years. Teach For America recruits outstanding recent college graduates and professionals to teach for at least two years in high-need schools, and has grown to include more than 6,000 corps members serving in over 50 urban and rural regions. After her success with Teach For America, Kopp co-founded Teach For All in 2007 to create a global movement, working alongside leaders worldwide who understand their local education needs and developing independent organisations to address their communities' specific challenges.

OCTOBER 19

"Are there sufficient safeguards against advancing more change than people can properly absorb?"
- Daryl Conner[295]

---

[295] *The Board's Role in Major Change: Mechanics and Mindsets for Successful Change Execution*, Daryl Conner, conneradvisory.com, November 2022.

Daryl Conner is a pioneering change management expert and founder/chairman of Conner Partners, best known for his groundbreaking book "Managing at the Speed of Change". Conner identified that "the single most important factor to managing change successfully is the degree to which people demonstrate resilience: the capacity to absorb high levels of change while displaying minimal dysfunctional behaviour." He introduced influential concepts to the change management field, including the "burning platform" metaphor that has been used for nearly 30 years to describe high urgency regarding change initiatives. For over forty-five years, Conner has educated and advised strategic leaders and veteran change practitioners in many of the world's most successful organisations, helping them understand and navigate transformational change challenges. His work focuses on how organisations and individuals can build resilience to thrive during periods of intense change rather than simply survive them. Conner's approach emphasises that successful change management is less about what to change and more about how to change, making resilience the cornerstone of effective organisational transformation.

OCTOBER 20

"Alternative Questions to asking "how" -
How do you do it? becomes
What refusal have I been postponing?
How long will it take? becomes
What commitment am I willing to make?
How much does it cost? becomes
What is the price I am willing to pay?
How do you get those people to change? becomes
What is my contribution to the problem I am
concerned with?
How do we measure it? becomes
What is the crossroad at which I find myself at this
point in my life/work?
How are other people doing it successfully? becomes
What do we want to create together?"
- Peter Block[296]

---

296 *The Answer to How Is Yes: Acting on What Matters*, Peter Block, 2018.

Peter Block is an organisational development consultant, author, and speaker known for his work on empowerment, community building, and transformational change in organisations. He's written several influential books including "Flawless Consulting," "The Empowered Manager," and "Community: The Structure of Belonging." Block focuses on shifting organisational cultures from dependency and control toward accountability and partnership, emphasizing the importance of engaging people's commitment rather than just their compliance. His approach centres on the belief that sustainable change happens when individuals take personal responsibility and when organisations create conditions for authentic engagement and shared ownership of outcomes.

OCTOBER 21

"What resources and assets do I have to dedicate to this project? Do I have enough kindling to burn this log?"
- Seth Godin[297]

---

[297] *The Strategy Questions*, Seth Godin, seths.blog, October 22, 2024.

Seth Godin is a bestselling author, entrepreneur, and marketing guru who has fundamentally changed how people think about marketing, leadership, and the spread of ideas. He's written over 20 books, including influential titles like "Purple Cow," which popularised the concept that businesses must be remarkable to succeed, "The Tipping Point" predecessor "Unleashing the Ideavirus," and "Linchpin," which argues that indispensable employees are those who bring creativity and humanity to their work. Godin founded several companies, including Yoyodyne (one of the first internet marketing companies, sold to Yahoo!) and Squidoo, and the altMBA, an intensive online leadership workshop. His daily blog, which he's maintained for decades, reaches millions of readers with insights on marketing, culture, and human behaviour. Godin is known for coining terms like "permission marketing" (marketing to people who want to be marketed to) and advocating for authentic, story-driven approaches over traditional advertising. His philosophy emphasises that in the modern economy, playing it safe is actually the riskiest strategy, and that success comes from being different, generous, and willing to make a difference. He's also a sought-after speaker who challenges conventional business wisdom and encourages people to embrace change and lead rather than follow.

OCTOBER 22

"What would 'going all in' look like?"
- Michael Bungay Stanier[298]

---

[298] "First, identify your leverage point, the place where effort will make a difference." Stanier writes. "Then think about the resources you have. Here's a list to start you off: Time, people, money, attention, courage, relationships, favours owed, expertise within and without the team, leverage over, physical space, technology, reputation, credibility ... Then, imagine if you will ... Saying no to the other projects, and pulling resources away from them. Putting all your people on this, rather than spreading them thin. Leaving some fires to burn. Not doing business as usual, as usual. Spending all your budget. Bringing in the very best expertise. Cashing in reciprocity, and asking for favours owed. Showing up with confidence and swagger. It's a little scary, isn't it? And probably madness to go all the way. Probably. But perhaps a little less spreading your bets, CYA[cover your ass]-ing, and timidness might be the play that will shake things up and make a difference. But often, seeing and sharing what's hard can bring its own measure of relief."
What would "going all in" look like?, thechangesignal.com, April 17, 2025.

Michael Bungay Stanier is an author, leadership coach, and business consultant best known for his bestselling book "The Coaching Habit: Say Less, Ask More & Change the Way You Lead Forever." He founded Box of Crayons, a learning and development company that helps organisations transform from advice-driven to curiosity-led, and currently leads MBS.works, a place where people find clarity, confidence and community to be a force for change. His work focuses on helping leaders develop better coaching skills through practical, science-backed approaches that emphasise asking powerful questions rather than giving advice. His philosophy is captured in his haiku-like summary: "Tell less and ask more. Your advice is not as good as you think it is." Known as a compelling speaker and facilitator who combines practicality, humour, and high audience engagement, Stanier has become a prominent voice in the leadership development space, helping countless managers and executives shift from being advice-givers to becoming more effective coaches who unlock potential in their teams through curiosity and thoughtful questioning.

OCTOBER 23

"Creation or change: What's your language?"
- David Lancefield[299]

---

[299] "Language really matters." Michael Bungay Stanier explains. "When I started in this world, it was all "change management," and since then it's moved on to "change," flirted with "transformation," doubled down on "digital transformation," and seems to have come back to "change." Or maybe not. Maybe now it's just "everything." And if we're confused, imagine what it's like when you're not in it so much as being subjected to it! So what do you call this thing we do? When we say "change" or "transformation," it's useful to know we might just be triggering resistance from everyone we hope will be on our side. David tells us: 'I tend to use more words that focus on creation rather than change. If you talk about 'How do we create something? How do we make something which will involve change?' I think it triggers different emotions.'"

What Are Your Top Three Decisions?: The Change Signal with David Lancefield, thechangesignal.com, 7 May 2025.

David Lancefield is the founder of Strategy Shift and a strategic leadership consultant who has worked with more than 50 CEOs and hundreds of C-suite executives across over 30 countries to design bold strategies, supercharge leadership, and transform culture. He has led 15 digital transformations with major organisations including the BBC, Royal Mail, NHS, and Vodafone. As a strategist, catalyst, and coach, Lancefield writes for prestigious publications like Harvard Business Review, MIT Sloan Review, and Strategy+Business, and serves as a guest lecturer at London Business School. A former senior partner at Strategy&, PwC's strategy consulting business, he focuses particularly on helping organisations in the media and entertainment sector transform for the digital age, though his expertise extends across health, energy, transport, and financial services. He also hosts the interview series "Lancefield on the Line" and publishes the Strategic Leader newsletter, establishing himself as a recognised thought leader on strategy, leadership, and organisational culture transformation.

OCTOBER 24

"How much of what you did today was simply due to inertia?"
- Steph Smith[300]

---

[300] This question echoes former Intel CEO Andy Grove who warned against mistaking inertia—the "light from dying stars"—for impetus and initiative. Companies often cling to outdated strategies or successes, even as their relevance fades. Leaders can be blinded by past achievements, when the environment has already shifted. Grove believed that companies must recognise when they're at a strategic inflection point, moments when fundamental change is needed to survive. If they don't adapt, they risk becoming obsolete, even if things still look successful on the surface. This idea is central to Grove's management philosophy. He argued that leaders must be hyper-aware of changes in technology, competition, and market dynamics, because by the time the decline is obvious, it may be too late to recover.

3-2-1 Newsletter, James Clear, May 6, 2021.

Steph Smith is an entrepreneur, content creator, and growth marketer who has made significant impacts across multiple tech companies and media platforms. She currently works as a podcast host for Andreessen Horowitz (a16z), having previously led The Hustle's product Trends to millions in annual recurring revenue and directed HubSpot's creator program. Smith is known for her expertise in remote work, continuous growth, and technology, with over 350,000 people having read her articles on these topics. Her career trajectory includes building and scaling content products, particularly during The Hustle's acquisition by HubSpot where she transitioned from leading the Trends newsletter to overseeing creator initiatives. Beyond her corporate roles, Smith has established herself as an indie maker and writer, maintaining a popular blog and sharing insights about entrepreneurship, content creation, and business growth. She's also notable for her philanthropic efforts, having launched scholarship programs and actively supporting aspiring entrepreneurs through her content and mentorship.

OCTOBER 25

"What would happen to our change practices if we began all our work with the positive presumption that organizations, as centers of human relatedness, are alive with infinite constructive capacity?"
- David Cooperrider[301]

---

[301] *Appreciative Inquiry: A Positive Revolution in Change*, David L. Cooperrider and Diana Whitney, 1999.

David L. Cooperrider is an American organisational theorist and professor at Case Western Reserve University's Weatherhead School of Management, best known for developing Appreciative Inquiry (AI), a revolutionary approach to organisational change and development. Rather than focusing on problems and deficits, Appreciative Inquiry emphasises identifying and building upon an organisation's strengths, successes, and positive potential. This methodology has been widely adopted by corporations, nonprofits, and government agencies worldwide as an alternative to traditional problem-solving approaches to organisational change. Cooperrider has worked with numerous Fortune 500 companies and global organisations, helping them transform their cultures and achieve sustainable change through AI principles. He's authored and co-authored several influential books on the subject, including "Appreciative Inquiry: A Positive Revolution in Change" and "The Strengths Revolution." His work extends beyond business into areas like social innovation and positive organisational scholarship. Cooperrider is also involved in various global initiatives focused on sustainable development and social change. His approach has influenced fields ranging from management consulting to community development, offering a more positive and strengths-based framework for creating organisational and social transformation.

OCTOBER 26

"Are you building something that the future you will thank you for?"
- Brad Feld[302]

---

[302] It is unlikely that anyone will remember our work achievements, irrespective of how impressive they might seem. What will be remembered is your presence in the lives of others. The real legacy will involve passing on traces of ideological DNA. Businessman and author Ricardo Semler notes, "It injects fundamental ideas and processes into the bloodstream of an organization and of individuals who see things the same way but lack the leverage to carry them out on their own. As a one-man or one-woman protectorate of a humane, sustainable business process, the leader sees to it that new ideas emerge and bloom when the timing is right. Dictators come and go, and when they go the dictatorship goes with them. When a true leader departs, the company he leaves behind is healthy, self-governing, vibrant, and intact." The Seven-Day Weekend: Changing the Way Work Works, Ricardo Semler, 2003.

30 Minutes of Awesome With Seth Godin, Brad Feld Thoughts, June 11, 2025.

Brad Feld is a venture capitalist, entrepreneur, and author based in Boulder, Colorado. He's a partner at Foundry Group, which he co-founded with Seth Levine, Ryan McIntyre, and Jason Mendelson, and has been an early-stage investor and entrepreneur for over 30 years. Feld was an early investor in successful companies like Harmonix, Zynga, MakerBot, and Fitbit. He's perhaps best known for co-authoring "Venture Deals: Be Smarter Than Your Lawyer and Venture Capitalist" with Jason Mendelson, which has become a definitive guide for entrepreneurs navigating venture capital funding. Feld is also a prolific blogger at "Feld Thoughts," an active speaker on entrepreneurship and venture capital topics, and has written several other books including "Startup Boards" and "Startup Opportunities." He's been instrumental in building the Boulder startup ecosystem and is known for his "give first" philosophy in the entrepreneurial community.

OCTOBER 27

"Are you with me?"
- Dan Heath[303]

---

[303] After Heath asks this question Michael Bungay Stanier adds, "I think it's a question we often forget to ask as change leaders. We just hope for the best. Or we assume. Or we stay in denial. So for your executive team. For your change sponsor. For your change team. For the people you're inviting to change. Are you with me? Remember, wait and hear the answer. Yes, we're with you. Or maybe no, we're not with you yet. Because that tells you what should happen next."

You're Over-Flexing This Change Muscle, The Change Signal with Dan Heath, thechangesignal.com, April 8, 2025.

Dan Heath is a bestselling author, speaker and fellow at Duke University's CASE center who has co-authored four New York Times bestsellers with his brother Chip: "Decisive," "Switch," "Made to Stick," and "The Power of Moments," with their books selling over 3 million copies worldwide and being translated into 33 languages. A Senior Fellow at Duke University's CASE center, he holds an M.B.A. from Harvard Business School and a B.A. from the Plan II Honors Program at the University of Texas at Austin. Beyond his collaborative work with Chip, Dan wrote his first solo book, "Upstream: The Quest to Solve Problems Before They Happen," which became an instant Wall Street Journal bestseller. He also hosts the award-winning podcast "What It's Worth" and focuses his work on helping organizations and individuals solve problems more effectively, often emphasising prevention over reaction and the power of creating memorable moments.

OCTOBER 28

"Did we come out of this stronger or weaker?"
- Marshall Ganz[304]

---

[304] "Many times, what really matters, what may be even more important than the goal is, *did we come out of this stronger or weaker?*" Ganz explains. "Have you ever had a "success" where you never want to see anybody ever again who was involved? You have to ask yourself: What did we *build*?"
Are You Building Something?, Stanford Social Innovation Review, February 13, 2025.
Marshall Ganz is the Rita E. Hauser Senior Lecturer in Leadership, Organizing, and Civil Society at Harvard Kennedy School, where he teaches, researches, and writes on leadership, narrative, strategy, and organisation in social movements and civic associations. He left Harvard College in 1964, a year before graduating, to volunteer as a civil rights organiser in Mississippi and then joined Cesar Chavez and the United Farm Workers in 1965, where he spent 16 years gaining experience in union, community, and political organising and eventually became director of organising. During the 1980s, he worked with grassroots groups to develop effective organising programs and designed innovative voter mobilisation strategies for electoral campaigns. After returning to complete his Harvard degree in 1991, he has become a leading authority on community organising and public narrative, coaching and advising social, civic, educational, and political groups worldwide on organising, training, and leadership development.

OCTOBER 29

"Are we putting those who have helped make change happen in leadership roles? Have the scouts been rewarded?"
- John Kotter[305]

---

[305] In their famous Culture Deck (2009), Netflix made it clear that "The *actual* company values, as opposed to the *nice-sounding* values, are shown by who gets rewarded, promoted, or let go."
Our Iceberg Is Melting: Changing and Succeeding Under Any Conditions, John P. Kotter, 2006.
John P. Kotter is a Harvard Business School professor emeritus and one of the world's foremost authorities on organisational change and leadership. Kotter is best known for his influential 8-step change process, outlined in his seminal book "Leading Change", which provides a systematic approach to managing organisational transformation. His model emphasises creating urgency, building guiding coalitions, developing vision and strategy, communicating the vision, empowering broad-based action, generating short-term wins, sustaining acceleration, and anchoring new approaches in culture. Kotter's research distinguishes between management (maintaining order and consistency) and leadership (creating change and movement), arguing that successful change requires strong leadership rather than just good management. He has authored numerous bestselling books including "Our Iceberg Is Melting" and "The Heart of Change," and his work has been translated into dozens of languages. Through his consulting firm Kotter International, he has helped organisations worldwide navigate complex transformations, making him one of the most cited and practically applied change theorists in business.

OCTOBER 30

*"What's this all for?
What are we working toward?"
- Daniel Coyle[306]*

---

[306] After examining what makes exceptional teams tick, Coyle revealed clarity was central to their performance. "When I visited the successful groups," Coyle writes, "I noticed that whenever they communicated anything about their purpose or their values, they were as subtle as a punch in the nose."

The Culture Code: The Secrets of Highly Successful Groups, Daniel Coyle, 2018.

Daniel Coyle is a New York Times bestselling author known for books including "The Culture Code," "The Talent Code," "The Little Book of Talent," and "The Secret Race." He works as a contributing editor for Outside magazine and serves as a special advisor to the Cleveland Guardians baseball team. Coyle specialises in studying high-performing teams and talent development, spending years observing elite groups around the world to understand how they build culture, develop skills, and achieve success. Winner of the 2012 William Hill Sports Book of the Year Prize (with Tyler Hamilton), he splits his time between Cleveland, Ohio during the school year and Homer, Alaska in the summer with his wife Jen and their four children. His work focuses on translating the science of skill acquisition and team dynamics into practical insights for coaches, leaders, and organisations seeking to unlock human potential and build stronger cultures.

OCTOBER 31

"How will the world be different when you've succeeded?"
- Seth Godin[307]

---

[307] A vision of what will be different and better is a prerequisite to lead. The clearer the vision is, the more compelling it will be for followers. Psychologist David McClelland explains, "Whatever the source of the leader's ideas, he cannot inspire his people unless he expresses vivid goals which in some sense they want. Of course, the more closely he meets their needs, the less 'persuasive' he has to be, but in no case does it make sense to speak as if his role is force submission. Rather it is to strengthen and uplift, to make people feel that they are the origins, not the pawns, of the socio-political system." *Leadership: what every leader should know about people*, Robert A. Portnoy, 1986.

16 questions for free agents, Seth Godin, seths.blog, June 2, 2010.

Seth Godin is a bestselling author, entrepreneur, and marketing guru who has fundamentally changed how people think about marketing, leadership, and the spread of ideas. He's written over 20 books, including influential titles like "Purple Cow," which popularised the concept that businesses must be remarkable to succeed, "The Tipping Point" predecessor "Unleashing the Ideavirus," and "Linchpin," which argues that indispensable employees are those who bring creativity and humanity to their work. Godin founded several companies, including Yoyodyne (one of the first internet marketing companies, sold to Yahoo!) and Squidoo, and the altMBA, an intensive online leadership workshop. His daily blog, which he's maintained for decades, reaches millions of readers with insights on marketing, culture, and human behaviour. Godin is known for coining terms like "permission marketing" (marketing to people who want to be marketed to) and advocating for authentic, story-driven approaches over traditional advertising. His philosophy emphasises that in the modern economy, playing it safe is actually the riskiest strategy, and that success comes from being different, generous, and willing to make a difference. He's also a sought-after speaker who challenges conventional business wisdom and encourages people to embrace change and lead rather than follow.

NOVEMBER

OVERCOME CHALLENGES

NOVEMBER 1

"What part of this situation is under my control?"
- James Clear[308]

---

[308] Clear echoes the stoic philosopher Epictetus who writes, "The chief task in life is simply this: to identify and separate matters so that I can say clearly to myself which are externals not under my control, and which have to do with the choices I actually control. Where then do I look for good and evil? Not to uncontrollable externals, but within myself to the choices that are my own . . .". *Discourses*, 2.5.4–5, Epictetus.
3-2-1 Newsletter, James Clear, November 5, 2020.
James Clear is an author, speaker, and entrepreneur best known for his book "Atomic Habits," which became a bestseller and popularised the concept of making small, incremental changes to build better habits and break bad ones. Clear focuses on the science of habit formation, emphasising how tiny improvements compound over time to create remarkable results. His approach centres on four key principles: making habits obvious, attractive, easy, and satisfying. Before his writing career took off, Clear was a successful entrepreneur and has a background in photography and business. He writes regularly about habits, decision-making, and continuous improvement on his website and newsletter, which has attracted millions of readers. Clear's work draws from psychology, neuroscience, and behavioural economics to provide practical strategies for personal and professional development, making complex research accessible to everyday readers seeking to improve their lives through better systems and habits.

NOVEMBER 2

*"Why did the idea or effort fail?
What if I could take what I've learned from this
failure and try a revised approach?
How might I do that?"*
- Warren Berger[309]

---

309 *A More Beautiful Question: The Power of Inquiry to Spark Breakthrough Ideas*, Warren Berger, 2014.

Warren Berger is an innovation expert and "questionologist" who has dedicated his career to exploring the transformative power of inquiry. He is the author or co-author of more than 12 books on innovation, including the bestseller "A More Beautiful Question: The Power of Inquiry to Spark Breakthrough Ideas" and the internationally acclaimed "Glimmer," which was named one of Business Week's Best Innovation and Design Books of the Year. Berger has studied hundreds of the world's foremost innovators, entrepreneurs, and creative thinkers to learn how they ask questions, generate original ideas, and solve problems. His work appears in prestigious publications including Fast Company, Harvard Business Review, Psychology Today, and The New York Times, and he has keynoted conferences for major organisations while serving as a guest lecturer at universities across the country. At the core of his philosophy is the belief that "questions are more important than answers," positioning questioning as a fundamental skill for breakthrough thinking and problem-solving in both business and personal contexts.

NOVEMBER 3

"How personal is it - does it affect only you?
How pervasive is it - does it effect every area
of your life?
How permanent is it - will it have lasting
consequences?"
- Martin Seligman[310]

---

[310] These questions have been paraphrased from Seligman's work on learned optimism. "The optimists and the pessimists: I have been studying them for the past twenty-five years." Seligman writes. "The defining characteristic of pessimists is that they tend to believe bad events will last a long time, will undermine everything they do, and are their own fault. The optimists, who are confronted with the same hard knocks of this world, think about misfortune in the opposite way. They tend to believe defeat is just a temporary setback, that its causes are confined to this one case. The optimists believe defeat is not their fault: Circumstances, bad luck, or other people brought it about. Such people are unfazed by defeat. Confronted by a bad situation, they perceive it as a challenge and try harder."

Learned Optimism: How to Change Your Mind and Your Life, Martin E. P. Seligman, 1990.

Dr. Martin E.P. Seligman is the Director of the Penn Positive Psychology Center and Zellerbach Family Professor of Psychology in the Penn Department of Psychology at the University of Pennsylvania. Commonly known as the founder of positive psychology, Seligman is a leading authority in the fields of positive psychology, resilience, learned helplessness, depression, optimism, and pessimism. American psychologist Martin Seligman initiated research on learned helplessness in 1967 at the University of Pennsylvania, and his groundbreaking and rigorously-tested theory of learned helplessness — which argued that a major component of human depression consisted of a "learned" pessimistic attitude — led to major breakthroughs in treating and preventing depression. In 2003, Seligman founded the Positive Psychology Center at the University of Pennsylvania, shifting his focus from what makes people mentally ill to what makes them flourish and thrive.

NOVEMBER 4

*"How have I been complicit in creating the
conditions I say I don't want?"*
- Jerry Colonna[311]

---

[311] Colonna explains that the origin of this concept came from in his mid-30s when, despite experiencing material success, he was miserable. His psychoanalyst was a tough, experienced therapist who grew tired of his constant complaining. She repeatedly asked: 'How have you been complicit in creating these conditions you say you don't want?' This question was transformative because it forced Colonna to examine his role as an accomplice in his own problems. The distinction between 'complicit' and 'responsible' is crucial. When we tell ourselves we're completely responsible for all our problems, we paradoxically avoid the deeper work. Being complicit means acknowledging how you've participated in creating unwanted patterns without shouldering all the blame, and that's where real change becomes possible.

Reboot: Leadership and the Art of Growing Up, Jerry Colonna, 2019.

Jerry Colonna is an executive coach, venture capitalist, and author who has become a prominent voice in bringing mindfulness and emotional intelligence to the world of entrepreneurship and leadership. Known as the "CEO Whisperer," he co-founded Flatiron Partners, one of New York's most successful early-stage venture capital firms, before transitioning to executive coaching and founding Reboot.io, a company focused on helping leaders develop self-awareness and authentic leadership skills. His book "Reboot: Leadership and the Art of Growing Up" combines his business experience with insights from Buddhism and psychology, advocating for a more compassionate and introspective approach to leadership that addresses the emotional and psychological challenges of running companies. Colonna's work emphasises the importance of examining one's own patterns, traumas, and unconscious behaviours as a path to becoming a more effective and fulfilled leader. Through his coaching practice, writing, and speaking, he has helped shift the conversation in Silicon Valley and beyond toward recognizing that sustainable success requires not just business acumen but also personal growth and emotional maturity.

NOVEMBER 5

"Did you collaborate in your own defeat?"
- John Gardner[312]

---

[312] "Of course failures are a part of the story too." Gardner writes. "Everyone fails, Joe Louis said 'Everyone has to figure to get beat some time.' The question isn't did you fail but did you pick yourself up and move ahead? And there is one other little question: 'Did you collaborate in your own defeat?' A lot of people do. Learn not to."

Personal Renewal, John W. Gardner. Speech delivered to McKinsey & Company on November 10, 1990. Transcript originally published on PBS.org.

John W. Gardner (1912-2002) was an influential statesman, educator, and social reformer who served as Secretary of Health, Education, and Welfare under President Lyndon Johnson and became known as "the father of campaign finance reform" after founding Common Cause in 1970. A Stanford University graduate with a Ph.D. in psychology from UC Berkeley, he served as president of the Carnegie Corporation of New York and the Carnegie Foundation for the Advancement of Teaching from 1955 before joining Johnson's Great Society administration, where he helped launch Medicare and expand federal education programs. Gardner authored several influential books on leadership and social excellence, including "Excellence: Can We Be Equal and Excellent Too?" and "On Leadership", and founded the prestigious White House Fellows program. His legacy continues through the John W. Gardner Center at Stanford University and fellowship programs that encourage public service among young leaders.

NOVEMBER 6

"What are you going to do about it?"
- Edith Eger[313]

---

[313] The complete quotation is, "What are you going to do about it? I believe in the power of positive thinking - but change and freedom also require positive action. Anything we practice, we become better at."
The Choice: Embrace the Possible, Edith Eger, 2017.

Edith Eger is a Czechoslovakian-born psychologist, a Holocaust survivor and a specialist in the treatment of post-traumatic stress disorder. At 97, she is a gymnast turned psychologist turned public speaker and author who uses her experience as a Holocaust survivor to offer guidance to her readers on how heal and thrive. At the age of sixteen, a trained ballet dancer and gymnast, she was sent to Auschwitz concentration camp, where she survived the horrors of the Holocaust while losing her parents. After immigrating to America, Eger earned her doctorate in psychology and became a world-renowned clinical psychologist specialising in post-traumatic stress disorder or PTSD. Her memoir entitled "The Choice: Embrace the Possible" became an international bestseller, combining her Holocaust survival story with insights on healing and resilience. She has also written "The Gift: 12 Lessons to Save Your Life," continuing to share her wisdom about overcoming trauma, finding freedom through forgiveness, and choosing hope over victimhood even in the face of unimaginable suffering.

NOVEMBER 7

"One of the best questions you can ask when something negative happens is this: What does this experience make possible?"
- Michael Hyatt[314]

---

[314] Hyatt echoes Navy Seal Commander and author Jocko Willink who trained himself to respond to all bad news with "good", immediately reframing the situation in a positive light. Every challenge is re-imagined as an opportunity. "When things are going bad there is going to be some good that comes from it. " Willink says. "Mission got cancelled? Good – we can focus on another one. Didn't get promoted? Good – more time to get better. Didn't get funded? Good – we own more of the company. Didn't get the job you wanted. Good – you get more experience and build a better resume. Got beat? You learned. Unexpected problems? Good – we have the opportunity to figure out a solution. When things are going bad, don't get all bummed out, don't get startled, don't get frustrated. Just look at the issue and say "good". Move forward. And lastly if you can say the word good, it means you are still alive. It means you still have some fight left in you. So get up, dust off, reload, recalibrate, re-engage and go out on the attack".

Living Forward: A Proven Plan to Stop Drifting and Get the Life You Want, Michael Hyatt, 2016.

Michael Hyatt is an author, blogger, and business coach who specialises in leadership, productivity, and goal achievement. He's the founder and CEO of Michael Hyatt & Company, a leadership coaching and development firm. Hyatt is best known for his books including "Platform: Get Noticed in a Noisy World," "Living Forward," and "Your Best Year Ever," which focus on helping people build their personal brand, increase productivity, and achieve their goals systematically. Before becoming an entrepreneur and coach, Hyatt served as chairman and CEO of Thomas Nelson Publishers (now part of HarperCollins), one of the largest Christian publishing companies in the world. He's known for his systematic approach to goal-setting and productivity, developing frameworks like the "Full Focus Planner" system and teaching concepts around what he calls "double your productivity." Hyatt maintains a popular blog and podcast where he shares insights on leadership, business, and personal development. His work emphasises the importance of intentional living, work-life balance, and creating systems that help people achieve both professional success and personal fulfillment. He's particularly focused on helping leaders and entrepreneurs scale their businesses while maintaining their values and priorities.

NOVEMBER 8

"Where's the good in what I'm going through?"
- Scott Mautz[315]

---

[315] "One powerful way to increase your emotional flexibility is to always find the "agreeable adversity" in any situation." Mautz writes. "This is about seeing adversity as a challenge or opportunity versus a threat. You do so by asking yourself three questions in particular:
– 'Where's the good in what I'm going through?'
– 'What possibilities does it present?'
– 'How might this lead to self-discovery and growth?'"
The Secret to Becoming More Adaptable: The three forms of flexibility you need, and how to improve each, Scott Mautz, scottmautz.com, April 7, 2021.

Scott Mautz is a leadership expert, bestselling author, and keynote speaker who combines corporate experience with practical leadership insights. A former Procter & Gamble senior executive who successfully ran four of the company's largest multi-billion dollar businesses all while transforming organisational health scores along the way. Mautz transitioned from corporate leadership to become a sought-after speaker and trainer. He's a multi award-winning author whose books include: Leading from the Middle, Find the Fire, and Make It Matter, with his work focusing on leadership, employee engagement, peak performance, and creating meaning at work. Scott is a popular instructor on LinkedIn Learning where his courses have been taken over 1.5 million times and serves as faculty at Indiana University's Kelley School of Business for Executive Education. His approach emphasises practical, actionable strategies for leaders at all levels, drawing from his extensive corporate experience to help organisations and individuals achieve what he calls "profound performance." Mautz is particularly known for his expertise in middle management leadership and helping leaders influence effectively across organisational hierarchies.

NOVEMBER 9

"What's the positive interpretation of this situation?"
- Naval Ravikant[316]

---

[316] "If I catch myself judging somebody," Ravikant writes, "I can stop myself and say, "What's the positive interpretation of this?" I used to get annoyed about things. Now I always look for the positive side of it. It used to take a rational effort. It used to take a few seconds for me to come up with a positive. Now I can do it sub-second."
The Almanack of Naval Ravikant: A Guide to Wealth and Happiness, Eric Jorgenson, 2020.

Naval Ravikant is a Silicon Valley entrepreneur, angel investor, and philosopher who has become one of the most influential voices on wealth creation, happiness, and decision-making. He's the co-founder and former CEO of AngelList, the platform that democratized startup investing and job matching in tech. As an angel investor, Naval has backed numerous successful companies including Twitter, Uber, Yammer, and Postmates, establishing himself as one of the most successful early-stage investors in Silicon Valley. Beyond his business success, he's gained a massive following for his philosophical insights on wealth, happiness, and life, often shared through Twitter threads, podcasts, and interviews. His thoughts were compiled into the popular book "The Almanack of Naval Ravikant," compiled by Eric Jorgenson. Naval is known for his aphoristic wisdom and his emphasis on building specific knowledge, taking accountability, and leveraging technology to create value. He advocates for principles like reading voraciously, thinking independently, and focusing on long-term compounding in both wealth and knowledge. His blend of practical business acumen with Eastern philosophy and rational thinking has made him a guru figure for entrepreneurs and investors seeking financial success and personal fulfillment.

NOVEMBER 10

"Is stress inflicted on you - or created by you?"
- Frank Sonnenberg[317]

---

[317] "On an average day, do you control your agenda, or do unplanned events control you?" Sonnenberg asks. "Are things manageable, or do you constantly feel under the gun? Do you manage the daily pressure well, or do you feel as though you carry the weight of the world on your shoulders? Stressed out? What's the cause? Stress and anxiety have a detrimental impact on your health, your relationships, and the quality of your life. Unforeseen events and external forces beyond our control create some of the stresses that we experience every day; other times we're simply doing it to ourselves. Is stress inflicted on you — or created by you?"
Soul Food: Change Your Thinking, Change Your Life, Frank Sonnenberg, 2018.
Frank Sonnenberg is an award-winning author and a well-known advocate for moral character, personal values, and personal responsibility. He has written 12 books and has been named one of "America's Top 100 Thought Leaders" and one of "America's Most Influential Small Business Experts." His books focus on ethical leadership, personal integrity, and character development, with titles including "Follow Your Conscience," "Listen to Your Conscience: That's Why You Have One," and "Soul Food: Change Your Thinking, Change Your Life." Sonnenberg's writing emphasises the importance of making conscience-driven decisions and developing self-awareness to become a better person. He works as a speaker and consultant, helping individuals and organisations align their actions with their values and build stronger ethical foundations. His work combines practical wisdom with moral philosophy, encouraging readers to take personal responsibility for their choices and to use their conscience as a guide for living a more meaningful and principled life.

NOVEMBER 11

"What's great about this?"
- Derek Sivers[318]

---

[318] Sometimes this is a very difficult question to answer in the moment. "Most of the time," Sivers writes, "I feel smart, successful, and driven — like I've got it all figured out. But last month a bunch of stuff knocked me on my ass. I've never felt so wrong. ... Usually I find an answer. But this time, my only answer was, 'Nothing. This just sucks.' I tried asking it again every day or two, but the answer was the same. Eventually, I had an epiphany. I actually love being wrong, even though it cracks my confidence, because that's the only time I learn. I actually love being lost, even though it fuels fears, because that's when I go somewhere unexpected. I pursue being wrong and lost in small doses. I love little lessons that surprise my expectations and change my mind. If we're not surprised, we're not learning. So I finally figured out what's great about this. Getting knocked on my ass made me humble as hell. It'd been years since I'd called for help. It'd been years since I was so open to advice."

Hell Yeah or No: what's worth doing, Derek Sivers, 2022.

Derek Sivers is an entrepreneur, author, and philosopher best known for founding CD Baby, which became the largest seller of independent music online before he sold it for $22 million and gave the proceeds to charity. Born a musician himself, Sivers created CD Baby in 1998 to help independent artists sell their music online when few platforms existed for that purpose. His book "Anything You Want" chronicles the unconventional business lessons he learned while building CD Baby, emphasizing customer service, simplicity, and purpose over profit maximisation. Sivers is known for his minimalist lifestyle, contrarian thinking, and practical philosophy about business and life, which he shares through his popular blog, TED talks, and books. After selling CD Baby, he moved to Singapore and later New Zealand, focusing on writing, programming, and sharing insights about entrepreneurship, decision-making, and living deliberately. His approach often challenges conventional wisdom, advocating for doing what feels right rather than what's expected, and he's become a respected voice in the startup and creative communities for his thoughtful, experience-based advice on building businesses that serve both customers and personal values.

NOVEMBER 12

*"How can you reframe failure as growth ...?
How can you reframe the entire experience as you
are not failing; you are growing?"*
- Jim Collins[319]

---

[319] Collins recounts his discussion with free climber Tommy Caldwell, who after four years of trying, had been unable to scale the Dawn Wall on El Capitan, a 3000-foot granite monolith in Yosemite. Collins said, "It's been four years. You just are failing and failing and failing. Why do you go back? You're the most accomplished free climber of your generation and now all you're getting is failure." Caldwell responded, "You don't understand, Jim. I am not failing. I'm growing. And that is the point of the climb. It is making me stronger. What is the other side of the coin from success? It's not failure; it's growth."

Jim's Seven Questions: Learning From Young Leaders Full Talk, Global Leadership Summit, 2015.

Jim Collins is a bestselling author, business researcher, and management consultant who has spent decades studying what makes companies transition from good to great performance. He's best known for his book "Good to Great," which identified key principles that distinguish exceptional companies from merely good ones, including concepts like Level 5 Leadership, the Hedgehog Concept, and getting the right people on the bus. Collins has written several other influential business books including "Built to Last" (co-authored with Jerry Porras), "How the Mighty Fall," and "Great by Choice." His research methodology involves rigorous data analysis and long-term studies of companies, often spanning decades to identify patterns and principles that drive sustained success. Before his writing career, Collins worked as a faculty member at Stanford Graduate School of Business and served as a consultant to corporations and social sector organisations. His work extends beyond the corporate world to nonprofits and educational institutions through books like "Good to Great and the Social Sectors." Collins is known for his disciplined approach to research, his ability to distil complex business concepts into memorable frameworks, and his focus on timeless principles rather than fleeting management fads.

NOVEMBER 13

*"How can I become strong enough
to be useful in a crisis?"*
- Jordan Peterson[320]

---

[320] *What are some deep, profound, thought-provoking questions to ponder over?*, Jordan B. Peterson, Quora, 2014.

Jordan B. Peterson is a clinical psychologist, professor, and author who gained international prominence for his views on free speech, political correctness, and personal responsibility. He taught at Harvard University and the University of Toronto, specialising in personality psychology, psychopathology, and the psychology of religious and ideological belief. His bestselling book "12 Rules for Life: An Antidote to Chaos" combines psychology, philosophy, and personal anecdotes to offer practical advice for living a meaningful life, emphasizing individual responsibility, self-improvement, and traditional values. His second book, "Beyond Order: 12 More Rules for Life," continues these themes. Peterson's lectures and online content focus on topics like mythology, religion, personal development, and the psychological significance of stories and archetypes.

NOVEMBER 14

"What's the worst that's going to happen if this doesn't work out? If it doesn't work out, what will I do to mitigate that I went all in? What is the probability that this bad event will occur? What would I be willing to give up or suffer from to achieve my plan?"
- Matt Higgins[321]

---

[321] Higgins lists the four questions he uses to alleviate concerns and reduce his own catastrophising impulses. The approach is similar to the one used by entrepreneur and author Tim Ferriss who has a process called "fear setting" where you fully envision and write down your fears in order to understand what you can control and what you cannot. Ferriss asks, "where in your lives right now might defining your fears be more important than defining your goals". Ferris ends by quoting stoic philosopher Seneca who writes, "We suffer more in our imagination more often than in reality." *Why you should define your fears instead of your goals*, Tim Ferriss, TED 2017.
The Learning Leader Show, Episode 154, Ryan Hawk.
Matt Higgins is a serial entrepreneur and growth equity investor who serves as co-founder and CEO of private investment firm RSE Ventures. Beginning in 2018, Higgins has appeared as a guest investor on the series Shark Tank, and his debut book, "Burn the Boats," landed on the Wall Street Journal bestseller list in 2023. His remarkable journey includes going from selling flowers on a street corner to becoming the youngest mayoral press secretary in New York City, and later serving as executive vice president of the New York Jets. Through RSE Ventures, he incubates and invests in businesses focused in sports, entertainment, food, lifestyle, and technology, working with everyone from David Chang to the Miami Dolphins.

NOVEMBER 15

"Whose perspective can I get if I'm having a particular challenge?"
- Tasha Eurich[322]

---

[322] Your view of the world is just one version of reality. What you see depends not only on what you are looking at, but also on where you look from. The problem is that we see things from one angle. The solution is to acquire fresh eyes. Writer Blas Moros says fresh eyes are "those outside your system due to age, experience,

background, expertise and/or wisdom". In anthropology the "emic" approach is

an insider's perspective, which looks at the beliefs, values, and practices of a culture from the perspective of the people who live within it. The "etic" approach is an outsider's perspective, which looks at a culture from the perspective of an outside observer or researcher.

Insight: The Surprising Truth About How Others See Us, How We See Ourselves, and Why the Answers Matter More Than We Think, Tasha Eurich, 2017.

Tasha Eurich is an organisational psychologist, researcher, and bestselling author who specialises in self-awareness and its impact on leadership and success. She's best known for her book "Insight: The Surprising Truth About How Others See Us, How We See Ourselves, and Why the Answers Matter More Than We Think," which presents research showing that while most people believe they are self-aware, only 10-15% actually are. Eurich's work distinguishes between internal self-awareness (understanding our own values, passions, and impact on others) and external self-awareness (understanding how others see us), arguing that both are crucial for effective leadership and personal fulfilment. She conducts extensive research on leadership effectiveness, emotional intelligence, and workplace dynamics, and works as a consultant helping executives and organisations develop greater self-awareness. Eurich is a popular keynote speaker and has been featured in Harvard Business Review, where she's written about the myths and realities of self-awareness. Her approach combines rigorous research with practical tools and strategies, helping people bridge the gap between how they see themselves and how others actually perceive them, ultimately leading to better relationships and more effective leadership.

NOVEMBER 16

"How can I be stronger for this?"
- Ryan Holiday[323]

---

[323] "There is a Scandinavian saying which some of us might well take as a rallying cry for our lives: The north wind made the Vikings!" pastor Harry Emerson Fosdick writes. "Wherever did we get the idea that secure and pleasant living, the absence of difficulty, and the comfort of ease, ever of themselves made people either good or happy? Upon the contrary, people who pity themselves go on pitying themselves even when they are laid softly on a cushion, but always in history character and happiness have come to people in all sorts of circumstances, good, bad, and indifferent, when they shouldered their personal responsibility. So, repeatedly the north wind has made the Vikings."

What If I Said No? (And Other Questions to Consider Daily), Ryan Holiday, Medium, August 21, 2019.

Ryan Holiday is the bestselling author of "Trust Me, I'm Lying", "The Obstacle Is the Way", "Ego Is the Enemy", "Conspiracy", and other books about marketing, culture, and the human condition. Holiday grew up in Sacramento, California, with his father as a police detective and his mother a high school principal. He dropped out of the University of California, Riverside in his sophomore year to pursue marketing and writing. He has written 12 best-selling books, covering topics including philosophy, marketing, history, and how to live well, with his work particularly focused on making ancient Stoic philosophy accessible to modern readers. His work has been translated into over 30 languages and has appeared everywhere from the New York Times to Fast Company. His company, Brass Check, has advised companies such as Google, TASER, and Complex, as well as multiplatinum musicians and some of the biggest authors in the world. Holiday opened The Painted Porch Bookshop in Bastrop, Texas with his wife during the pandemic, supporting local independent bookstores while continuing his mission to popularise Stoic wisdom.

NOVEMBER 17

"Did you make meaning out of your hardships?"
- Diane Coutu[324]

---

[324] Effective leaders learn to transmute difficulties into fuel. "Of all the virtues we can learn no trait is more useful," psychologist Mihaly Csikszentmihalyi explains, "more essential for survival, and more likely to improve the quality of life than the ability to transform adversity into an enjoyable challenge."

How Resilience Works, Diane Coutu, Harvard Business Review, May 2002.

Diane L. Coutu is a distinguished journalist and editor best known for her groundbreaking work on resilience at Harvard Business Review. She was named a Rhodes Scholar at Oxford after graduating with honors from Yale University, where she studied literature at Yale and then philosophy, politics and economics at Oxford. She worked at RAND before returning to Europe as a foreign correspondent with TIME and The Wall Street Journal Europe, then moved to McKinsey's European office/think tank in Brussels during the integration of the Single Market. As HBR senior editor, she became the magazine's first psychology editor and authored the seminal 2002 article "How Resilience Works," which identified three key characteristics of resilient people: a lucid acceptance of reality, a will to give meaning to things, and an ability to improvise. Her work on resilience has been widely cited and has significantly influenced how organisations and individuals understand coping with adversity and change.

NOVEMBER 18

"How do we build anti-fragile human systems and mindsets that benefit from volatility?"
- Graham Duncan[325]

---

[325] Anti-fragility is the property of systems that become stronger when exposed to stress, volatility, or disorder, rather than merely surviving or breaking under pressure. Unlike resilience, bouncing back to your original state, anti-fragility means you actually improve and gain from challenges. Examples include muscles that grow stronger from exercise stress, immune systems that develop resistance through exposure to pathogens, or businesses that adapt and thrive during market turbulence by becoming more efficient and innovative.

Current questions I find interesting, Graham Duncan, grahamduncan.blog.

Graham Duncan is a successful investor and talent spotter who co-founded East Rock Capital, a multi-family office investment firm that manages $2 billion for a small number of families and their charitable foundations. Before starting East Rock, Duncan worked at two other investment firms and started his career by co-founding an independent Wall Street research firm. A Yale graduate with a degree in ethics, politics, and economics, Duncan has become known as a "talent whisperer" for his unique ability to identify and nurture emerging investment talent. Duncan's unusual ability to wait out the moment is one of his defining characteristics as an investor, with colleagues noting that he's "not susceptible to impatience the way most people are" when it comes to seeding new investment managers. He also co-chairs The Sohn Investment Conference, which raises money for paediatric cancer research. Duncan maintains an active presence as a thoughtful writer and commentator on investment philosophy, human development, and talent identification, sharing insights through his blog and social media about the intersection of psychology and investing. His approach emphasises patience, deep understanding of human potential, and the importance of allowing talent to develop naturally rather than forcing growth.

NOVEMBER 19

"Do I truly understand—and accept—the reality of my situation?"
- Diane Coutu[326]

---

[326] Coutu's question echoes "The Stockdale Paradox", an idea coined by Jim Collins. The concept is named after Admiral James Stockdale who survived eight years of imprisonment in the Hanoi Hilton after being shot down during the Vietnam War. Explaining to Collins that the optimists perished in prison because they were crushed after not being released when they hoped, Stockdale told Collins, "This is a very important lesson. You must never confuse faith that you will prevail in the end—which you can never afford to lose—with the discipline to confront the most brutal facts of your current reality, whatever they might be."

How Resilience Works, Diane Coutu, Harvard Business Review, May 2002.

Diane L. Coutu is a distinguished journalist and editor best known for her groundbreaking work on resilience at Harvard Business Review. She was named a Rhodes Scholar at Oxford after graduating with honors from Yale University, where she studied literature at Yale and then philosophy, politics and economics at Oxford. She worked at RAND before returning to Europe as a foreign correspondent with TIME and The Wall Street Journal Europe, then moved to McKinsey's European office/think tank in Brussels during the integration of the Single Market. As HBR senior editor, she became the magazine's first psychology editor and authored the seminal 2002 article "How Resilience Works," which identified three key characteristics of resilient people: a lucid acceptance of reality, a will to give meaning to things, and an ability to improvise. Her work on resilience has been widely cited and has significantly influenced how organisations and individuals understand coping with adversity and change.

NOVEMBER 20

"What would I tell my best friend to do in this situation?"
- Chip Heath[327]

---

[327] The question is also one asked by author Dan Pink who explains that "we are often better at solving other people's problems than our own". The technique is called "self-distancing" and it helps bypass emotional biases. By imagining you're advising a friend, you can gain perspective and make more objective choices.

Decisive: How to Make Better Choices in Life and Work, Chip Heath, 2013.

Chip Heath is the Thrive Foundation for Youth Professor of Organizational Behavior at Stanford Graduate School of Business. He graduated from Texas A&M University with a Bachelor of Science degree in industrial engineering and subsequently earned a PhD in psychology from Stanford University before teaching at the University of Chicago Graduate School of Business and Duke University's Fuqua School of Business. His research examines why certain ideas — ranging from urban legends to folk medical cures, from Chicken Soup for the Soul stories to business strategy myths — survive and prosper in the social marketplace of ideas. Heath is best known for co-authoring three New York Times bestselling books with his brother Dan Heath: "Made to Stick: Why Some Ideas Survive and Others Die", which explores the anatomy of memorable ideas, "Switch: How to Change Things When Change is Hard", and "Decisive: How to Make Better Decisions in Life and Work". His work focuses on understanding how to make ideas more effective in organisational and social contexts.

NOVEMBER 21

"What is it trying to teach me?"
- John Gardner[328]

---

[328] "Learn all your life." Gardner advises. "Learn from your failures. Learn from your successes, when you hit a spell of trouble, ask "What is it trying to teach me?" The lessons aren't always happy ones, but they keep coming. It isn't a bad idea to pause occasionally for an inward look. By midlife, most of us are accomplished fugitives from ourselves."

Personal Renewal, John W. Gardner. Speech delivered to McKinsey & Company on November 10, 1990. Transcript originally published on PBS.org.

John W. Gardner (1912-2002) was an influential statesman, educator, and social reformer who served as Secretary of Health, Education, and Welfare under President Lyndon Johnson and became known as "the father of campaign finance reform" after founding Common Cause in 1970. A Stanford University graduate with a Ph.D. in psychology from UC Berkeley, he served as president of the Carnegie Corporation of New York and the Carnegie Foundation for the Advancement of Teaching from 1955 before joining Johnson's Great Society administration, where he helped launch Medicare and expand federal education programs. Gardner authored several influential books on leadership and social excellence, including "Excellence: Can We Be Equal and Excellent Too?" and "On Leadership", and founded the prestigious White House Fellows program. His legacy continues through the John W. Gardner Center at Stanford University and fellowship programs that encourage public service among young leaders.

NOVEMBER 22

"What if I could only subtract to solve problems?"
- Tim Ferriss[329]

---

[329] "From 2008 to 2009 I began to ask myself, "What if I could only subtract to solve problems?" when advising startups." Ferriss recalls. "Instead of answering, "What should we do?" I tried first to home in on answering, "What should we simplify?" For instance, I always wanted to tighten the conversion fishing net (the percentage of visitors who sign up or buy) before driving a ton of traffic to one of my portfolio companies. One of the first dozen startups I worked with was named Gyminee. It was rebranded Daily Burn, and at the time, they didn't have enough manpower to do a complete redesign of the site. Adding new elements would have been time consuming, but removing them wasn't. As a test, we eliminated roughly 70% of the "above the fold" clickable elements on their homepage, focusing on the single most valuable click. Conversions immediately improved 21.1%. That quick-and-dirty test informed later decisions for much more expensive development. The founders, Andy Smith and Stephen Blankenship, made a lot of great decisions, and the company was acquired by IAC in 2010. I've since applied this "What if I could only subtract . . . ?" to my life in many areas, and I sometimes rephrase it as "What should I put on my not-to-do list?"

17 Questions That Changed My Life, Tim Ferriss, tim.blog.

Tim Ferriss is an entrepreneur, author, podcaster, and angel investor best known for his bestselling book "The 4-Hour Workweek," which popularised concepts including lifestyle design, automation, and geographic arbitrage. Ferriss has written several other influential books including "The 4-Hour Body," "The 4-Hour Chef," "Tools of Titans," and "Tribe of Mentors," all focused on optimisation, efficiency, and learning from high performers. He hosts "The Tim Ferriss Show," one of the most popular podcasts, where he interviews world-class performers from various fields to deconstruct their habits, routines, and strategies. Ferriss is known for his systematic approach to "hacking" different areas of life, from business and fitness to learning new skills, often using unconventional methods to achieve maximum results with minimum input. As an angel investor, he has invested in companies like Uber, Facebook, Shopify, and Duolingo. His work emphasises the importance of asking better questions, testing assumptions, and designing life around one's priorities rather than defaulting to conventional paths. Ferriss has become a leading voice in the productivity and self-optimisation space, helping millions of people rethink how they approach work, learning, and personal development.

NOVEMBER 23

*"To solve any problem, here are three questions to ask yourself:
First, what could I do?
Second, what could I read?
And third, who could I ask?"*
- Jim Rohn[330]

---

[330] *How to Solve Any Problem That Gets in Your Way,* Jim Rohn, jimrohn.com, October 29, 2017.

Jim Rohn (1930-2009) was an entrepreneur, author and motivational speaker who became one of the most influential figures in the personal development industry. His parents owned and worked a farm in Caldwell, Idaho, where Rohn grew up as an only child. A successful entrepreneur, author, and motivational speaker, he achieved his first million by 31, thanks to his dedication, resilience, and keen insights. His rags to riches story played a large part in his work, which influenced others in the personal development industry, and he was the recipient of the 1985 National Speakers Association CPAE Award for excellence in speaking. He frequently stressed the notion that in order to attain success an individual must continually strive to improve themselves, firmly believing that investing in self-education, self-reflection, skill development is the gateway to unleashing a person's capabilities. Rohn is remembered for his philosophy of personal responsibility and his famous quote: "Formal education will make you a living; self-education will make you a fortune."

NOVEMBER 24

*"Over the course of my lifetime,
how important is this?"*
- Chip Conley[331]

---

[331] Effective leaders keep things in perspective. "When you arise each morning," Janet Sternberg writes, "remind yourself that today you do not have to go to a gas oven with your sisters, brothers, children, and friends. This thought may help you to deal more courageously with the fact that it is raining and your paper is late." Nystrom's Nugget #3 (named after Christine Nystrom), Janet Sternberg, from *Neil Postman's Advice on How to Live the Rest of Your Life*.

Learning to Love Midlife: 12 Reasons Why Life Gets Better with Age, Chip Conley, 2024.

Chip Conley is a hospitality entrepreneur, author, and business consultant best known for founding Joie de Vivre Hospitality, which became California's largest boutique hotel company. After selling his hotel empire, he joined Airbnb as Head of Global Hospitality and Strategy during the company's rapid growth phase, helping to professionalize their host experience and scale their operations. Conley has written several books on business and personal development, including "Peak: How Great Companies Get Their Mojo from Maslow," and is recognized for applying psychological principles like Maslow's hierarchy of needs to business strategy. He later founded the Modern Elder Academy, focusing on wisdom and experience in the workplace, and has become a prominent speaker on topics ranging from hospitality excellence to midlife reinvention.

NOVEMBER 25

*"Do you look to the future more with
anticipation or anxiety?"*
- Gregory Stock[332]

---

[332] Napoleon Bonaparte is often credited with saying, "A leader is a dealer in hope." "The optimist is right." writer and philosopher Ralph Waldo Trine writes. "The pessimist is right. The one differs from the other as the light from the dark. Yet both are right. Each is right from his own particular point of view, and this point of view is the determining factor in the life of each. It determines as to whether it is a life of power or of impotence, of peace or of pain, of success or of failure."
The Book of Questions: Revised and Updated, Gregory Stock, 2013.

Gregory Stock is a biotech entrepreneur, bioethicist, best-selling author and public communicator who is a leading authority on the broad impacts of genomic and other advanced technologies in the life sciences. He founded the influential Program on Medicine, Technology and Society at UCLA's School of Medicine in 1997 and served as its director for ten years while leading a broad effort to explore critical technologies poised to reshape medical science, Stock is the co-founder and former CEO of Signum Biosciences and has held academic positions at institutions including the University of California, Los Angeles (UCLA) and the Icahn School of Medicine at Mount Sinai. Gregory Stock is a scholar in the evolution of humanity as it is and will be, aided by technology. He is in the forefront of the debate on biotech policy, is a frequent speaker at conferences that study the issue, and contributes to scientific journals in the United States and abroad. His work focuses on the intersection of technology and human enhancement, exploring ethical questions around genetic engineering, life extension, and the future of human evolution. His insight at where technology and ethics connect have made him a popular guest on TV and radio, and he has been a prominent voice in discussions about biotechnology policy and the implications of emerging life sciences technologies for society, medicine, and human development.

NOVEMBER 26

"When you don't know what to do in a situation, ask yourself, 'What would the person I want to be do in this situation?' Then do that."
- Drew Dudley[333]

---

[333] "Decide the type of person you want to be," author James Clear advises, "and then you prove it to yourself with small wins. And the more small wins, the more small habits that you perform, the more votes that you cast for that identity, the more you build up evidence of being that kind of person. And eventually you start to take pride in that aspect of your identity."
This Is Day One: A Practical Guide to Leadership That Matters, Drew Dudley, 2018.

Drew Dudley is a leadership speaker, author, and educator who focuses on redefining leadership as everyday acts of positive impact rather than grand gestures. He gained widespread recognition through his popular TED Talk "Everyday Leadership," which has been viewed millions of times and challenges the traditional notion that leadership requires formal authority or dramatic moments. Dudley is the author of "This Is Day One" and has built his career around the concept of "lollipop moments"—small actions that can profoundly change someone's life without the actor even realizing it. As a former university administrator and founder of Day One Leadership, he works with organisations to help people recognise their capacity for leadership in daily interactions. His approach emphasises accessibility and authenticity in leadership, arguing that everyone has the potential to be a leader through simple acts of kindness, recognition, and positive influence on others.

NOVEMBER 27

*"Resolve dilemmas with greater ease.
Ask "What could I do?" rather than
"What should I do?"*
- Caroline Webb[334]

---

[334] *How To Have A Good Day: The Essential Toolkit for a Productive Day at Work and Beyond*, Caroline Webb, 2016.

Caroline Webb is CEO of Sevenshift, a firm that shows people how to use insights from behavioural science to improve their working life and a senior adviser to McKinsey, where she was previously a partner. She graduated from the University of Cambridge in economics, and received her MPhil from the University of Oxford in economics. Before McKinsey, Webb spent the 1990s working in public policy as an economist at the UK's central bank, the Bank of England, where her work included working closely with the Monetary Policy Committee as author of the Inflation Report and global economic forecasting. She is best known for her book "How to Have a Good Day," which shows how to use recent findings from behavioural economics, psychology and neuroscience to transform the quality of our everyday lives, at work and beyond. She is a founding fellow of the Harvard-affiliated Institute of Coaching and founded McKinsey's flagship leadership development course for senior female executives.

NOVEMBER 28

"If I had 10x the agency I have, what would I do?"
- Nick Cammerata[335]

---

[335] Writer and entrepreneur George Mack distils the concept of agency down to a question. "You wake up in a 3rd world jail cell." Mack writes. "You're only allowed to call one person you know to get you out of there. Who do you call?" *High Agency*, George Mack, highagency.com.

3-2-1 Newsletter, James Clear, January 30, 2025.

Nick Cammarata is a leading AI researcher specialising in neural network interpretability at OpenAI, where he focuses on understanding how artificial intelligence systems actually work internally. His research concentrates on neural network interpretability, seeking to demystify the "black box" nature of modern AI models by analysing how individual neurons and circuits function within large language models. Cammarata has contributed to significant OpenAI projects including work on multimodal neurons and OpenAI Microscope, tools that help visualise and understand what neural networks learn. His research is part of the broader mechanistic interpretability movement, which aims to reverse-engineer AI systems to make them more transparent, predictable, and safe. With his research works and hundreds of citations, Cammarata represents a new generation of researchers working to ensure that as AI systems become more powerful, we maintain the ability to understand and control their behaviour—a critical challenge as these systems become increasingly integrated into society. He also writes essays.

NOVEMBER 29

"How much worse it must've been in the past? What do I owe to my grandparents and great-grandparents, and great-great-grandparents who suffered and toiled, who barely managed to survive to produce another generation? What do I owe to them?"
- Martine Rothblatt[336]

---

[336] "In times when people don't see a way out of their circumstances," Polina Pompliano writes, "Rothblatt recommends staying in touch with your ancestors." If you are feeling lost, Rothblatt asks these questions to instantly shift perspective. Rothblatt added, "I owe it to them to make the absolute most possible out of my life and that's what I'm going to do."

The Profile Dossier: Martine Rothblatt, the Futurist Creating Life-Saving Technology, Polina Pompliano, August 3, 2022.

Martine Rothblatt is an entrepreneur, biotech pioneer, and futurist who has built multiple groundbreaking companies. She founded GeoStar (the GPS-based navigation system) in the 1980s, then Sirius in 1990, and later the biotech company United Therapeutics. Her transition from satellite technology to biotechnology was deeply personal. After her daughter Jenesis was diagnosed with a fatal lung disease, she founded United Therapeutics to develop drugs that ended up saving her daughter's life and those of thousands of others. United Therapeutics specialises in lung disease treatment and the manufacture of organs for transplants, helping those with pulmonary hypertension live longer than ever. Beyond her business success, Rothblatt is a prominent transhumanist thinker who explores concepts like digital immortality and "mindclones" - she even commissioned an artificially intelligent robot based on her wife. She transitioned in 1994 at age 40 and has become a visible advocate for transgender rights while pushing the boundaries of biotechnology, organ transplantation, and the future of human consciousness.

NOVEMBER 30

*"Survivors don't have time to ask, 'Why me?'
For survivors, the only relevant question is,
'What now?'"*
- Edith Eger[337]

---

[337] *The Choice: Embrace the Possible*, Edith Eger, 2018.

Edith Eger is a Czechoslovakian-born psychologist, a Holocaust survivor and a specialist in the treatment of post-traumatic stress disorder. At 97, she is a gymnast turned psychologist turned public speaker and author who uses her experience as a Holocaust survivor to offer guidance to her readers on how heal and thrive. At the age of sixteen, a trained ballet dancer and gymnast, she was sent to Auschwitz concentration camp, where she survived the horrors of the Holocaust while losing her parents. After immigrating to America, Eger earned her doctorate in psychology and became a world-renowned clinical psychologist specialising in post-traumatic stress disorder or PTSD. Her memoir entitled "The Choice: Embrace the Possible" became an international bestseller, combining her Holocaust survival story with insights on healing and resilience. She has also written "The Gift: 12 Lessons to Save Your Life," continuing to share her wisdom about overcoming trauma, finding freedom through forgiveness, and choosing hope over victimhood even in the face of unimaginable suffering.

DECEMBER

LEAVE A LEGACY

DECEMBER 1

"What truly matters?"
- James Ryan[338]

---

[338] Ryan says this is one of five truly essential questions that you should regularly ask yourself and others. If you get in the habit of asking these questions Ryan believes you will have a very good chance of being successful and happy. "'What truly matters?' You can tack on 'to me' as appropriate." Ryan says. "This is the question that forces you to get to the heart of issues and to the heart of your own beliefs and convictions. Indeed, it's a question that you might add to, or substitute for, New Year's resolutions. You might ask yourself, in other words, at least every new year: what truly matters to me?"

Harvard Graduate School of Education Commencement Address, James E. Ryan, May 28, 2016.

James E. Ryan is a legal scholar who was the President of the University of Virginia from 2018 to 2025, having previously served as dean of Harvard Graduate School of Education and formerly the Matheson and Morgenthau Distinguished Professor at the University of Virginia School of Law. A leading expert on law and education, James Ryan has written extensively about how law structures educational opportunity. He is the author of several influential books, including "Wait, What?: And Life's Other Essential Questions" and "Five Miles Away, A World Apart: One City, Two Schools, and the Story of Educational Opportunity in Modern America". His book "Wait, What?" became a New York Times self-help best-seller, and describes the art of asking good questions, distilling them to five "essential" ones, and how they lead to better answers. Ryan is known for his thoughtful approach to leadership and education policy, emphasising the importance of asking the right questions to strengthen connections and deepen understanding.

DECEMBER 2

"What did you do to make a difference in the world?"
- Bill George[339]

---

[339] This question relates to another question, one that fighter pilot and military strategist John Boyd would ask young and impressionable colleagues. "Tiger, one day you will come to a fork in the road," Boyd said. "And you're going to have to make a decision about which direction you want to go." He raised his hand and pointed. "If you go that way you can be somebody. You will have to make compromises and you will have to turn your back on your friends. But you will be a member of the club and you will get promoted and you will get good assignments." Then Boyd raised his other hand and pointed another direction. "Or you can go that way and you can do something - something for your country and for your Air Force and for yourself. If you decide you want to do something, you may not get promoted and you may not get the good assignments and you certainly will not be a favorite of your superiors. But you won't have to compromise yourself. You will be true to your friends and to yourself. And your work might make a difference." He paused and stared into the officer's eyes and heart. "To be somebody or to do something. In life there is often a roll call. That's when you will have to make a decision. To be or to do. Which way will you go?"

True North, Bill George, Talks at Google, October 23, 2008.

Bill George is a prominent business leader, author, and Harvard Business School professor who is widely recognised as one of the foremost authorities on authentic leadership. He was the CEO of Medtronic from 1991 to 2001 where he achieved remarkable success. George is the author of best-selling books including "Authentic Leadership" and "True North" which have become foundational texts in leadership development. His concept of authentic leadership emphasises that effective leaders must be true to themselves, understand their values and purpose, and lead from a place of genuine conviction rather than trying to emulate others. His speeches convey powerful principles: organisations can only achieve their full potential by developing authentic leaders inside them; each individual must cultivate True North, a moral compass to successfully navigate the challenges of leadership. After leaving Medtronic, George became a professor at Harvard Business School where he teaches leadership courses and continues his research on authentic leadership development. He has served on the boards of Goldman Sachs, Novartis, Target, ExxonMobil, and Mayo Clinic. His work focuses on helping leaders discover their authentic selves, develop their moral compass, and create organisations where people can find meaning and purpose in their work. George's influence extends beyond academia, as he's sought after as a speaker and advisor for his insights on leadership in an era where trust and authenticity are increasingly valued in business.

DECEMBER 3

"How will I know I've done a great job?"
- Peter Drucker[340]

---

[340] "I pondered what Drucker would say," Collins writes, "and then answered: 'Identify one big thing that would most contribute to the future of the university and orchestrate getting it done. If you make one distinctive contribution—a key decision that would not have happened without your leadership (even if no one ever credits you for your catalytic role)—then you will have rendered a great service.' Drucker applied this idea to his own consulting. When I asked him what he contributed to his clients, he modestly said, "I have generally learned more from them than they learned from me." Then, pausing for effect, he added, 'Of course, in each case there was one absolutely fundamental decision they would not have made without me.' What is your one absolutely fundamental contribution that would not happen without you?"

Ten Lessons I Learned from Peter Drucker, Jim Collins, Foreword to the 50th Anniversary Edition of The Effective Executive, May 17, 2016.

Peter Drucker (1909-2005) was a management consultant, educator, and author widely regarded as the founder of modern management theory. Drucker wrote over 30 books and countless articles that fundamentally shaped how we think about business, leadership, and organisational effectiveness. He coined many concepts that are now management staples, including "management by objectives," "knowledge worker," and the idea that the purpose of business is to create customers. His most influential works include "The Practice of Management" and "The Effective Executive". Drucker emphasised that management is both an art and a science, focusing on people rather than just processes, and he predicted many major business trends including the rise of the information economy and the importance of innovation. Beyond business, he was a prolific social commentator who wrote about democracy, society, and the role of institutions. His insights remain remarkably relevant today, and he's remembered for his practical wisdom and his belief that effective management could make organisations more productive while also making work more meaningful for people.

DECEMBER 4

"You may have a success in life, but then just think of it - what kind of life was it?"
- Joseph Campbell[341]

---

[341] "What good was it - you've never done the thing you wanted to do in all your life." Campbell explains. "I always tell my students, go where your body and soul want to go. When you have the feeling, then stay with it, and don't let anyone throw you off..." Campbell's advice to those seeking fulfilment and happiness was simple. "The way to find out about your happiness is to keep your mind on those moments when you feel most happy, when you really are happy – not excited, not just thrilled, but deeply happy." Campbell says. "This requires a little bit of self-analysis. What is it that makes you happy? Stay with it, no matter what people tell you. This is what I call "following your bliss"... There's something inside you that knows when you're in the center, that knows when you're on the beam or off the beam. And if you get off the beam to earn money, you've lost your life. And if you stay in the center and don't get any money, you still have your bliss."

Joseph Campbell and the Power of Myth, PBS documentary with Bill Moyers, 1988.

Joseph Campbell (1904 - 1987) was a mythologist, writer, and lecturer who became one of the most influential scholars of comparative mythology and religion in the 20th century. He's best known for his theory of the "monomyth" or "Hero's Journey," which he outlined in "The Hero with a Thousand Faces", arguing that heroic narratives from cultures worldwide follow a similar underlying pattern. Campbell spent decades studying mythologies, religions, and folklore from around the globe, seeking to identify universal themes and structures that reveal shared human experiences and psychological truths. His work gained popular recognition through his televised interviews with Bill Moyers in "The Power of Myth", where he explored how ancient myths remain relevant to modern life. Campbell's ideas have profoundly influenced storytelling in literature, film, and popular culture, with creators like George Lucas citing his work as inspiration for Star Wars.

DECEMBER 5

"If you could write your own eulogy, what would it say?"
- Sahil Bloom[342]

---

[342] Bloom's question echoes Warren Buffett whose advice is to "Write your obituary and then try and figure out how to live up to it."
The Curiosity Chronicle, Sahil Bloom, July 27, 2023.

Sahil Bloom is an entrepreneur, writer, and content creator who captivates millions of people every week through his insights and biweekly newsletter, The Curiosity Chronicle. He's the author of "The 5 Types of Wealth" and graduated from Stanford University with an MA in public policy and a BA in economics and sociology. Bloom is the owner of SRB Holdings, a personal holding company currently comprised of seven cash-flowing businesses, and the Managing Partner of SRB Ventures, a venture investment firm. Bloom's approach focuses on using his creator experience to understand and serve other creators' needs, rather than just being a traditional content creator. He shares frameworks and insights on personal development, entrepreneurship, and building wealth across multiple dimensions.

DECEMBER 6

*"If you are a boss, ask yourself:
When you look back at how you've treated followers,
peers, and superiors, in their eyes, will you have
earned the right to be proud of yourself?
Or will they believe that you ought to be ashamed of
yourself and embarrassed by how you have trampled
on others' dignity day after day?"*
- Robert Sutton[343]

---

[343] The question is reminiscent of Greek stateman and general Pericles who explained, "What you leave behind is not what is engraved on stone monuments, but what is woven into the lives of others."
Good Boss, Bad Boss: How to Be the Best... and Learn from the Worst, Robert I. Sutton, 2010.
Robert I. Sutton is an organisational psychologist and Professor Emeritus of Management Science and Engineering at Stanford University. Sutton studies innovation, leaders and bosses, evidence-based management, the links between knowledge and organisational action, and workplace civility. He is best known for his provocative and influential book "The No Asshole Rule: Building a Civilized Workplace and Surviving One That Isn't", which won the Quill Award for best business book in 2007 and sold more than 115,000 copies. He has written eight books, including (with Huggy Rao) "The Friction Project: How Smart Leaders Make the Right Things Easier and the Wrong Things Harder". Sutton's work focuses on practical organisational psychology, exploring how toxic workplace behaviour destroys productivity and morale, while providing evidence-based strategies for creating more civilised and effective work environments. His research combines academic rigor with accessible, often humorous writing that addresses real workplace challenges.

DECEMBER 7

"When you look back on your experiences in life and think of those things that you regret, what would you say you regret more, those things that you did, but wish you hadn't, or those things that you didn't do, but wish you had?"
- Chip Conley[344]

---

[344] "Mark Twain didn't dabble in psychological focus groups," Conley explains, "but he certainly knew something about human nature when he wrote, 'Twenty years from now you will be more disappointed by the things that you didn't do than by the ones you did do. So throw off the bowlines. Sail away from the safe harbor. Catch the trade winds in your sails. Explore. Dream. Discover.' A series of surveys explored the premise that time is an important variable in this equation. Researchers asked a random sampling of people, 'When you look back on your experiences in life and think of those things that you regret, what would you say you regret more, those things that you did, but wish you hadn't, or those things that you didn't do, but wish you had?' The results found that regrettable 'failures to act' outnumbered 'regrettable actions' by a two-to-one margin and that this was true for both sexes." *Emotional Equations: Simple formulas to help your life work better*, Chip Conley, 2012.

Chip Conley is a hospitality entrepreneur, author, and business consultant best known for founding Joie de Vivre Hospitality, which became California's largest boutique hotel company. After selling his hotel empire, he joined Airbnb as Head of Global Hospitality and Strategy during the company's rapid growth phase, helping to professionalize their host experience and scale their operations. Conley has written several books on business and personal development, including "Peak: How Great Companies Get Their Mojo from Maslow," and is recognized for applying psychological principles like Maslow's hierarchy of needs to business strategy. He later founded the Modern Elder Academy, focusing on wisdom and experience in the workplace, and has become a prominent speaker on topics ranging from hospitality excellence to midlife reinvention.

DECEMBER 8

"Would your successor thank you?"
- Michael Lombardi & George Raveling[345]

---

[345] Lombardi and Raveling say the mark of a secure leader is building something that works without them. Ask yourself -

Are you building something that's only strong when you're in the room-or something that gets even stronger when you're not?

Would your successor say you left things better than you found them?

Can you root for [support] what comes next, even if you're not part of it?

Lombardi and Raveling say while some leaders leave a mark, the best ones leave momentum.

The Daily Coach May 29, 2025.

Michael Lombardi is a three-time Super Bowl champion as an executive with over 30 years of experience in NFL front offices who recently joined the North Carolina football program as General Manager in December 2024. He has spent 35 years working for the New England Patriots, San Francisco 49ers, the Oakland Raiders and the Cleveland Browns, and has the distinction of the being the only person to make it to the Super Bowl with both the Patriots and 49ers. Beyond his front office work, Lombardi has been a prominent media personality as an NFL analyst, author, and cofounder with George Raveling of The Daily Coach, a newsletter that shares sports and organisational leadership lessons.

George Raveling is a Basketball Hall of Fame coach and Nike executive who has had an extraordinary impact on both basketball and sports marketing. After a successful college coaching career at schools including Washington State, Iowa, and USC, he joined Nike at the request of Phil Knight, where he played an integral role in signing a reluctant Michael Jordan. Raveling has worked as the Director for International Basketball for Nike since his retirement from USC and is known as "the iconic leader who brought Michael Jordan to Nike". Beyond basketball, he has a unique connection to civil rights history and having a personal connection to Martin Luther King Jr.'s "I Have a Dream" speech. Raveling was present at the March on Washington on August 28, 1963, and after Dr. King delivered his speech, King handed Raveling the original typewritten copy.

The two co-founded The Daily Coach newsletter, sharing leadership wisdom from sports and business.

DECEMBER 9

*"What do we want to leave behind?
What do we want to support, maintain, in the limited
time we are here?"*
- Jenn Shapland[346]

---

[346] Whilst it is tempting to think of legacy in terms of your accomplishments, it should include those things that live on in the hearts of others you have touched. "If something comes to life in others because of you," Norman Cousins writes, "then you have made an approach to immortality."
Thin Skin: Essays, Jenn Shapland, 2023.

Jenn Shapland is a writer and archivist. She received her PhD in English from the University of Texas at Austin and works as an adjunct instructor in the Creative Writing Department at the Institute of American Indian Arts in Santa Fe, as well as an archivist for a visual artist. Shapland is best known for her memoir "My Autobiography of Carson McCullers," which was a finalist for the 2020 National Book Award. The book is a hybrid of memoir and biography that emerged from her discovery of novelist Carson McCullers' love letters while working as an intern in archives. Her essay "Finders, Keepers" won a Pushcart Prize in 2017, and her non-fiction has appeared in publications like Tin House and Outside magazine.

DECEMBER 10

"Are you getting what you want out of life?"
- Rebecca Solnit[347]

---

[347] The following is paraphrased from Billy Oppenheimer. Throughout her career, writer Rebecca Solnit has been persistently "interrogated" and "hounded" about her choice not to have children—during book tours, interviews, and even casual conversations. The relentless questioning prompted her to examine why society so predictably demands explanations when someone diverges from conventional life paths. "Maybe part of the problem is that we have learned to ask the wrong things of ourselves," Solnit reflects in *The Mother of All Questions*. "Our culture is steeped in a kind of pop psychology whose obsessive question is: Are you happy? ... Questions about happiness generally assume that we know what a happy life looks like. Happiness is understood to be a matter of having a great many ducks lined up in a row—spouse, offspring, private property, erotic experiences—even though a millisecond of reflection will bring to mind countless people who have all those things and are still miserable." Solnit suggests that perhaps the fundamental question we should ask isn't about conformity to prescribed happiness templates but rather: "Are you getting what you want out of life?" This reframing acknowledges the profound diversity of human fulfillment. Though her path diverges from mainstream expectations, Solnit affirms with quiet conviction, "I have done what I set out to do in my life", a powerful testament to defining success on one's own terms rather than through society's limiting lens.

The Mother of All Questions, Rebecca Solnit, 2017.

Rebecca Solnit is a prolific writer and cultural critic whose work spans twenty-five books on feminism, environmental and urban history, popular power, social change and insurrection, wandering and walking, hope and catastrophe. She's perhaps best known for coining the term "mansplaining" in her influential essay collection Men Explain Things to Me, and for her foundational work Hope in the Dark, which examines how social change happens in unexpected ways. Her books include this year's No Straight Road Takes You There, as well as Orwell's Roses, Recollections of My Nonexistence, and A Paradise Built in Hell, which explores how communities come together during disasters. Solnit's writing consistently weaves together personal narrative, political analysis, and cultural observation, making her a distinctive voice in contemporary discussions about power, gender, environmental justice, and the nature of hope itself.

DECEMBER 11

"Would the people you serve miss you when you're gone?"
- Seth Godin[348]

---

[348] "When I say 'missed when you're gone,'" Godin explains, "I'm not talking about having a lot of people come to your funeral. I'm talking about creating a reputation where you get asked back, where people seek out your product, where a store or a conference or an agenda isn't complete without you." *The best way to be missed when you're gone*, Seth Godin, seths.blog, August 10, 2012.
This Is Marketing: You Can't Be Seen Until You Learn to See, Seth Godin, 2018.
Seth Godin is a bestselling author, entrepreneur, and marketing guru who has fundamentally changed how people think about marketing, leadership, and the spread of ideas. He's written over 20 books, including influential titles like "Purple Cow," which popularised the concept that businesses must be remarkable to succeed, "The Tipping Point" predecessor "Unleashing the Ideavirus," and "Linchpin," which argues that indispensable employees are those who bring creativity and humanity to their work. Godin founded several companies, including Yoyodyne (one of the first internet marketing companies, sold to Yahoo!) and Squidoo, and the altMBA, an intensive online leadership workshop. His daily blog, which he's maintained for decades, reaches millions of readers with insights on marketing, culture, and human behaviour. Godin is known for coining terms like "permission marketing" (marketing to people who want to be marketed to) and advocating for authentic, story-driven approaches over traditional advertising. His philosophy emphasises that in the modern economy, playing it safe is actually the riskiest strategy, and that success comes from being different, generous, and willing to make a difference. He's also a sought-after speaker who challenges conventional business wisdom and encourages people to embrace change and lead rather than follow.

DECEMBER 12

"Will I be an ancestor or a ghost?"
- Ryan Holiday[349]

---

[349] "Will you be a ghost or an ancestor to your children?" Holiday asks. "Will you be the kind of example they need? Will you leave the kind of legacy that will guide them? That will inspire them to be decent and disciplined, great and good? Or will you haunt them with your mistakes, with the pain you inflicted on them, with the things left unsaid or unresolved?"

15 Questions That Will Make You A Better Parent (And Person), Ryan Holiday.

Ryan Holiday is the bestselling author of "Trust Me, I'm Lying", "The Obstacle Is the Way", "Ego Is the Enemy", "Conspiracy", and other books about marketing, culture, and the human condition. Holiday grew up in Sacramento, California, with his father as a police detective and his mother a high school principal. He dropped out of the University of California, Riverside in his sophomore year to pursue marketing and writing. He has written 12 best-selling books, covering topics including philosophy, marketing, history, and how to live well, with his work particularly focused on making ancient Stoic philosophy accessible to modern readers. His work has been translated into over 30 languages and has appeared everywhere from the New York Times to Fast Company. His company, Brass Check, has advised companies such as Google, TASER, and Complex, as well as multiplatinum musicians and some of the biggest authors in the world. Holiday opened The Painted Porch Bookshop in Bastrop, Texas with his wife during the pandemic, supporting local independent bookstores while continuing his mission to popularise Stoic wisdom.

DECEMBER 13

*"Is the life you're living worth the price
you're paying to live it?"*
- Tony Schwartz[350]

---

[350] *Is the Life You're Living Worth the Price You're Paying to Live It?*, Tony Schwartz, Harvard Business Review, July 6, 2011. Also refer to *The way we're working isn't working*, Tony Schwartz, TEDxMidwest, June 27, 2012, and *The Way We're Working Isn't Working: The Four Forgotten Needs That Energize Great Performance*, Tony Schwartz, Jean Gomes, Catherine McCarthy, 2011.

Tony Schwartz is an author, business consultant, and entrepreneur who has dedicated his career to transforming how people approach work and productivity. In 2003, Schwartz founded The Energy Project, a consulting firm that focuses on the improvement of employee productivity and counts Facebook as one of its clients, after previously co-authoring "The Power of Full Engagement: Managing Energy Not Time" with Jim Loehr. His groundbreaking philosophy centres on the idea that managing energy, rather than time, is the key to peak performance and sustained productivity. Through his years of intensive work consulting to companies including Procter & Gamble, Sony, Toyota, Microsoft, Ford and Ernst & Young, with his firm The Energy Project, Schwartz has developed a powerful program for changing the way we are working that greatly boosts our engagement and our satisfaction with our work and increases our performance. His bestselling book "The Way We're Working Isn't Working" argues that the modern workplace model is counterproductive, sapping employees of their physical, emotional, mental, and spiritual energy. Schwartz's approach focuses on four core human needs that he believes organisations must address to create high-performing, engaged workforces. His work has influenced countless companies to rethink their approach to employee well-being, productivity, and organisational culture, making him a leading voice in the movement toward more sustainable and human-centered approaches to work.

DECEMBER 14

"Did you do your best?"
- Hyman Rickover[351]

---

[351] The title of the book by US President Jimmy Carter is sometimes misattributed as a quotation of Rickover; though the title was inspired by a job interview Carter had with Rickover. Carter explains, "I had applied for nuclear submarine program, and Admiral Rickover was interviewing me for the job... Finally he asked me a question and I thought I could redeem myself. He said, 'How did you stand in your class at the Naval Academy?' ... I swelled my chest with pride and answered, 'Sir, I stood 59th in a class of 820!' I sat back to wait for the congratulations — which never came. Instead the question: 'Did you do your best?' I started to say, 'Yes, sir,' but I remembered who this was... I finally gulped and said, 'No sir, I didn't always do my best.' He looked at me for a long time, and then turned his chair around to end the interview. He asked one final question, which I have never been able to forget — or to answer. He said, 'Why not?'"
Why Not the Best?, Jimmy Carter, 1975.

Admiral Hyman G. Rickover (1900-1986) was a transformational leader known as the "Father of the Nuclear Navy" who revolutionised naval warfare and power generation through nuclear technology. In his 63 years of service, Admiral Rickover took nuclear power "from an idea to the present reality of more than 150 U.S. naval ships under nuclear power, with a record of 3,000 ship-years of accident-free operations." Rickover was notorious for his exacting standards, rigorous interview processes, and demanding leadership style that pushed subordinates to achieve unprecedented levels of excellence and safety. He simultaneously held positions directing the Naval Reactors program and overseeing civilian nuclear power development, including the world's first commercial nuclear power plant at Shippingport, Pennsylvania. His approach to organisational change was characterised by absolute personal accountability, meticulous attention to detail, and an unwavering commitment to nuclear safety that established the foundation for both military and civilian nuclear programs. Rickover's legacy demonstrates how a single leader with clear vision and uncompromising standards can drive fundamental technological and organisational transformation across entire industries.

DECEMBER 15

"How will you use your gifts? What choices will you make? Will inertia be your guide, or will you follow your passions? Will you follow dogma, or will you be original? Will you choose a life of ease, or a life of service and adventure? Will you wilt under criticism, or will you follow your convictions? Will you bluff it out when you're wrong, or will you apologize? Will you guard your heart against rejection, or will you act when you fall in love? Will you play it safe, or will you be a little bit swashbuckling? When it's tough, will you give up, or will you be relentless? Will you be a cynic, or will you be a builder? Will you be clever at the expense of others, or will you be kind?"

- Jeff Bezos[352]

---

[352] *We are What We Choose*, Remarks by Jeff Bezos as delivered to the Class of 2010, Princeton University, May 30, 2010.

Jeff Bezos is an entrepreneur and business magnate who founded Amazon in 1994 and transformed it from an online bookstore into one of the world's largest and most influential companies. Bezos worked on Wall Street before starting Amazon from his garage in Bellevue, Washington, initially focusing on selling books online. Under his leadership as CEO until 2021, Amazon expanded into virtually every sector of commerce, revolutionising retail through innovations like one-click purchasing, Prime membership, and same-day delivery, while also becoming a dominant force in cloud computing through Amazon Web Services. Beyond Amazon, he founded the space exploration company Blue Origin in 2000 with the goal of making space travel more accessible, and he's been involved in various philanthropic efforts including climate change initiatives. Known for his long-term thinking, customer obsession, and willingness to experiment and fail, Bezos has been credited with fundamentally changing how people shop and businesses operate in the digital age.

DECEMBER 16

*"Should you live for your resume ...
or your eulogy?"*
- David Brooks[353]

---

[353] Brooks contrasts "resume virtues" and "eulogy virtues" to highlight the two distinct sets of values that shape a person's life. Resume virtues are the skills and accomplishments emphasised in professional settings and on résumés, often focused on external success and career advancement. Eulogy virtues, on the other hand, are the deeper, more personal qualities that are remembered and celebrated at a person's funeral, such as kindness, honesty, and the capacity for love.
Should you live for your résumé ... or your eulogy, David Brooks, TED March 2014.

David Brooks is a prominent journalist, political commentator, and author who writes for The New York Times, where he has been an op-ed columnist since 2003. Known for his thoughtful analysis of American politics, culture, and society, Brooks often takes a moderate conservative perspective while focusing on themes like community, character, and moral development. He's written several influential books including "The Social Animal," which explores human behaviour and decision-making, "The Road to Character," which examines the difference between résumé virtues and eulogy virtues, and "The Second Mountain," about finding deeper meaning and purpose in life. Before joining the Times, Brooks worked at publications like The Wall Street Journal, The Weekly Standard, and The Atlantic. He's also a regular commentator on PBS NewsHour and NPR, and teaches at Yale University. Brooks is known for his ability to bridge political divides and his interest in how psychology, sociology, and moral philosophy intersect with public policy and everyday life.

DECEMBER 17

*"What might our descendants wish
we had done better for them?"*
- Roman Krznaric[354]

---

[354] "There is an Apache saying," Krznaric explains, "'We do not inherit the land from our ancestors; we borrow it from our children.' In the end it is not just our own children, but all children who will judge us from the future."

The Good Ancestor: A Radical Prescription for Long-Term Thinking, Roman Krznaric, 2020.

Roman Krznaric is a public philosopher who writes about the power of ideas to change society, with internationally bestselling books including "The Good Ancestor," "Empathy," "The Wonderbox," and "Carpe Diem Regained" published in more than 25 languages. A popular speaker and co-founder of The School of Life, he has travelled the world researching and lecturing on the subject of empathy, and serves as Senior Research Fellow at Oxford. Krznaric became known for his work on empathy as a force for social transformation, exploring what he calls the "Six Habits of Highly Empathic People." He came up with the innovative idea of an Empathy Museum and created the touring art exhibit "A Mile in My Shoes", a shoe shop where visitors are invited to literally walk a mile in someone else's shoes, demonstrating his commitment to making philosophical concepts tangible and experiential.

DECEMBER 18

*"What do I want to be remembered for?
Why do I want to be remembered at all?"*
- Ricardo Semler[355]

---

[355] "I taught MBAs at MIT for a time and I ended up, one day, at the Mount Auburn Cemetery." Semler recalls. "It is a beautiful cemetery in Cambridge. And I was walking around. It was my birthday and I was thinking. And the first time around, I saw these tombstones and these wonderful people who'd done great things and I thought, what do I want to be remembered for? And I did another stroll around, and the second time, another question came to me, which did me better, which was, why do I want to be remembered at all? And that, I think, took me different places. When I was 50, my wife Fernanda and I sat for a whole afternoon, we had a big pit with fire, and I threw everything I had ever done into that fire. This is a book in 38 languages, hundreds and hundreds of articles and DVDs, everything there was. And that did two things. One, it freed our five kids from following in our steps, our shadow ... And the second thing is, I freed myself from this anchor of past achievement or whatever. I'm free to start something new every time ..." Semler echoed Marcus Aurelius who penned, "So many who were remembered already forgotten, and those who remembered them long gone." *Meditations - A New Translation*, Gregory Hays, 2003.
Ricardo Semler: Radical wisdom for a company, a school, a life, TED, February 2015.
Ricardo Semler is the chief executive officer and majority owner of Semco Partners, a Brazilian company best known for its radical form of industrial democracy and corporate re-engineering. Semler took over the Semco Group from his father at age 21, transforming what was originally a marine pump manufacturer into a pioneering example of workplace democracy. At Semco, Semler implemented radical changes such as profit sharing, workplace flexibility, and radical transparency to empower employees and foster a culture of innovation. He is the author of "Maverick" and has written influential Harvard Business Review articles including on managing without managers. Semler's revolutionary approach to corporate democracy has made him a sought-after speaker and consultant, and he became so successful at democratising his company that it eventually held a party to celebrate the tenth anniversary of the last time he made a decision about anything.

DECEMBER 19

"The question is - if you die today, what ideas, what dreams, what abilities, what talents, what gifts, would die with you?"

- Les Brown[356]

---

[356] Brown prefaces this question with the following context: "Imagine if you will being on your death bed - and standing around your bed - the ghosts of the ideas, the dreams, the abilities, the talents given to you by life. And that you for whatever reason, you never acted on those ideas, you never pursued that dream, you never used those talents, we never saw your leadership, you never used your voice, you never wrote that book. And there they are standing around your bed looking at you with large angry eyes saying 'we came to you, and only you could have given us life! Now we must die with you forever.'"

Live Your Dreams, Les Brown, 1992, and *It's Not Over Until You Win* from circa 1992. The speech is also referred to by actor Denzel Washington in his University of Pennsylvania Commencement Address on May 16, 2011.

Leslie Calvin "Les" Brown is a renowned motivational speaker, author, and former politician. Born into poverty and adopted by a single mother who worked as a cafeteria attendant, Brown overcame significant early challenges including being labelled "educable mentally retarded" in grade school and being placed in special education classes. After starting his speaking career in 1986 while broke and sleeping on his office floor, he transformed his life to become one of the highest-paid motivational speakers in the nation by the early 1990s. For over three decades, Brown has worked with Fortune 500 CEOs, small business owners, and community leaders across all sectors of society, studying and mastering the science of achievement while delivering his empowering message to diverse audiences ranging from corporate executives to prison inmates. He also served in the Ohio House of Representatives from 1977 to 1981, demonstrating his commitment to public service alongside his motivational speaking career.

DECEMBER 20

"Close your eyes, you're dead (sorry!).
Imagine you're at your own funeral.
People are walking in, crying, hugging each other.
Everyone sits down.
Who's in the front row?
Those are the people that really matter.
What are you doing today to cherish them?"
- Sahil Bloom[357]

---

[357] *33 Life Learnings from 33 Years*, Sahil Bloom, The Curiosity Chronicle, Episode 175, sahilbloom.com, January 5, 2024.

Sahil Bloom is an entrepreneur, writer, and content creator who captivates millions of people every week through his insights and biweekly newsletter, The Curiosity Chronicle. He's the author of "The 5 Types of Wealth" and graduated from Stanford University with an MA in public policy and a BA in economics and sociology. Bloom is the owner of SRB Holdings, a personal holding company currently comprised of seven cash-flowing businesses, and the Managing Partner of SRB Ventures, a venture investment firm. Bloom's approach focuses on using his creator experience to understand and serve other creators' needs, rather than just being a traditional content creator. He shares frameworks and insights on personal development, entrepreneurship, and building wealth across multiple dimensions.

DECEMBER 21

*"What do you want people to say about you?
Which people?"*
- Seth Godin[358]

---

[358] *8 questions and a why*, Seth Godin, seths.blog, December 15, 2009.

Seth Godin is a bestselling author, entrepreneur, and marketing guru who has fundamentally changed how people think about marketing, leadership, and the spread of ideas. He's written over 20 books, including influential titles like "Purple Cow," which popularised the concept that businesses must be remarkable to succeed, "The Tipping Point" predecessor "Unleashing the Ideavirus," and "Linchpin," which argues that indispensable employees are those who bring creativity and humanity to their work. Godin founded several companies, including Yoyodyne (one of the first internet marketing companies, sold to Yahoo!) and Squidoo, and the altMBA, an intensive online leadership workshop. His daily blog, which he's maintained for decades, reaches millions of readers with insights on marketing, culture, and human behaviour. Godin is known for coining terms like "permission marketing" (marketing to people who want to be marketed to) and advocating for authentic, story-driven approaches over traditional advertising. His philosophy emphasises that in the modern economy, playing it safe is actually the riskiest strategy, and that success comes from being different, generous, and willing to make a difference. He's also a sought-after speaker who challenges conventional business wisdom and encourages people to embrace change and lead rather than follow.

DECEMBER 22

"Jump ahead to the end of your life.
...
What one-sentence inscription would you like to see on your tombstone that would capture who you really were in your life?"
- Jim Loehr[359]

---

[359] This question echoes one asked by Michael Lombardi & George Raveling: "What do you need to do in order to arrive to your deathbed proud of yourself?"
The Power of Full Engagement, Managing Energy, Not Time, Is the Key to High Performance and Personal Renewal, Jim Loehr and Tony Schwartz, 2003.

Dr. Jim Loehr, renowned performance psychologist and author of 16 books, has spent over three decades studying human achievement. A member of the American Psychological Association with masters and doctorate degrees in psychology, Dr. Loehr's research has led him to a powerful conclusion: character strength is the fundamental driver of success, personal fulfillment, and life satisfaction. His evidence-based insights, drawn from extensive work with high achievers, demonstrate that ethical behaviour and personal integrity are essential to sustained performance in any field.

DECEMBER 23

"In everything you choose, you must first ask: but what will this do to my soul?"
- Michael Lombardi & George Raveling[360]

---

[360] Do not do anything out of alignment with your values. "The wounds of conscience" Latin writer Publilius Syrus explains, "always leave a scar."
Sunday Thinking, The Daily Coach, November 5, 2023.

Michael Lombardi is a three-time Super Bowl champion as an executive with over 30 years of experience in NFL front offices who recently joined the North Carolina football program as General Manager in December 2024. He has spent 35 years working for the New England Patriots, San Francisco 49ers, the Oakland Raiders and the Cleveland Browns, and has the distinction of the being the only person to make it to the Super Bowl with both the Patriots and 49ers. Beyond his front office work, Lombardi has been a prominent media personality as an NFL analyst, author, and cofounder with George Raveling of The Daily Coach, a newsletter that shares sports and organisational leadership lessons.

George Raveling is a Basketball Hall of Fame coach and Nike executive who has had an extraordinary impact on both basketball and sports marketing. After a successful college coaching career at schools including Washington State, Iowa, and USC, he joined Nike at the request of Phil Knight, where he played an integral role in signing a reluctant Michael Jordan. Raveling has worked as the Director for International Basketball for Nike since his retirement from USC and is known as "the iconic leader who brought Michael Jordan to Nike". Beyond basketball, he has a unique connection to civil rights history and having a personal connection to Martin Luther King Jr.'s "I Have a Dream" speech. Raveling was present at the March on Washington on August 28, 1963, and after Dr. King delivered his speech, King handed Raveling the original typewritten copy.

The two co-founded The Daily Coach newsletter, sharing leadership wisdom from sports and business.

DECEMBER 24

"What is success?"
- Paulo Coelho[361]

---

[361] The question is similar to Harvard professor Howard Stevenson's: What do you mean by success? Well, what do I really care about? Am I doing the things that I care about? Will I be proud of my life at the end?" Coelho's answer: "It is being able to go to bed each night with your soul at peace". What is yours?

Manuscript Found in Accra, Paulo Coelho, 2013.

Paulo Coelho is an author who became one of the world's most widely read writers through his international bestseller "The Alchemist". "The Alchemist" sold 35 million copies and is the most translated book in the world by a living author. Before achieving worldwide fame, Coelho experienced a turbulent early life - his parents committed him to a mental hospital three times as a teenager when he expressed his desire to become a writer, leading him to later drop out of law school and become a "globetrotting hippie" through the 1960s and 70s. Before dedicating his life completely to literature, he worked as theatre director and actor, lyricist and journalist. In 1986, he did the pilgrimage to Saint James of Compostella, an experience that deeply influenced his spiritual writing. His masterpiece tells the mystical story of Santiago, an Andalusian shepherd boy whose quest for worldly treasure becomes "a discovery that the most valuable treasures are those found within" and serves as "an eternal testament to the transforming power of our dreams." Coelho's work combines spirituality, personal transformation, and the pursuit of one's "Personal Legend," making him a significant voice in contemporary inspirational literature.

DECEMBER 25

*"What kind of imprint did you leave
on the lives of others?"
- Scott Mautz*[362]

---

[362] "In the corporate world," Mautz writes, "it's easy to spend too much time worrying about how you come across in meetings or what your boss (or boss's boss) thinks of you. I certainly got caught here at times. But I see more clearly than ever that it's not what people think of you that counts. It's what they say about you, from the heart, when no one is looking. What kind of person are you? What kind of imprint did you leave on the lives of others? Find ways to broaden your platform for making a difference to others. Chase authenticity, not approval."

I left my corporate job and these 8 things became clear, Scott Mautz, scottmautz.com, March 11, 2020.

Scott Mautz is a leadership expert, bestselling author, and keynote speaker who combines corporate experience with practical leadership insights. A former Procter & Gamble senior executive who successfully ran four of the company's largest multi-billion dollar businesses all while transforming organisational health scores along the way. Mautz transitioned from corporate leadership to become a sought-after speaker and trainer. He's a multi award-winning author whose books include: Leading from the Middle, Find the Fire, and Make It Matter, with his work focusing on leadership, employee engagement, peak performance, and creating meaning at work. Scott is a popular instructor on LinkedIn Learning where his courses have been taken over 1.5 million times and serves as faculty at Indiana University's Kelley School of Business for Executive Education. His approach emphasises practical, actionable strategies for leaders at all levels, drawing from his extensive corporate experience to help organisations and individuals achieve what he calls "profound performance." Mautz is particularly known for his expertise in middle management leadership and helping leaders influence effectively across organisational hierarchies.

DECEMBER 26

*"What pain do you want in your life?
What are you willing to struggle for?"
- Mark Manson*[363]

---

[363] Manson recounts how he fantasized about being a rock star when he was young. "I was in love with the result—the image of me onstage, people cheering, me rocking out, pouring my heart into what I'm playing—but I wasn't in love with the process." he explains. "And because of that, I failed at it. Repeatedly. Hell, I didn't even try hard enough to fail at it. I hardly tried at all." He wanted the reward, but not the struggle. "Sometimes I ask people," Manson writes, "'How do you choose to suffer?' and 'What is the pain that you want to sustain?'"
The Most Important Question of Your Life, Mark Manson, markmanson.net.

Mark Manson is a bestselling author, blogger, and entrepreneur who has become one of the most influential voices in modern self-help through his irreverent, no-nonsense approach to life's challenges. Manson initially gained attention through his popular blog challenging conventional wisdom about happiness and success with psychology, philosophy, and profanity-laced humour. His breakthrough came with the 2016 publication of "The Subtle Art of Not Giving a F*ck," which became an international bestseller by arguing that the key to a better life is choosing what to care about more carefully and accepting that struggle is inevitable. His writing combines academic research with accessible language and contrarian thinking that challenges typical positive psychology approaches. Instead of promoting endless optimism, Manson advocates for embracing negative emotions, accepting responsibility, and focusing on what truly matters. His work has particularly resonated with those who appreciate his honest, unvarnished take on life's difficulties and rejection of superficial solutions.

DECEMBER 27

*"Whatever one does for a living, three questions need to be confronted before it is too late:
What really matters to me?
What price do my spouse and kids pay for my career success?
What price does my soul pay?"*
- Dennis Prager[364]

---

[364] Prager's questions echoes philosopher and author Roman Krznaric who asks, "What is your current work doing to you as a person – to your mind, character and relationships?" Be aware of the true cost. "The cost of a thing" Henry David Thoreau reminds us, "is the amount of what I call life which is required to be exchanged for it, immediately or in the long run."
Think a Second Time, Dennis Prager, 1995.

Dennis Prager is a conservative radio host, author, and founder of PragerU who has been a prominent voice in American conservative media for decades. In 2009, Prager and his producer Allen Estrin started a website called PragerU, which creates five-minute videos on various topics from a conservative perspective. BuzzFeed News described PragerU as "one of the biggest, most influential and yet least understood forces in online media." Prager also hosts the conservative radio talk show The Dennis Prager Show in Los Angeles. His work focuses on promoting what he describes as Judeo-Christian values and traditional conservative principles through accessible digital content. Prager is also an author of nine books and has built a substantial following through his radio show and online content, making him a significant figure in contemporary conservative thought and media.

DECEMBER 28

"How would you spend your days differently if you didn't care so much about seeing your actions reach fruition?"
- Oliver Burkeman[365]

---

[365] Burkeman's question reflects a quote by Leo Tolstoy who writes, "If you care too much about being praised, in the end you will not accomplish anything serious. Let the judgments of others be the consequence of your deeds, not their purpose."

Four Thousand Weeks: Time Management for Mortals, Oliver Burkeman, 2021.

Oliver Burkeman is an author and journalist known for his thoughtful, often contrarian approach to productivity and happiness. He wrote the popular "This Column Will Change Your Life" for The Guardian for over a decade, where he explored psychology, productivity culture, and the pursuit of well-being with a healthy dose of scepticism toward self-help orthodoxies. His most acclaimed book, "Four Thousand Weeks: Time Management for Mortals", challenges conventional productivity advice by arguing that our limited time on earth—roughly 4,000 weeks for the average human lifespan—should lead us to embrace our constraints rather than constantly seek optimisation. Burkeman's work stands out in the self-improvement space for its philosophical depth, dry humour, and willingness to question whether the relentless pursuit of efficiency and happiness might actually be counterproductive, offering instead a more realistic and accepting approach to human limitations.

DECEMBER 29

"Imagine you could fast-forward to the very last moments of your life, when it is time for you to pass on.
Now look back on your life's journey as a whole.
What would you want to see at that moment?
What footprint do you want to leave behind on the planet?
What would you want to be remembered for by the people who live on after you?"
- Otto Scharmer[366]

---

[366] These questions are part of a broader self-inquiry process that Scharmer outlines to help individuals and teams connect with their deepest sources of inspiration and purpose.
Theory U: Learning from the Future as It Emerges, Otto Scharmer, 2009.
Otto Scharmer is a Senior Lecturer at MIT and Founding Chair of the Presencing Institute. He focuses on awareness-based action research with leaders across various sectors, anchored in the concept of presencing, a method of "learning from the emerging future". Scharmer is the author of several influential books including "Theory U" and "Presence", the latter co-authored with Peter Senge and others, which introduced the groundbreaking concept of "presencing". His Theory U methodology provides a framework for transformational change that moves beyond downloading habitual patterns to accessing deeper sources of knowing and creativity. He chairs the MIT IDEAS program for cross-sector innovation and through the Presencing Institute works with leaders worldwide to address complex social, environmental, and organisational challenges using awareness-based approaches to systems change and regenerative leadership.

DECEMBER 30

"How will you measure your life?"
- Clayton Christensen[367]

---

[367] Christensen's recommendation is to, "think about the metric by which your life will be judged, and make a resolution to live every day so that in the end, your life will be judged a success." Warren Buffett has a closely related idea. "The big question about how people behave is whether they've got an Inner Scorecard or an Outer Scorecard." Buffett says. "It helps if you can be satisfied with an Inner Scorecard." An inner scorecard tracks what is most important ... to you. Be very deliberate what goes on your scorecard. In the words of author and entrepreneur Scott Galloway, "the metrics we value are the guardrails of our intentions, actions, and values".

How will you measure your life?, Clayton M. Christensen, Harvard Business Review, July-August 2010.

Clayton M. Christensen (1952 - 2020) was a Harvard Business School professor and influential business theorist best known for developing the concept of "disruptive innovation." His groundbreaking 1997 book "The Innovator's Dilemma" explained how established companies often fail not because they do things poorly, but because they focus too heavily on existing customers and high-margin products, leaving them vulnerable to simpler, cheaper alternatives that eventually improve and capture the market. Christensen wrote several other influential books including "The Innovator's Solution," "How Will You Measure Your Life?" and "Competing Against Luck," which introduced the "jobs-to-be-done" framework for understanding customer motivation. Beyond business strategy, he was deeply interested in education, healthcare, and personal values, often integrating his Mormon faith into his teachings about leadership and life purpose. Christensen taught at Harvard for over two decades, consulted with major corporations worldwide, and co-founded several companies including Innosight. He passed away in 2020, leaving behind a legacy as one of the most cited business thinkers of his generation, with his theories continuing to influence how leaders think about innovation and competitive strategy.

DECEMBER 31

*"And did you get what you wanted from
this life, even so?"*
- James Ryan[368]

---

[368] Ryan says this is one of five truly essential questions that you should regularly ask yourself and others. If you get in the habit of asking these questions Ryan believes you will have a very good chance of being successful and happy. "'What truly matters?' You can tack on 'to me' as appropriate." Ryan says. "This is the question that forces you to get to the heart of issues and to the heart of your own beliefs and convictions. Indeed, it's a question that you might add to, or substitute for, New Year's resolutions. You might ask yourself, in other words, at least every new year: what truly matters to me?"

Harvard Graduate School of Education Commencement Address, James E. Ryan, May 28, 2016.

James E. Ryan is a legal scholar who was the President of the University of Virginia from 2018 to 2025, having previously served as dean of Harvard Graduate School of Education and formerly the Matheson and Morgenthau Distinguished Professor at the University of Virginia School of Law. A leading expert on law and education, James Ryan has written extensively about how law structures educational opportunity. He is the author of several influential books, including "Wait, What?: And Life's Other Essential Questions" and "Five Miles Away, A World Apart: One City, Two Schools, and the Story of Educational Opportunity in Modern America". His book "Wait, What?" became a New York Times self-help best-seller, and describes the art of asking good questions, distilling them to five "essential" ones, and how they lead to better answers. Ryan is known for his thoughtful approach to leadership and education policy, emphasising the importance of asking the right questions to strengthen connections and deepen understanding.

AFTERWORD

Leadership development isn't about accumulating answers, it is about cultivating the discipline of inquiry. The most effective leaders understand that questions can create breakthrough moments and lasting transformation. Poet and leadership consultant David Whyte captures this beautifully. "The ability to ask beautiful questions," Whyte explains, "often in very unbeautiful moments, is one of the great disciplines of a human life." He continues, "And a beautiful question starts to shape your identity as much by asking it, as it does by having it answered. You just have to keep asking. And before you know it, you will find yourself actually shaping a different life, meeting different people, finding conversations that are leading you in those directions that you wouldn't even have seen before." Questioning is more than information-gathering, it is a transformative practice that reshapes who we are and where we are headed.

Surround yourself with people who embody curiosity. "Look for people who have lots of great questions." investor Ray Dalio urges. "Smart people are the ones who ask the most thoughtful questions, as opposed to thinking they have all the answers. Great questions are a much better indicator of future success than great answers." When you encounter these questions, resist the urge to rush toward solutions. Instead, sit with the inquiry itself. The most profound insights often emerge not from quick responses, but from the silence that follows a penetrating question. Deep listening amplifies the power of inquiry, creating space for unexpected insights to emerge. Musician Robert Breault captured this wisdom. "If

I had it to do again," he writes, "I'd ask more questions and interrupt fewer answers."

The path of leadership development through questioning demands courage—the courage to inhabit uncertainty without rushing toward comfort, to resist the seductive pull of easy answers, and to trust that wrestling with the right questions can help forge us into the leaders our organisations and communities desperately need. This journey requires us to embrace the uncomfortable truth that our most transformative growth emerges not from what we know, but from our willingness to sit with what we don't yet understand, and allowing those spaces to become fertile ground for authentic leadership to take root. The engagement with uncertainty isn't passive, it is active exploration that opens new possibilities we couldn't have imagined from our current vantage point.

The deepest questions don't demand immediate answers, they invite us into a different way of being. "Live the questions now." poet Rainer Maria Rilke wrote. "Perhaps then, someday far in the future, you will gradually, without even noticing it, live your way into the answer."

"And what greater might do we possess as human beings than our capacity to question and to learn?"
- Ann Druyan

www.ingramcontent.com/pod-product-compliance
Lightning Source LLC
Chambersburg PA
CBHW070135100426
42743CB00013B/2714